A 'Toxic Genre'

A 'TOXIC GENRE'

The Iraq War Films

Martin Barker

PlutoPress

www.plutobooks.com

First published 2011 by Pluto Press
345 Archway Road, London N6 5AA

www.plutobooks.com

Distributed in the United States of America exclusively by
Palgrave Macmillan, a division of St. Martin's Press LLC,
175 Fifth Avenue, New York, NY 10010

British Library Cataloguing in Publication Data
A catalogue record for this book is available from the British Library

ISBN   978 0 7453 3130 0   Hardback
ISBN   978 0 7453 3129 4   Paperback

Library of Congress Cataloging in Publication Data applied for

This book is printed on paper suitable for recycling and made from fully managed
and sustained forest sources. Logging, pulping and manufacturing processes are
expected to conform to the environmental standards of the country of origin.

10   9   8   7   6   5   4   3   2   1

Designed and produced for Pluto Press by Chase Publishing Services Ltd
Typeset from disk by Stanford DTP Services, Northampton, England
Simultaneously printed digitally by CPI Antony Rowe, Chippenham, UK and
Edwards Bros in the United States of America

Contents

List of Figures and Tables

FIGURES

TABLES

Acknowledgements

The research I have done for this book owes a great deal to many individuals, who have helped me both by pointing me to materials and by being willing to discuss my emergent ideas with me. I hope and believe that I have thanked all of you already. But in all the more than 30 years that I have researched and published, I have never directly acknowledged the value and enjoyment that my wife Judith has brought into my life. I do this now, knowing that this book, along with all the others I have produced, may have benefited from particular conversations and shared experiences, but they were made possible at all in far more ways by a long-shared life. For exactly the same reason, I want to name and thank the rest of my family who have put up with a father/grandfather who becomes easily distracted, has weird interests and just cannot see what is really important. So, love and apologies to Garrick, Siân and Rosie, and love and hope to Alice, Oscar and Owen – to whom the future belongs.

1
The disappearing Iraq war films

On 3 March 2010, the British Broadcasting Coorporation's (BBC's) evening news carried a lengthy item about the impending release of the film *The Green Zone*, Paul Greengrass's dramatisation of the search for Weapons of Mass Destruction following the 2004 invasion of Iraq. Presenter Huw Edwards prefaced the filmed report with the comment that this was a new development in Hollywood. Up until this point, he declared, few films bar *The Hurt Locker* had yet tackled the Iraq conflict. How wrong he was. Between 2005 and 2008, at least 23 such fiction films emerged from in and around Hollywood, and most of them claimed a base in the real events and circumstances of the war. But the BBC could be forgiven for not knowing about this lengthy list of films. All of them, until the very last one in the cycle, bombed at the box office, if they made it there at all – and just about all of them vanished without trace. Indeed, for a time, the most important topic of debate about the films was precisely their failure.[1] Known collectively simply as the 'Iraq war movies', they were, to quote one report, 'box office poison' (Everhart 2009). This book is a study of these films.

These films were actually being awaited. Quite a few commentators were asking how long it would take Hollywood, this time, to get round to saying something about the war. Hollywood's 'cowardice' over Vietnam was well-remembered, but there was a feeling that this time, perhaps, the studios might live up to their (partly-deserved) reputation for liberalism, and opposition to George W. Bush and his cronies. The expectations were, of course, different according to your politics. In 2004, the *Washington Post* ran an article about Jim Deutsch, a historian interested in the scars that wars leave on returning veterans, and the ways these are hidden from view:

> The popular portrayals run contrary to the image of postwar boom and optimism that many people think of today. According to Deutsch, 1946 had the highest divorce rate until the 1970s. The disaffected vet from the Vietnam War is familiar, but World War II? Deutsch says it's a recurring element of American culture

after all wars. Bleak post-Iraq war movies and literature are next. 'Some of these people literally went through hell,' Deutsch says. 'A common theme is the civilians back home don't understand what they went through.' (Montgomery 2004)

It was mostly assumed that the films, when they came, would be unlike the boosterist films of previous periods. But there were exceptions. The Democratic Underground, a forum on the left of the Democratic Party, feared that the studios were capable of delivering only military-friendly dross:

> Now that the War against those Dastardly Saddam-backed 911 terrorists and the Enshrinement of Glorious Democratic Values in the Backwards Middle East and the Freeing of the latent American who resides inside every Iraqi has gone on longer than WWII where are the war films? Where is the Iraq equivalent of the *Sands of Iwo Jima*? Perhaps we could call it the *Streets of Hadithah*? ... The DoD learned its lessons from Vietnam very well, they will not allow the unvarnished truth to make its way from Iraq. Service members are being censored in theater and at home. (Democratic Underground 2007)

Others on the Right saw 'Hollywood' quite differently – as a nest of radical vipers.

The cycle began with a little-noticed film from director Sidney Furie, whose credentials were good – he had directed *The Boys in Company C* (1978), one of the critical films about the Vietnam War. But *American Soldiers: A Day in Iraq*, where noticed at all, was judged by most early reviewers (professional or otherwise) to be a total disappointment. As others began to emerge, a pattern quickly emerged. Films would be reviewed in groups. Or if the focus was on one, it was examined for whether it looked any different from the flops that preceded or surrounded it.

In researching this book, there came a point where I had to make some hard decisions about which films to include in my list of 'Iraq war movies'. I tried to include only those that were included in those comparative lists, for reasons which will become clear (see Chapter 5). Others could have been added. Some commentators have argued, with reason, that the cycle of 'torture porn' movies owes much to the revelations about Abu Ghraib and Guantánamo. As an example, consider this web report:

It's hard to imagine that for every 15-year-old reading this article right now, the war has really been with them since they have probably been conscious of current events. This war has now run longer than World War II. Like the Vietnam War, which definitely influenced horror films of the early 1970s, the Iraq War had a real impact on the horror films of the past half decade. Filmmakers are all influenced by the current events they are operating in, so it's no surprise that horror films have been affected too. So here are the Top 10 best Iraq War-influenced horror films. *Hostel* (2005): Eli Roth's mega-hit horror film was undeniably influenced by the goings on at Abu Ghraib – whether Roth is conscious of it or not. Iraqi soldiers dehumanized, forced into naked human pyramids – vs. Americans dehumanized and cut up by twisted businessmen. Truth is often stranger than fiction ... *28 Weeks Later* (2007): With smiling faces, American troops take over a war ravaged nation – then attempt to exterminate that nation's citizens when they lose control. This is what happens in Juan Carlos Fresnadillo's superior sequel to *28 Days Later*. The horror of *28 Weeks Later* is actually quite real for a nation run by friendly, smiling occupiers – and it's happening now. (Anon 2009)

The writer goes on to add *Land of the Dead* (dir. George A. Romero, 2005), *The Hills Have Eyes* (dir. Alexandre Aja, 2006), *Planet Terror* (dir. Robert Rodriguez, 2007), *The Signal* (dir. David Bruckner & Dan Bush, 2008), *Diary of the Dead* (dir. George A. Romero, 2007) and *The Mist* (dir. Frank Darabont, 2007) as further examples of Iraq-influenced horror. But this is Iraq-as-metaphor. Horror, fantasy and the like mark a distance from their topics. The films discussed here frequently made claims of direct relevance and – every bit as importantly – were seen by many commentators as contributions to the debate over the war. The 23 films in Table 1, then, constitute my primary focus.

The figures show the evident financial straits they all encountered. Although there are many important differences among them, we will see that there is a core set of themes, motifs and aesthetic choices which the films veer towards – and do so the more strongly, the more they seek to provide direct commentary on the Iraq War. Those which go elsewhere – *The Marine*, for instance, or *The Objective* – ditch those themes and tell their stories differently. And through those very differences we can still learn much.

Table 1   Details of films in the Iraq War film cycle

Title	Director/date	Maximum screens[2]	Budget	US gross
American Soldiers	Sidney J. Furie, 2005	0	No info.	$0
The Jacket	John Maybury, 2005	1,331	$29 million	$7 million
Home of the Brave	Irwin Winkler, 2006	120	$12 million	$41,000
The Situation	Philip Haas, 2006	2	$1 million	$48,000
GI Jesús	Carl Colpaert, 2006	12	$2 million	$8,000
The Marine	John Bonito, 2006	2,545	$20 million	$18 million
Badland	Francesco Lucente, 2007	2	$10 million	$1,900
Battle for Haditha	Nick Broomfield, 2007	2	$3 million	$7,000
Grace Is Gone	James C. Strouse, 2007	7	$2 million	$50,000
In the Valley of Elah	Paul Haggis, 2007	978	$23 million	$6.7 million
The Kingdom	Peter Berg, 2007	2,836	$80 million	$47 million
Lions for Lambs	Robert Redford, 2007	2,216	$35 million	$15 million
The Mark of Cain	Marc Munden, 2007	0	'Low'	$0
Redacted	Brian de Palma, 2007	49	$5 million	$65,000
Rendition	Gavin Hood, 2007	2,250	$27 million	$9 million
Day Zero	Bryan Gunnar Cole, 2007	2	No info.	$13,800
Conspiracy	Adam Marcus, 2008	0	$18 million	$0
The Lucky Ones	Neil Burger, 2008	425	$15 million	$183,000
Stop-Loss	Kimberley Pierce, 2008	1,291	$29 million	£11 million
War, Inc.	Joshua Seftel, 2008	33	$10 million	$578,000
Body of Lies	Ridley Scott, 2008	2,710	$70 million	$39 million
The Objective	Daniel Myrick, 2008	1	$4 million	$95
The Hurt Locker	Kathryn Bigelow, 2008	535	$11 million	$12.5 million

HOLLYWOOD POST-9/11

Histories such as this do not have starting points. But they can have turning points. And there is little doubt that the 11 September 2001 attacks on New York and Washington set in train many of the circumstances that shaped this cycle of films. Shortly after the attacks, on 17 October 2001, the White House announced the formation of an 'Arts and Entertainment Task Force' to help align Hollywood's money and talents with the Bush Administration's needs for films appropriate to this new era of 'terror'. The announcement produced astonishment: was Hollywood 'getting into bed with Bush'? In an overview of subsequent developments, David Chambers recalls the brief history and impact of this Task Force:

Between October 17 and December 6, there were a series of high-profile meetings in Los Angeles and Washington featuring Karl Rove, senior presidential advisor, and Jack Valenti, the long-time head of the Motion Picture Association of America (MPAA), the lobbying group for the major studios. The major outcome of these meetings was a repeated question from Hollywood, how can we help? while the White House, to avoid accusations of co-opting Hollywood into propaganda, could only answer, we can't tell you how. (Chambers 2002)

Chambers details a number of small but significant developments that might be attributed to Valenti's group: for example, free provision of films to American soldiers overseas; special programmes on MTV; the promulgation of exchanges and debates about terrorism among students across a number of countries. In the reverse direction, federal actions against Hollywood over 'sex and violence' were largely suspended. Just as importantly, incipient moves to challenge the increasing media monopolisation were transferred to the Federal Trade Commission, and stalled.

The impact on film-making itself was much more muted – not least because, as Chambers notes, the 'creatives' were not really part of the Task Force. A number of films (all 2002) were delayed and adjusted to the 'new sensibilities'. This could involve altering New York skylines (*Spiderman* [dir. Sam Raimi, 2002]), or re-editing to reflect the 'new mood' (an airplane hijack was removed from *Collateral Damage* [dir. Andrew Davis, 2002]), while *Black Hawk Down* (dir. Ridley Scott, 2001) was substantially revised in ways which, it has been argued, dehumanised the Somali 'enemy' whilst cleaning up the American soldiers.

Films which came close to criticising American policies and motives got pulled back. Philip Noyce's remake of *The Quiet American* (2002) made uncomfortable viewing, with its emphasis on American duplicity over war preparations. Due for distribution just days after the attacks, it was stopped; only a campaign by Michael Caine, who smelt a possible Oscar for his performance as world-weary journalist Thomas Fowler, got it a limited release. Even where a film was not it itself political, it could become edgy by dint of the politics of those in it. The UK's *Guardian* quoted Peter Rainer, of the American society of film critics, on the makeup of the list of Oscar nominees: 'If Susan Sarandon was nominated for *The Banger Sisters*, this would definitely be an issue' (Campbell 2003). Sarandon was among the most vocal Hollywood star critics of Bush's preparations for war. In the end, that year, the Oscars played safe with eleven awards to *The Lord of the Rings* (dir. Peter Jackson, 2001–03) where choosing sides and making wars happened safely in a fantasy world.[3]

Older films that had briefly been discussed for their uncanny prefiguration of the 9/11 attacks (where had they got such insightful storylines from?) dropped surprisingly out of view:

> There seems to be little talk about recent, prophetic films such as *The Siege* (1998). In *The Siege*, director Ed Zwick and screenwriter Lawrence Wright unfolded their story as if they had glimpsed Osama bin Laden's master plan. In the movie, Middle Eastern terrorists attack New York City by blowing up a bus, a theater, and the office tower housing the FBI's New York headquarters. The terrorists are portrayed as Arab, Islamic militants, largely Palestinian and under the leadership of one mysterious 'Sheikh Ahmed bin Talal.' At its release, the Arab-American community roared in indignation, while film critics lambasted the plot's unlikely scenarios. Now, there is just silence. (Chambers 2002)

However, if at an overt level the new Hollywood/Washington cuddling did not lead to a great deal, at other levels there were new strategic collaborations. Jonathan Burston (2003) caught some of the early forms of this, in the partnerships forged between studios and the military, particularly over the training potentials of new technologies. Resonantly-named new but secretive organisations were set up: Future Combat Systems; CADRE (College of Aerospace, Doctrine, Research, and Education) and the Institute of Creative Technologies – the last funded by a $45 million US military grant to the University of Southern California with the aim to 'enlist the resources and talents of the entertainment and game development industries and to work collaboratively with computer scientists to advance the state of immersive training simulation' (Burston 2003:166). Burston's powerful argument is overstated in as much as he tends at crucial moments to speak of 'Hollywood' as if a single entity – without divisions, cautions and countervailing tendencies.

It was not in fact long before the general discomfort felt by many Hollywood liberals at the idea of working with the Bush Administration flared into renewed distrust, as the Republicans' war plans became clear. The spread of conspiracy theories about (for example) Saudi involvement in 9/11, suspicions about government and military incompetence, revelations that an invasion of Iraq had long been on the political agenda all fuelled a fearful antagonism: a will to resist and decry, but an awareness that the charge of being soft on terror would easily stick. The challenge was undertaken by two 2006 films: *United 93* (dir. Paul Greengrass, 2006) and *World Trade Center* (dir. Oliver Stone, 1996). The careful insulation of the attacks on New York from the surrounding penumbra of 'the war on terror' was an achievement in itself.[4]

But the film-maker who more than anyone threw down the gauntlet to the Republicans was of course Michael Moore. Many people have discussed the nature of Moore's interventions, and I do not need to rehearse their accounts here. What does need emphasising is the way in which Moore's *Fahrenheit 9/11* (2004) became, for a time, a beacon for radical Democrats – to the point of believing that with this film they might tip the balance and defeat the Republicans in the 2004 Presidential election. Ben Dickensen's 'insider' book on the history of the Hollywood Left captures this aspect very well. He describes the re-emergence of activism following the deep disappointment after Bill Clinton emerged as an anti-labour technocrat (Dickensen 2006). Despite their disappointment with him, attempts to impeach Clinton over his sex scandals were resisted by activists, including through the organisation MoveOn – which then evolved into an anti-war coalition alongside others such as ANSWER (Act Now to Stop War and End Racism), and Not In Our Name. Far from united, there were divisions over what *kinds* of anti-war position should be taken. It was these organisations which did much to promote Moore's documentary:

> MoveOn's election activity was eye catching, and often required much effort on the part of the creative community. A cacophony of television adverts was produced by Hollywood talent: director Richard Linklater interviewed disgruntled Texans; Donal Logue exposed the 9/11 terrorists to be Saudi Arabians; actor Woody Harrelson hammered corruption in the decision to choose corporate oil giant Halliburton to rebuild Iraq; director Robert Reiner cut press conferences in which Bush denied mistakes with evidence of his errors. On 11 July the biggest grossing documentary of all time, *Fahrenheit 9/11*, became a campaign tool. Fifty-five thousand volunteers organised house parties where *Fahrenheit 9/11* could be watched. In New York, Edie Falco, star of HBO's hit series *The Sopranos*, joined movie actor Bull Pullman in the best publicised of these events. Outside, popular musicians including Pearl Jam, the Dixie Chicks, Bonnie Raitt and

REM performed on the 'Vote For Change' tour, that peppered the country with politically-charged gigs. (Dickensen 2006:196)

But for all of the boost that Moore gave to the arguments and morale of the anti-Bush campaign, Bush, with much election finagling, won again. And Moore's film came under intense fire, to the extent that it was even sometimes mooted that it backfired – angering and turning out Republican voters who might otherwise have abstained.[5] In retrospect, therefore, the film was seen by many as a mixed blessing.[6]

2004 was in many ways the critical year. It was the year of Bush's hugely controversial victory. It was the year of Moore's film. But it was also the year when, for all kinds of reasons, public opinion was seen to be turning against Bush's post-9/11 triumphalism and the associated major shifts in domestic policy – most notably the Patriot Acts and their infringements of civil rights. The shift is well caught in an essay by Jarice Hanson, citing a 2004 *Village Voice* article:

> One year after 9/11, National Public Radio did a poll and found that only 7 per cent of Americans felt that they had given up important liberties in the war on terrorism. Two years after 9/11, NBC or CBS did a very similar poll and they found that now 52 per cent of Americans report that their civil liberties are being infringed by the Bush administration's war on terrorism. That's a huge shift. (Hanson 2008:56)[7]

But while public opinion was widely *felt* to be shifting, it simply didn't turn into the kind of electoral shift radicals were looking for. Defeat in the election hurt, deeply.

Battered by the impact of 9/11, hurt by their failure to unseat Bush in 2004, Hollywood's Left entered 2005 looking for ways to continue their propaganda struggle against the war machine. Some turned to documentary. A spate of important ones did what documentaries are good at: uncovering hidden aspects of the American war. Robert Greenwald's *Uncovered: the War on Iraq* (2004) brought out many of the lies on which the war was based, and then again in *Iraq for Sale: The War Profiteers* (2006) he exposed the workings of companies like Halliburton and Blackwater. Eugene Jarecki's *Why We Fight* (2005) drew ironically on the World War II propaganda series to expose some of the propaganda tricks being used now. James Longley's *Iraq in Fragments* (2006) gave voice to the views of ordinary Iraqis about what the war meant, and had done, to them. Many others began to give voices to American soldiers, drawing out their thoughts on why they were there, and what the war was doing to them. These included Civia Tamarkin's *Jerabek* (2007), which went on to show the impact on one American family of the death of their son in Iraq, and the self-questioning this entrained.[8]

But documentaries carried that risk of evidential challenges. Others chose a fiction route. But their makers were still desperately aware of the difficult atmosphere into which any films would emerge. Just how difficult is indicated in the next chapter, as I look at the fate of one planned film which would have been decidedly *not* anti-war.

THE HOLLYWOOD WAR FILM TRADITION

There is nothing at all new in film-makers finding themselves severely constrained. Since Hollywood's beginnings, war films have been expected to play the patriotic game. But this became regularised after the 1940s. Since that time, Washington and Hollywood have been in a close and institutionalised embrace. They remain separate domains, but there are such strong and long-standing ties that it makes no sense to try to understand the production of war films, or their narratives, without reference to that context. Koppes and Black (1987) explain in great detail how the embrace began, as the Roosevelt administration readied itself for entry to World War II – and realised two things. They had no machinery of propaganda. And they had a large draft army that, they soon realised, neither knew nor cared about America's 'war aims'. A crucial step, therefore, was the creation of the Office of War Information (OWI) in 1940, among whose remits was the development of strategies for using film (identified as the medium most likely to reach soldiers and the general population) to propagate its messages.

Koppes and Black discuss the rising tensions between Hollywood, the Justice Department, Roosevelt, and America's leading isolationists (led by Senator Gerald Nye). The occasion for these early battles was the late 1930s release of a series of anti-Nazi films from Hollywood, and accusations that these constituted illegal propaganda for American involvement in the war. But the isolationists' case dissolved the moment news of the Japanese attack on Pearl Harbor reached America. From this point on, OWI's mission was to work to build 'national unity and morale' at a time when many Americans suspected they might well lose the war – and in one poll 49 per cent of African–Americans in Harlem thought they would be no worse off under Japanese rule. This became the subject of intense research and intervention effort (about which I say more in Chapter 7).

The problem for the OWI was their real nervousness about giving any ammunition to Axis propaganda, which was already playing on racial hypocrisy over America's claims to be a 'free' society. This nervousness fed into early negotiations between Washington and Hollywood over the planned film *Tennessee Johnson* (dir. William Dieterle, 1942). MGM were advised of a 'major concern' because of the film's handling of the issue of race through its portrayal of Andrew Johnson and Thaddeus Stevens. But it was not only overtly political issues such as this which bothered the OWI. As Koppes and Black found, even a film like *Palm Beach Story* (dir. Preston Sturges, 1942), a fluffy upper-class romance set in that year, worried the OWI because of its 'giddy disregard for war sacrifices' (Koppes & Black 1987:91). When sacrifices were being demanded and when America needed friends to believe it was committed to the war, such a film could do no good.

The OWI wanted to intervene early, at the script development stage. But the risk was of producing utterly worthy films which audiences would reject, and thus antagonise Hollywood. When, therefore, in 1943, the OWI began talking of barring films it judged 'bad for America's image' from export, a major Hollywood revolt began. The resultant battle redrew the lines and restricted the administration's ability to intervene in films' development. What emerges from Koppes and Black's research is a picture of competing forces gradually evolving (under wartime conditions) arrangements that all sides could live with. This necessary pragmatism nonetheless gave rise to what they call 'two core myths':

> Wartime movies fused two powerful myths that had deep roots in American popular and political discourse. One was the division of the world into slave and free. They divided the world of total peril into either ultimate evil or righteousness. [...] The other myth was a newly universalised version of the idea of regeneration through war. [...] In OWI/Hollywood's vision, the war produced unity. Labor and capital buried their differences for a greater cause; class, ethnic and racial divisions evaporated in the foxholes and on the assembly-lines; even estranged family members were reconciled through the agency of war. (Koppes & Black 1987:325)

This pragmatism by and large worked and, with variations, remained in place after the war ended. Under conditions of peacetime, the

OWI was replaced by more informal bodies and eventually by the Pentagon's Film Office.

The later cloak-and-dagger activities of this Office have been exposed in a recent book by investigative journalist David Robb (2004). Using the benefits of Freedom of Information enquiries, supplemented by interviews with key players, Robb recounts many instances in which branches of the Pentagon successfully steered film scripts in some very precise directions, or effectively prevented others from being made, by threats to withhold access to bases, equipment, uniforms and so on. Robb recounts how thorough this became, with the Pentagon Film Office regularly reviewing script-ideas and laying down detailed requirements for cooperation. In particular, he shows that the Pentagon regularly overruled historically accurate elements of films in favour of what would enhance the military image. Three phrases capture the Pentagon's line: unfavourable scripts were automatically judged 'inaccurate' (Robb 2004:232, here relating to Clint Eastwood's attempts to get support for *Heartbreak Ridge* [1986]); military personnel were to be 'normal but dedicated' (Robb 2004:330, addressing *Air Strike* [1955], which sought to deal with racial discrimination in the Navy); and overriding all, 'not the image we wish to project' (Robb 2004:262, regarding a film addressing the role of the National Guard shortly after the Kent State killings). The Pentagon's set goals were, first and foremost, that films should boost recruitment, benefit Congressional funding considerations and support military interests abroad.

What shines through Robb's account is that, because of this history, studio films have mainly become virtual advertisements for 'America' and its military. Whilst books might truthfully reveal the scabs and sores of American military behaviour (for example Philip Caputo's *A Rumor of War* [1976], which recounts Vietnam soldiers' traumas, but also shows their wild behaviour in Mexico), films of those books could not. What also show through are the continuing tensions between military (and even between different branches thereof), politicians and film-makers. The point is that any understanding of the 'genre' of Hollywood war movies has to begin by seeing the conditions of their production as an institutionalised compromise, of course constantly renegotiated, but insistently kept within the frame of those two heavily-invested, 'balancing' myths. Any who try to escape these can expect to pay a heavy price. So, if by the new millennium 'Hollywood' was expected to be anti-Bush, their relations with the military could prove crucial.

THE QUESTION OF 'VIETNAM'

The other major defining context for films about the Iraq conflict was undoubtedly Vietnam. Notoriously, Hollywood shied away from addressing the Vietnam War precisely because America was so riven with conflict over it. John Wayne's absurd *The Green Berets* (1968) apart, no film directly and substantively addressed the war until it was safely over. That failure was oddly coupled with the continuing accusation that 'the media' – in particular television – lost the war for the Americans.[9] So, when George Bush Sr declared that victory in the first Gulf War meant that America had once and for all 'kicked the Vietnam syndrome', the stakes piled even higher. If 'Hollywood' spoke out on Iraq, anything it produced would instantly be examined for its political position – with the expectation of being damned as anti-war, thence anti-American. The issue of taking sides was inescapable, including for film academics.

To date, there has been little attention to the films I address here – with one exception. Douglas Kellner's *Cinema Wars* (2009) ranges widely across Hollywood's response to the 'Bush–Cheney Era', discussing films produced from 2000 onward, and covering documentaries (both television and cinema), directly political commentaries (for example, *Three Kings* [dir. David O. Russell, 1999]), and allegoric framings (for example, the later *Star Wars* and *Saw* horror series). Kellner includes brief forays into nine of my 23 films. Since Kellner's accounts of these are so different from mine, I have taken time to explore his accounts and offer a critique of his approach.

Kellner's book is in line with his earlier (1988) collaboration with Michael Ryan. He sees Hollywood films as offering 'transcodings' of political events and processes. The key question to be asked is: which side are they on? Two key assumptions underpin his approach. First, that there are three clearly separable 'sides'– conservative, and liberal, with a rare radical third. The mapping of these onto the standard structure of American politics (Republican, Democrat and fringe Left) is uncanny. Second, placing films under each of these labels is a quite simple process. One looks, describes the 'events' and dialogue of a film, and bingo! – its politics are clear. The result is a constant repetition of phrases such as 'is an analogue to', 'can be read as a metaphor for' and 'as an allegory for'. This has a tendency to lose specificities and squash differences. So, for instance, *Good Night and Good Luck* (2005) 'provides critical reflection on the Bush–Cheney rightwing extremist regime' (Kellner 2009:28). In the

Saw (2004–09) series, 'the lunatic killer Jigsaw can therefore be read as a metaphor for Dick Cheney and his subordinates, a group of fanatical, warped, and vicious advocates of torture and murder, believing that their torturing and murdering is in the cause of good because it is punishing evil' (Kellner 2009:8). The fact that the first film is set in the 1950s and constitutes a quiet, measured evocation of one man's courage, while the latter are set contemporaneously in various Eastern European countries and operate at the fringes of the horror genre, apparently hardly matters.

This means that filmic elements take on slippery significance. Writing of the *Bourne* franchise, Kellner says:

> The US intelligence agencies in the trilogy evoke fears of an out-of-control Bush–Cheney administration. In *The Bourne Ultimatum*, the CIA's deep cover New York City office has an image of Donald Rumsfeld visible on a computer monitor. In a deleted scene featured on the DVD, there is a picture of Bush on the wall behind the evil Noah Vosen, thus evoking the real people who were doing vile and immoral deeds in real life. (Kellner 2009:168)

What are we supposed to make of this as an example? Would the showing of the Rumsfeld image constitute an *exposure* of the association (as opposed to a conceivable 'reading' of this as covert referencing)? In which case, does the cutting of the Bush image now constitute a *hiding*? Or does its presence in the DVD recuperate the film? The decision, to be frank, seems quite arbitrary.

With these parallelist accounts of the films come hints of a kind of late mass-society critique. Films, however distanced, are to be evaluated almost as if they were documentaries, judged for their truthfulness or 'distortion'. They are seen as impacting through 'manipulation' on 'the masses'. Hints at impact abound, but paradoxically. Where films have been popular (assessed crudely by box office tallies), that is evidence of their impact – and of the force of the ideologies he is locating. Yet where they are minority sport or box-office weaklings, that is not taken as a sign of the failure of ideological transport. Of the *Saw* series again, he writes in a way that anything they might do is bad:

> Many viewers may identify with the torture sequences and obtain sadomasochistic pleasure from watching them, pointing to a propensity to take pleasure in others' misfortunes and suffering.

The *Saw* films may also convince viewers that guilty individuals are worthy of punishment and torture. The *Saw* franchise's popularity and continuation is thus an index of a pathological society riven with unmastered aggression and violence. (Kellner 2009:9)

There is much to be said about this and others in the 'torture porn' mini-genre, but this reveals little more than an analyst's fears.

Kellner adopts an instant explanation for the failure of the Iraq war movies: '[F]ilms dealing with Iraq and terrorism did not do well at the box office, suggesting audience fatigue with Bush–Cheney politics' (Kellner 2009:233). As I argue in Chapter 5, film 'failure' is a vastly more complicated issue than this. It is tempting to argue that the problem with Kellner's book is that it simply tries to cover too much. I would argue that the problem with this account is much deeper. Kellner has one criterion for evaluating films: do they overtly share my politics? If not, they are preaching against them, and constitute a component in the evil 'Bush–Cheney' ideological array. It becomes clear just how much there is a pre-established 'measure' for the films when he discussed the Iraq War fiction films. Writing of *The Situation*, he says:

Although a love triangle and melodrama detract somewhat from the politics, the film makes clear that the various factions will probably not be able to come together and resolve their conflicts, and that the US is condemned to make unholy alliances with unsavory forces in an impossibly muddled and violent situation (Kellner 2009:220)

There is clearly less interest in what the films are than in what they should have been. And that takes us to the heart of this book's matter: what does it mean to be 'anti-war'? My argument will be that the main available definitions of pro- and anti-war get in the way of understanding these films.

THE TASKS AND SCOPE OF THIS STUDY

In this book, I try to answer four large questions:

1. How has it come about that 'Hollywood' (a term itself requiring scrutiny) has produced so many films about the Iraq conflict

while that is still continuing, yet all of which have been judged 'failures'?

2. How have the highly-charged contexts enclosing them both driven and constrained the ways the films make their arguments?
3. How have the films negotiated the comparison with Vietnam, and the images and accusations associated with memories of that war?
4. What is new and specific to these films? What in particular is achieved through the adoption of fictional forms?

Each of these large questions will spawn smaller and more specific ones, as the book proceeds.

This book studies one complex phenomenon, which in itself causes a problem. Although focusing on a brief period and flurry of film-making, I have found myself pushed out to puzzle over much wider issues. And I can honestly say that for this book I have found myself forced to review issues and debates across a wider terrain than for any previous research. For this reason, the structure of the book has been a challenge. For example, in Chapter 3 I present a table which is necessary to guide the examination of individual films. But its full meaning can only be understood once those examinations occur in subsequent Chapters. I hope readers will be willing to check back as the argument unfolds.

Two issues do need flagging from the outset. This book continues my interest in methods of 'textual' research.[10] Textual analysis of films often depends upon mounting claims about what 'the audience' might or must do as they watch and engage. In recent years such 'figures of the audience' have become a topic of concern for me and a number of other critics, for the work they do in warranting claims about the meanings and potential impacts of films and other cultural forms.[11] These figures are especially a problem with this cycle of films, because of the penumbras of politics and 'failure' that hang over them. For instance, overarching debates about their failure often offer instant explanations about why audiences have disliked and rejected them. Yet for every one of the films, it is easy to find people who have welcomed and approved of them. The difficulty is that critics and approvers tend to see and attend to quite different features and qualities. A film as analysed by a critic can be almost unrecognisable to a person who has engaged positively.

What I am offering, I hope, is a way of analysing how these films work, which is compatible with looking at how actual (as against putative) audiences engage and respond. And to check this, I have drawn on one very handy source. The Internet Movie Database (IMDb) carries for every film a User Comments page where viewers leave their personal evaluations (frequently scoring out of ten stars). Cumulative responses can run into hundreds and even thousands. This is not about cherry-picking responses that agree with my analysis, or even looking for the most common. Rather, it involves two steps: (1) We need to consider first the *most positive* responses: a series of researches have shown that positive respondents engage more richly and complexly, and more readily perceive patterns and coherence in a film, than those who are hostile.[12] By looking at positive responses, therefore, it is possible to ask what kinds of engagement, pleasure and understanding are attainable with a film's resources. (2) A comparison, then, of these with the most critical and negative commentators allows us to see the *terms of debate* over a film. This can throw more light on the issues at stake in these debates. Therefore, to the extent that space has allowed, for each of the 23 films considered here I have at least indicatively explored a sample range of positive and negative citizen reviews at IMDb.

2
No True Glory: the film that never was

On 16 December 2004, *Variety*, the insider's bible on Hollywood, carried an announcement about the 'first major feature project about the current war in Iraq' (Fleming 2004). The film was being developed by Universal Pictures' partner Double Features Films, who had optioned a yet-to-be-published book by ex-Marine Francis 'Bing' West about one vital battle during the 2004 American-led invasion of Iraq. With the same working title as the book (*No True Glory: the Battle for Fallujah* [2006]), key news was that Harrison Ford had 'attached' to the film to play General Jim Mattis who had commanded the assault on Fallujah. This story was picked up by many news sources across America and beyond, and became the basis for much discussion and debate. Over the next 5 years, the story continued to circulate. As late as 11 November 2009, the *San Diego Union-Tribune*, reporting a veterans' anniversary of the battle, reminded its readers that: 'Their combat is the subject of several books and documentaries, and film producer Michael Shamberg – whose credits include *Erin Brockovich* (dir. Steven Soderbergh, 2000), *Pulp Fiction* (dir. Quentin Tarantino, 1994) and *World Trade Center* – is interested in making a movie about the battle, with Harrison Ford playing the main character'. (Gardner 2009)

The rumours have persisted. However, not only has the film not yet emerged, it still bears a 'To be announced' marker.[1] There is, in one way, nothing unusual about this. It is the norm in Hollywood for film-projects to be floated, and even developed extensively, only to be denied a production green light.[2] But in this case, although we cannot know about the internal discussions at Double Features and Universal, a lot can be learnt by considering the ongoing noise around the war, this battle and the people around the film. In this Chapter, I use this non-released film to build a framework of contexts and to suggest how these shaped the movies that *did* come out.

Bing West was not simply 'a Marine'. He came from a military family. West had himself been assistant secretary of defence in the Reagan administration, had become a war correspondent, served as a Marine in Vietnam, and his books have won awards from military groups. West appears regularly on 'The News Hour' and 'Fox News', and on the Council on Foreign Relations (a 'nonprofit and nonpartisan membership organization dedicated to improving the understanding of US foreign policy and international affairs', according to its website). His son, Owen, also a Marine, was scheduled to produce the film's script with him. The book belongs to a clear oeuvre of military works, which combine what one review called 'an immersive experience for the reader' (Redd 2008) with a plea that soldiers be left to 'get on with war' without the disabling limits and delays that politicians impose. Indeed, the book was a major carrier of an argument widely pressed in America that Washington made a mistake in making American troops stop before they had completed their initial assault on the city. For when they had to go in again, insurgents had dug in, and that caused more American casualties.

This was never going to be just a film, therefore. It was even going to be more than just a pro-war film. West, in 2009, was still arguing his case:

> Abdicating responsibility for Fallujah's security was a major blunder, said Bing West, a retired Marine officer and author of *No True Glory*, an eyewitness account of the second Fallujah campaign. 'We, the coalition, backed off and surrendered the city ... we had to go back in with more casualties', said West, who lives in Newport, R.I., who said that more than 50 US troops died during the second battle, draws parallels to Fallujah as President Barack Obama weighs whether to send more troops to Afghanistan, particularly for the Morjah area of Helmand province, a Taliban and drug-lord stronghold. 'We've learned nothing from Fallujah. The longer we delay in Afghanistan, the tougher the fight in Morjah is going to be', West said. (Gardner 2009)

A film about the battle for Fallujah would thus inevitably have become part of political struggles over American tactics, politics and diplomacy. Even the rumours of the film did as much. As *Variety* put it, the film would 'explore the dangerous intersections between war and politics' (Fleming 2004). They already had, in fact. A key incident that sparked the American assault was the killing of four people, whose bodies were put on display. How should they be described? Naming them as 'Blackwater employees' made visible that they were part of a virtual mercenary force, part of the simultaneous occupation and privatisation of Iraq. Naming them as 'Americans', as the early reports on book and film did, made them national representatives.

Given West's reputation, unsurprisingly we find oppositional groups readying themselves for a hostile film. The Democratic Underground, alert to all such interventions, exchanged thoughts on the likely meaning of this: '*The Battle for Fallujah* seems to be in production – this makes me sad that we are going to be seeing propaganda like this. It is rumored Harrison Ford will be in this movie. IMDb has it in their database but there is no information' (Anon 2005a). Capturing Harrison Ford was clearly a coup, although Ford clearly likes working with Shamberg – in the period of the non-appearance of the Fallujah film, he starred in another Double Features project, *Extraordinary Measures* (dir. Tom Vaughan, 2010). Ford's star-persona – from young cheeky semi-rebel to grumpy but determined American (who, in a number of more recent films, has played ultra-patriots) – looked a winner to play Mattis. As one report put it: 'the film has a title that may bring anguish to some ... even while its star, Harrison Ford, adds a tone of respectability to the project' (Derakshani 2004). But Ford quickly proved a problematic choice, not least in some key military quarters.

On military websites in the period after the project was announced, debates took place. Some loved it, but were aware of concerns. In 2007 one ex-soldier wrote thus:

> Look, it's no secret that I have a total man-crush on Marine General Mattis. So when I find out that one of my favorite actors is going to play one of my favorite generals in a film adaption of a book by one of my favorite authors... omg [sic], *swoon*. Translation, in order: Harrison Ford will play the role of General Mattis in *No True Glory: The Battle for Fallujah*. ... According to IMDb, *No True Glory* is slated for a 2008 release. I like the timing. One year after a shotgun blast full of Hollywood anti-war films tank at the BO, we get a nitty-gritty *Blackhawk Down* style flick that will (presumably) focus on the individual heroism and ultimate nobility of US Marines. If *No True Glory* does as well as *BHD* did, it'd send a pretty clear message to Hollywood. Courage sells. Weakness doesn't. What, you think *300* was a smash because of the costumes? Here's hoping they do this flick right. ('John' 2007)

The tensions in here ('I love Mattis, I love Ford, we need pro-troop movies to counter all these "liberal Hollywood movies" – but I've just heard about these rumours ...') are revealing. The 2004 blog to which 'John' referred was occasioned by Harrison Ford making a statement querying America's role in Iraq. That prompted two very contradictory responses. One army wife challenged Ford, insisting he should not play the role as Mattis unless he made clear he had changed his mind. Meanwhile a group of anti-war activists petitioned Ford not to play the role because of its jingoistic implications. As one said:

> I think Mr Ford would be making a terrible career move and a ghastly mistake that will lose him millions of fans if he makes this movie, and also, I believe firmly that he would be encouraging the growth of terrorist threat to our country by engaging in a one-sided, skewed version of history that is so false, it can only stir hatred in a land we invaded. I feel sure anyone who looks at the facts will agree with me. I feel prompted to return to the fray and try to stop this movie getting made, if just by making heard our voices over the yes man and military machine, and perhaps, over his personal desire to play a strong general. I wish to stir Mr Ford's conscience. (Blackfive 2004)

What this reveals are the closely-operating sensitivities which crowd round a film project of this kind.

Concerns about Ford added to problems aroused by some widely-reported remarks by General Mattis. Giving a talk in early 2005, this 'famously cantankerous' General crossed a line at a San Diego panel discussion hosted by the Armed Forces Communications and Electronics Association. 'Actually, it's a lot of fun to fight. You know, it's a hell of a hoot. It's fun to shoot some people. I'll be right upfront with you, I like brawling', he quipped, especially against people who 'ain't got no manhood'. Warned by a superior for being a bit too overt, the remarks nonetheless travelled the wires (Associated Press 2005).[3]

In the early days of the rumours about the film, few doubts were expressed about its viability. *USA Today* (as did several other publications) in a substantial article compared the present situation with Vietnam where America didn't have the courage to do it until long after the events:

Not since World War II has Hollywood so embraced an ongoing conflict. It took years for pop culture to tackle the Korean and Vietnam wars, and it took time before the country was ready to be entertained by those politically charged conflicts. With Iraq, however, and after 9/11, 'all bets are off', says film historian Leonard Maltin. 'Whatever happens in real life inspires and affects our storytellers'. With no resolution in sight, Iraq remains a timely backdrop. Audiences are hungry for glimpses of history in the making. March 19 is the war's second anniversary. But not any and every angle of the war is being depicted. One aspect is glaringly absent from most projects: negativity. The US soldier is the hero, his cause is just. Storylines featuring the Abu Ghraib prisoner-abuse scandal or war protests are no-nos. (Soriano & Oldenburg 2005)[4]

This fascinating report, with its intellectual gloss from Maltin, marks out the demarcations. Nothing 'policy-oriented', nothing 'political', just 'human experience' and 'grand natural human drama'. The executive producer of the intended *Battle for Fallujah* is then quoted: 'We will always be patriotic in our representations and will never take a political stand'. This puts on display a widely-assumed and utterly disabling discursive argument: that to be patriotic is above and beyond politics. 'Bad events' may happen, but they are 'policy' and 'politics', and films shouldn't deal with those. Now, go and try to make a film about that, if you dare ...

In fact, many documentarists did try, and Fallujah became one of the prime foci for attention. *Shootout! D-Day Fallujah* came from Tony Long in 2005. *Fallujah Uncensored: Operation Al-Fajr* (Operation Phantom Fury) came out in 2007. *Fight For Fallujah* (Millitary Channel, 2008) celebrated the way in which the battle 'forged new fighting Americans': 'Just as Somalia (*Blackhawk Down*) defined a generation of Army Rangers, Fallujah created a special breed of Marine for the 21st Century, one schooled in intense, hand-to-hand combat and urban warfare unlike anything that's engaged the US military since Vietnam' (from the DVD cover). Mark Manning and Rana Al-Aiouby's *Caught in the Crossfire: the Untold Story of Fallujah* (2006), produced on a shoestring budget and outside Allied control, told the stories of Iraqi citizens, and explained their increasing hostility to American presence. Manning's *The Road to Fallujah* (2009) tells his own story of going to Fallujah and teaming up with an Iraqi aid-worker, to try to uncover some truths about the situation in the face of all the conflicting accounts.

Books tended to be soldiers' memoirs. Patrick O'Donnell's 2007 book *We Were One: Shoulder to Shoulder with the Marines who Took Fallujah* was by an embedded author fighting alongside Marines, capturing 'not only the sights, sounds and smells of the battles, but the human drama of the young men from a close-knit platoon fighting and dying side-by-side' (from the cover description).

Some of the particular characteristics of this 'human drama' are well captured in one book: Colby Buzzell's *My War: Killing Time in Iraq*. Beginning as a blog, and then assembled into a 2005 book, Buzzell writes as an almost accidental insider to the war. He writes of the boredom, the routine, and the minute controls over soldiers' lives – and the 'seediness familiar to any soldier: the prevalence of pornography, the foul language, the gallows humor' (Fryer 2005). This ordinary nastiness authenticates both the soldiers and the author – these people are not there with a political purpose, therefore not to be judged, only to be admired for their courage. The emphasis on finding a human drama meant, almost always, finding an *American* drama within the war, even in the case of Australian short film *A Message from Fallujah* (dir. Richard Gibson, 2005):

> Daniel Crane is an American civil engineer who, nearing the end of a three month stint trying to help rebuild war torn Iraq, is intoxicated by the exotic people and surrounds. On the morning of his last day in Fallujah he stays for 'One more cup of habibi'. This is all it takes for Daniel to find himself beaten and alone, a hostage in the drama of war. As hope fades, he is left with one last wish, to tell his wife how much he really loves her. Lance Henriksen delivers a heart wrenching performance as Daniel Crane, taking the viewer on a deeply personal journey of heartfelt desire. *A Message From Fallujah* puts aside the politics and rationalisation of war, to show that in the end, it doesn't matter in what name the violence is committed. For the dead, the homeless and the orphans, the effect is still the same. (Anon 2005b)

'Putting aside the politics' here means that an American's suffering can stand in for 'human experience', made more poignant because here is a man who just loved (exotic) Iraq. And it is for this reason that it is hard to find mention of the one response to Fallujah which broke those rules, Jonathan Holmes' play *Fallujah*:

> The play *Fallujah*, written by Jonathan Holmes, starring Samantha Morton and with a score by Nitin Sawhney, is this

year's Guantánamo. In this extraordinary sourcebook, Holmes gathers together the testimony that formed the basis of his verbatim script, and which came from Iraqi civilians, NGOs, politicians, US and UK military, and journalists involved in the three attacks on Fallujah. It makes a strong case – using unpublished evidence collected by Nobel Peace Prize-nominee Dr Scilla Elworthy of Peace Direct – that the US military should be hauled up before the ICC [International Criminal Court] for war crimes. The documentary sources establish the facts that shaped the play's fictional form, while a new essay by Scilla Elworthy sets out the case behind the research and reveals the truth of the atrocities carried out by the USA. (Holmes 2007)

The emphasis on the evidential base underpinning its presentation presses the question: what is the benefit of doing this as a fiction? This is a question I return to, later.

Some things did not make it. One computer game, *Six Days in Fallujah*, was well into development before being killed:

The game was to be based on events as told by a group of Marines who fought in the battle, who were actually the driving force behind the idea of creating a game based on the battle. The game was originally meant to be a training simulator for the Marine Corps until this group of Marines brought the idea of making it into a game about the Battle of Fallujah to Atomic Games, the developer of the project. Naturally, much controversy has arisen from the public, anti-war groups, as well as veterans and family members of fallen soldiers, particularly from the UK, prompting Konami to pull out of the project. Atomic Games has said they want to keep working on the game but will need another publisher willing to face the heat. What do you think? Too soon to be making games about the war in Iraq? Or does the fact that soldiers want these stories to be told make it okay? (Anon 2007)

Notice the boundaries of sensitivity here, but notice just as much that each release is checked for appropriateness.

The point of quoting all these is to show two things: that the meanings of all these events were intensely debated; but that those debates were circumscribed, within limits set by two things: the need to remain 'patriotic' and the need not to be seen as 'anti-troops'. Tim Robbins, a leading anti-war figure in Hollywood, who features later for his role in *The Lucky Ones*, acknowledged this self-silencing when talking of the satire he was also involved in: *Embedded* (dir. Tim Robbins, 2005), which featured at the Sundance Festival. 'About the only thing we don't poke fun of is soldiers', *USA Today* quoted. Among the key points of reference – whether positive or negative – was Michael Moore's *Fahrenheit 9/11*. But while hated by the Right and sneered at by military commentators, Moore was at least excused from being "anti-soldier"' (Soriano & Oldenburg 2005). But however you viewed it, Fallujah was a risky, occupied topic.

The career of this non-film spans the entire period I am studying: 2004–09. It is not yet certain whether *No True Glory* will ever appear.[5] Universal Studios have since become involved in Paul Greengrass's *The Green Zone*, and that has not been a striking success, despite trying for a crossover appeal from the Jason Bourne/Matt Damon franchise.[6] Besides, part of the initial interest in taking on the project would surely have been, as some commentators noted at the time, to be the first to tackle the topic.[7] For a major studio to venture into much-contested territory, it would have to want to be seen to take a position. And the only position Universal have made sure that they are unequivocally seen to be taking is one of generalised sympathy and support for American soldiers.[8] The story of this non-appearance therefore reveals a great deal that is of relevance to films which *did* come out. In no special order, I list these elements:

1. The nature of the companies financing and producing these films: the changes in 'independent' Hollywood and its relations with the master-studios are well illustrated by Shamberg's history – from his early engagement with slightly alternative films (his first-ever role as producer was on a documentary on Indian gurus), through a period in independent comedies (for example, *A Fish Called Wanda* [dir. Charles Crichton,1988]) and then in 'cult' (the high point being his involvement in *Pulp Fiction*), via involvement in the serious drama of *World Trade Center*, to the current situation where his production company has a 'first refusal' relationship with Universal. Double Features Films dates from 2006, one of the most current crop of attached production outfits that work in close symbiotic relationship with one of the Majors. This is typical of wider changes that writers such as Geoff King have documented (see Chapter 8 for more on this).

2. The search for sources for films, since the industry generates few of its own narratives and scenarios. Essentially a parasitic

industry, Hollywood seeks sure-fire winners, stories with reputations upon which it can build, but hopefully without downsides. The striking thing, however, about the 23 Iraq war movies identified here is how few of them are based directly on existing published sources – yet how many of them, in other ways, put considerable effort into presenting themselves as 'based in reality'. This puts a curious question-mark over their status as fictions.

3. There is one striking differences between West's book and the corpus of films considered here. The book (and indeed a number of others[9]) addresses soldiers' experience of the invasion and its immediate aftermath. Only one – the very first – of my films touches on this stage at all: Sidney Furie's *American Soldiers*. Thereafter, it is as if the actual 2004 invasion is off bounds; it is not covered or even mentioned. In Furie's film, as we will see, the most striking feature is the soldiers' lament that they thought the war was over, and that they had won – so why is it, then, that they are so hated? My suggestion is that an unspoken criterion overarches these films: there can be no ambiguity attached to the idea of 'America winning'. If a film shows America not winning, it is classed as anti-war – and perhaps anti-troops. Wars can be 'mistakes', situations can be 'impossible'. But after Vietnam, defeat is inconceivable, so to conceive it is anti-patriotic. If a film shows America winning, it is acceptable, even if there are ambiguities over the Army's motives and the soldiers' behaviour. This will later help explain the peculiarities associated with one of my films, *The Kingdom*.

4. The overwhelming presence of rumours, leaks, testing of the waters, building of reputations – and, in the reverse direction, managing undermining stories – is important. Story development is never only about finding coherent cinematographic form for a given story. It is also about massaging stories into acceptable form, whilst appearing to be brave. Only mavericks such as Michael Moore manage to stand outside of these systems.

5. 'Hollywood' is itself an arena of intense meanings. Widely viewed as 'liberal' and hostile to what many regard as 'American values', the sheer fact of being presented as a film sets up requirements and expectations. But Hollywood also litters American culture with marks and signs of its past – when, for many, it was better. (A tiny marker of this is the naming of a modern military vehicle as 'Stryker', for many a small reminder of the 'proper heroism' of John Wayne [an iconic resource I consider in Chapter 4].) This combination – plus an overwhelming sense that Hollywood is more than anything else driven by money ('I would bet that 90 per cent

of Hollywood hates George Bush and they were against the war. However, the studios know where money can be made; war movies!' [Norris 2004]) – together surround all film production with a task of seeing-off cynicism, before any product ever sees a screen.

All of these lead to a picture of struggles to produce films which will challenge but not offend, find spaces but push few boundaries. This must be remembered as we begin to look at the films that *did* get made and released.

3
Constructing an 'Iraq war experience'

What kinds of stories do these films tell, and how do they tell them? There are many obvious differences among them, which we must not lose. While most take Iraq as their frame, one or two (*Lions for Lambs* and *The Objective*) also include Afghanistan, while two address the 'Middle East' in a more general way (*The Kingdom* and *The Situation*). While many include at least fragments of combat experience, several deal with the 'war back home' (*The Lucky Ones*), soldiers' return (*Home of the Brave* and *Badland*), civilian reception (*Grace Is Gone*, in particular), forced return (*Stop-Loss*), or threat of being drafted (*Day Zero*). The great majority focus on the American experience of the war, but occasionally films will consider what people of other origins undergo (although this is mostly through their association with Americans – see *The Situation*, and *Rendition*). Films not directly set in Iraq were widely treated as part of the same corpus. *Lions for Lambs*, for instance, was regularly reviewed as an 'Iraq war movie'. How, then, is it best to analyse them?

One way is to group them into a limited number of kinds, as Pat Aufderheide has done in a short study of the documentaries about the Iraq war. Aufderheide finds three main kinds. First, 'Why-We-Are-In-Iraq' documentaries 'analyse and extrapolate motives for the US's government's decision to invade Iraq' (Aufderheide 2007:57) – all of which, she argues, broadly share a critique of the invasion as a 'politics of empire'; second, 'Grunt' documentaries try to evoke the combination of boredom and frustration with the problems of combat with a faceless enemy, and often use new technologies to get close to soldiers' experience; and third, 'Learning From the Iraqis' documentaries go among the local population and try to give them voices. Perhaps most interesting, though, is her meta-question: how these documentaries seek to constitute kinds of publics, who are willing to be informed and educated. But her emphasis remains on the differences between them.

My approach is to that extent different. In the midst of all the differences, and connecting the various kinds of films, I aim to show that there are a number of shared elements – styles, themes, motifs and narrative moves – that go to make up a cinematic space within which film-makers feel that they can create an 'Iraq war experience'. These allow them to manage the constraints imposed by this contested period: 2005–08. The elements do not all necessarily appear in one film, but they cohere quite well. Where there are discordant elements and contrary cases, I have separated these out (see especially Chapter 8). These can be revealing in their own right. But mostly the shared threads assemble to construct a working ideological position, one which constructs an account of American soldiers and their actions.

Individual films participate in this 'Iraq war experience' rather in the way that Vladimir Propp showed individual Russian Wondertales to participate in an overall form, in his celebrated *Morphology of the Folktale* (1968). Propp discerned a sequence of 31 'functions' (that is, story-components carrying the narrative forward) across his corpus of Wondertales, but showed that individual stories might abridge some parts of the sequence, or loop and repeat certain elements. For Propp, the point was that these tales depict the reach and limits of the imaginative life of Russian peasants, among whom they originated. In a somewhat similar fashion, this cycle of films can reveal both the achievements and the limits of cinematic anti-war statements in this period. Of course, there are major differences between essentially formulaic folktales and films that always stress their distinctiveness. Even so, I hope to prove the analogy with Propp is helpful.

IN THE VALLEY OF ELAH

I begin with *Elah*. This film centres on a retired military policeman (Hank Deerfield, played by Tommy Lee Jones), a Vietnam vet and very precise man still heavily invested in the idea of the American army, its disciplines and its honour, searching for his son Mike who is reported as having gone AWOL. His wife Joan (Susan Sarandon) becomes the emotional weathervane of the film as Hank can only stare, horrified, at what he gradually sees and learns.

The film opens with some unexplained, crackly, voice-over sounds from Iraq. We only know that someone has got out of a combat vehicle, despite orders. We go to Tennessee, November 2004: Hank gets a phone call saying his son is missing. All he has to go on is a puzzling photograph emailed by Mike from Iraq, showing a crashed van and a distant body at a roadside. Unable to find out more,

Hank heads for his son's base. (On the way out of town, he pauses to correct a Latino man who is raising the town flag incorrectly – he has to tell him its meaning if upside down ['crisis'].) Arriving, everywhere he seeks information (at the base, around the town), he hits dead ends. Trying the police, he gets passed to Detective Emily Sanders, a sidelined policewoman given the shit jobs by her colleagues. When we first see her, she is dealing with a woman who says her husband has gone crazy and killed their dog (Sanders' colleagues laugh.) At first she will not become involved. At the base, Mike's platoon members are at a loss over what has happened to him. Hank manages to make off with Mike's mobile phone, and sees a specialist who can recover its corrupted files. The rest of the film is excerpted with the arrival of these almost incomprehensible bits of film.

Then, Mike's body is found, cut up and burnt, by the roadside. Hank gets Sanders to take him out to the site and, using his old MP skills, pieces together what happened. Gradually they put pressure on the military to let them interrogate the other members of Mike's platoon. Over the course of the rest of the film, their story unravels. Hank gains Sanders' trust, not least because on a visit to her house he tells a story to her nervy son. Hank chooses the story of David and Goliath, and this offers the boy a model on which he gradually builds, becoming sufficiently metaphorical to provide the title for the film. Sanders aside, the film is full of people – the police, the military, men at a strip club, some café owners – who simply do not care.

Evidence appears to point to a drug connection and to Mexican–American soldier Robert Ortiez, who goes on the run. He is chased and beaten up by Hank, who abuses Ortiez as a 'wetback prick'. But he proves to be innocent, a convenient target. Meanwhile, the body of the threatened woman is found, killed by her husband – who was an ex-Iraq soldier, stressed out. Sanders' colleagues are shamed.

Finally, the real story emerges – told in an entirely de-emotionalised way by one of Mike's platoon, who even offers, 'I'm sorry for your loss, sir', to Hank, like a formal military apology, after he describes how he and his platoon-mates butchered Mike. Hank now learns the meaning of the confusing images from inside the Humvee. His son had learned to enjoy torturing 'Haji' prisoners, pushing his hand into their wounds: 'It became a thing with Mike. That's how he got his name, Doc. It was just a way to cope. We all did stupid things.'

Hank, now knowing the truth, goes to see Ortiez to apologise to him. Ortiez describes how dehumanising Iraq was. And yet, 'after

two weeks back all I wanted was to go back – how fucked is that?'
From Ortiez, Hank finally learns the story behind Mike's emailed
photo. Standing Orders forbade them ever to stop on patrol. Mike
(as driver) had hit and driven over something in their first week in
Iraq. It was a small boy playing football. But Ortiez keeps telling
himself that it was just a dog, it is not allowed to be a child in his
head. As Hank heads home, we 'see' the events-as-live: of Mike
driving, seeing the road ahead blocked, speeding up, hitting the
child, then getting out to take the photograph – as what? Apology?
Trophy? Record? Memorial? We cannot be sure. Now we learn
through Hank's memory of a distressed phone-call from Mike

Figure 3.1   In the Valley of Elah: At the close of the film, following all the revelations
surrounding Mike's death, we are offered 'consolation' as we see him stepping tight-lipped
out of his Humvee to photograph (memorialise?) the body of a child he has just driven
over, because of orders not to stop for anything while on patrol. Mike's agony over this
becomes the post-facto explanation for his abusive behaviour towards prisoners, captured
in this 'impossible' shot of him taking this photograph.

Figure 3.2   Battle for Haditha: Awaiting his court-martial as sacrificial military victim when
a murderous assault on an Iraqi is exposed, Corporal Ramirez goes 'inside his head'. He
'sees' (truth? retrospective wish?) himself rescuing a young girl from the burning house.
This impossible self-filming becomes his epitaph.

asking his father to get him out, because 'something's happened'. Hank's refusal to help him makes his guilt very personal. Arriving home, he finds a last package from Mike's unit, with his old flag. He takes it out and instructs the Latino worker to mount it upside down, as a sign of how bad things now are. For a man entirely devoted to the military, this is a highly symbolic act. Over these final scenes, a slow ballad accompanies Hank's acts. It is a woman's lament that from the moment we are born we are touched by death. The final image is of a dead body in the road, captioned with the words 'For The Children'.

What needs to be noted about the construction of this powerfully-acted and emotionally-demanding film?

- Although fictionalised, part of its claim on our attention is the film's basis in real-life events. *Elah* emphasises its origin in the story of Richard T. Davis, who was murdered by his fellow troopers, and whose parents went on to establish a charity in his name committed to tackling stress among ex-soldiers. (This was emphasised in trailers and publicity, and on the DVD.) This *authenticates* and makes hard to question the shocking nature of the unfolding events. But it does again pose the question, what precisely is gained by addressing these issues through fiction when their factual basis is so important?
- The distorted and grainy clips of mobile phone footage are critical to disclosing what happened – including the terrible truth about Mike's predilection for casual torture. The soldiers' own filming comes to play an *evidential* role.
- Throughout the film, military officers are thoroughly duplicitous, motivated at best by protecting their own kind, at worst by excusing behaviours that they have effectively encouraged and instigated.
- Hank's own military (Vietnam) background inhabits his every move, from the way he wakes in the morning to how he makes his bed, presents himself and relates to other people. It is central to how he thinks, feels and investigates, and it ensures his trustworthiness. A sense of what an 'American soldier' is like invests every frame of the film.
- The film very cleverly shows us high levels of *apparent* normality in Mike's buddies. In the first half of the film, we see no overt signs of post-conflict trauma. In the end, their very fixedness and their incapacity to feel – caught best in the utterly detached way in which Mike's murder is ultimately

related – becomes the strongest evidence of just how disturbed they are.

- Civilian attitudes to the soldiers are dismissive, unconcerned and uncaring. They live mean and selfish lives, which serve to increase the sense of soldiers' self-sacrifice and mutual dependence. This is symbolised in the attitudes of the police, their dismissive response to the frightened woman, but then their embarrassment at her death.

- The film takes narrative turns, which work to throw us off-balance – and for those knowing its director Paul Haggis' other best-known work, *Crash* (2004), this is not surprising. Marketed as a 'thriller', *Elah* indeed appears for a while to be a complex murder mystery. We are led down explanatory blind-alleys, such that the truth, when it emerges, is all the more shocking. But the withholdings of information are more than a director's whim. They belong within the conspiracy of silence which the military authorities try to enact.

- Nowhere is this more true than in the prejudiced assumptions about Ortiez. A Latino, therefore presumed to be involved in drugs, he is the easy fall-guy – and Hank falls. Ortiez's doubled victimhood, coupled with his unhappy role in their crimes, mark him apart from the other troopers. Proven innocent, his evidence becomes a testimonial to a 'truth' about Iraq.

- This whole process of misleading and disclosing creates a space in which soldiers' cruel and inhuman treatment of Iraqis becomes *excusable*. We see their brutality simply as a mistake arising out of stress and sickness. One of the central ways this is achieved – although it is more strongly present in some other films, and mainly hinted at and implied in *Elah* – is by drawing a line between three aspects of soldiers' behaviour. There is parade-behaviour, which is disciplined, restrained and courteous – although that may be evidence of a silencing and suppression of stresses. There is barracks-behaviour, which is crude, macho, invested with sexism and pornography, and capable of crude racism. Finally, there is battle-behaviour, where American soldiers are constructed as confused, distressed and overwhelmed by experiencing hostility.

This last is critical. A central feature of the Iraq war films is the tensions between these three strands of 'being an American soldier'. In the least political films, we will see, the line dividing them is maintained. No matter how crude, misogynistic and racist the soldiers may appear when seen off-duty, the moment they step out onto the streets of Iraq they become innocent, bewildered and desperate. In these films, senior officers play almost no role at all. In the more political films, the line creaks if not breaks and – often licensed by officers who then turn their backs – elements of the bad behaviour cut loose in their treatment of civilians. The crisis over America's role in Iraq is being played out, more than anything, through cracks in the image of the 'American soldier'.

This shows starkly within debates over the film. Responses at IMDb were, as always, sharply divided. Against a background awareness that a lot of public commentary had attacked the film, praisers speak of the film's 'restraint', its 'remarkable absence of polemic' (countering claims that it is 'heavy-handed'). A lot hangs for its admirers on the texture of the acting – the characters come to *embody* distress, something that fiction of course can do but documentaries cannot. And this means that the film is seen, beneficially, to avoid being political. The narrative twist is recognised: 'I love how it starts as a genre movie and then transcends into something deeper and soul-searching'. Another expresses the same point in this way: 'Haggis did not turn this into a typical Hollywood crime thriller and also did not turn it into a political propaganda piece against the war and President Bush. Instead he mixes the two plots together seamless and subtle'. Notice, again, that sense of double-plotting. But perhaps the most telling comment is this: 'There are no speeches or lectures, but watching illusions and faith in old systems being peeled away is very powerful. And very, very sad'. This feels like a journey already undertaken by the viewer, now being relived. Both starting-point (what they used to believe) and end-point (what they now realise) are givens. And this is not 'political'. It is just the de-humanisation of soldiers back from war.

Dislikers of the film found the film and its acting styles too 'wallowing' and this theme in itself too political. One ex-soldier develops this, calling 'disgusting' the 'portrayal of practically every soldier in the movie as some drugged out, burned out, stressed out product of the war'. Another more angrily denounces the film as 'condescending leftist tripe':

> Haggis, the pioneer behind this tasteless, insidious piece of crap, crosses the line from anti-war to anti-military as he portrays all soldiers as monstrous perpetrators of war crimes, ultimately dehumanized by war to the point of victimhood. From the horrific portrayal of soldiers, to his successful attempts to turn a tragic

tale into a mockery completed with hanging the flag upside down, Haggis demonstrates his conspicuous hatred of the United States.

It is clear even from this small selection that the argument is over what will count as being pro- or anti-military, and thus pro- or anti-US. The typicality of the soldiers' suffering is one thing, the use of this as a ground of criticism crosses a line. A key way in which the film tries to navigate this kind of critique is by including signs of showing soldiers' own recordings of their experiences. A messy, grainy video aesthetic dominates this and other films, directly recalling the flux of videos which from late 2004 onwards flooded onto the internet, most notably onto YouTube, from soldiers in Iraq.

THE YOUTUBE WAR

As I emphasised at the beginning of this chapter, not all the films are set in Iraq. Yet the theme of Iraq combat experience – its look, and feel – is found in ten of the films (not including *The Marine*, whose off-pisteness I consider later), and is strongly hinted at in a further four. To understand the construction of this 'Iraq war aesthetic', it is necessary to consider the rise of soldiers' YouTube videos.

The near-simultaneous emergence of mobile phones with video capacity, cheap digital film cameras, laptop editing systems and wireless technologies meant that by 2005, when YouTube was established, many American soldiers serving in Iraq were able to make records of their lives there in a way never previously possible. From its inception, soldiers made use of YouTube, uploading large numbers of short films. A great deal has been written about YouTube. Much of the writing continues the vein of previous work on new technologies which promotes their new democratic potentials, how previously invisible identities have emerged and new networks flourished, despite the venture-capitalist origins of such sites.[1] This work tends to emphasise, if not celebrate, the 'amateur' status of films' makers, almost as a corrective to 'mainstream' media. But work specifically on soldiers' videos has gone in rather different directions. Two authors in particular have studied these postings closely.

Kari Andén-Papadopoulos (2009b) explores a large number of soldiers' videos. She notes that for a time the posting of these was hardly policed, nor were any official materials distributed by these routes. It was only in March 2007 that an official YouTube channel, 'Multi-National Force – Iraq', was created, followed in

May by a block on soldiers accessing popular sites from military computers – with limited success.[2] Soon, a number of the videos which had occasioned concern – videos showing evidence of soldiers' maltreatment of people and animals – were taken down by YouTube. Andén-Papadopoulos distinguishes four different kinds of videos. 'Combat Action' videos show the impact of air strikes and artillery fire, and are frequently boastful and openly aggressive ('See that car, I lit that fucker up! He got 30 rounds in that bitch!'). Often edited to hard rock tracks, these videos often 'contain imagery that originates from military surveillance devices such as night vision cameras and aerial surveillance technologies' (Andén-Papadopoulos 2009b:22). 'Operation Iraqi Boredom' displays life in camps or barracks, with plenty of Frat-style humour, and soldiers performing stupidly to camera. 'Tribute' videos put on display what the authorities tried to hide: the funerals, the flag-draped coffins and colleagues crying. Some even show the ruined bodies of the soldiers. The most complicated, she argues, are the 'Interactions with Iraqis' videos, which run from shots of innocent children and hand-shaking with civilians, to films of amused abuse (for example, teaching an Iraqi child to say, 'I fucked a donkey'). The key to these videos, whatever their contents and politics, is their *authenticity*, and this view of them circulated widely with them.

In related fashion, Christian Christensen (2008) compared 29 videos on the US's official YouTube channel with 13 unofficial ones. The official ones, he argues, make the war seem clean and purposeful, and show soldiers doing good to the local populace. Better filmed, they look and feel like propaganda films. The unofficial ones look 'dirty' by comparison, both aesthetically and in how they portray the conflict. Importantly, he shows these videos taking the piss out of the official ones. Christensen describes one such video, *Leaked Video of US Soldiers in Iraq* (2007):

> In one segment, the soldier is asked about being sent overseas, to which he sarcastically responds in a sweet voice: 'You know, it's great because you get to interact with the kids, to help them out a lot, and help other people that are poorer than you. You know, you feel like you are giving something back'. The soldier then ends the sarcastic tone and continues: 'Fuck that shit! I don't give a fuck! First week I felt love coming out of my heart helping those kids. The second week? Get the fuck out of here!' (Christensen 2008:162).

In a second essay, Christensen (2009) focuses on their use of popular music, looking particularly at the 'Get Some!' videos which try to evoke the excitement and terror of battle, using clips of gunfire, explosions, thermal imaging, aircraft target-sights and the like, sometimes along with images of Iraqi corpses, frequently intercut with memorial scenes of the Twin Towers in New York.

A more complicated story is told by Mark Astley (2010), who links soldiers' videos to the larger arena of death movies and websites. He notes the popularity of the 'torture porn' film series such as *Hostel* and *Saw* among soldiers, and the cultural proximity of the images of dead or damaged bodies to the short-lived series of beheading videos – many of which surfaced on one notorious website, Ogrish.com. For the soldiers, Astley argues, Abu Ghraib became aestheticised,[3] a source of horror counter-images; and this took on additional meanings when one website, nowthatsfuckedup. com, offered soldiers a free trade: good combat footage in exchange for hardcore porn.[4] A key issue around Ogrish in its main period (2002–06) was again the issue of authenticity, with postings of some evidently faked beheading videos. Even to look at these could pose threats. One such faked video carried a powerful Trojan virus to anyone tempted to open it – a deliberate punishment for voyeurism. Astley's overall argument is that such images of death and torture shift uneasily between being pure awful-carnivalesque spectacle and conveying cultural meanings about their victims and perpetrators.

The points I take from these important contributions are these. The Iraq occupation did indeed become a YouTube phenomenon, with a stream of soldiers' videos, as well as other circulated or leaked kinds of filming. These created a recognisable look to the conflict, among whose meanings was the question of the trustworthiness of those images. Who took them? What attitudes underpinned and accompanied them? Can there even be 'authentic' images when so much is clearly staged, posed and edited? And in the midst of so much damage, destruction and death, what is possible other than wringing one's hands in horror? The aesthetics of the filming, in other words, were much more than its hand-held quality, its grainy shooting, and the amateurishness of its 'performers'.

With these ideas to hand I want to look at the most controversial of all the films in this cycle, Brian de Palma's *Redacted*, because it is the film which takes most seriously not just the *look* of soldiers' videos, but also their implications for who is telling the stories, and what their accounts of the war may reveal or hide. But because it does it so directly – keeping the 'bad' as well as the 'sad' elements, turning the soldiers' recordings into evidence against the military – it was widely condemned.

REDACTED

Reviled by its critics, *Redacted* brought accusations of 'giving comfort to our enemies', and charges of treason. The venom was sufficient to persuade some cinema managers to take the film off – it was in its own turn redacted. *Redacted* is closely based on the true story of the rape and murder, in Samarra in March 2006, of a 14-year-old Iraqi girl, Abeer Qasim Hamza al-Janabi, whose body was burned along with other members of her family by US soldiers in a revenge mission for the death of their sergeant by an IED. Made on a shoestring budget of $5 million with an ambitious script, de Palma managed to find one company (HDNet/Magnolia) to back his determination. The price of their backing was, interestingly, a further degree of fictionalisation of events: changing people's names to defray possible legal actions, even though the events were not in question. The film's principle of construction is striking. *Redacted* is in effect constructed entirely from faux found footage, of 13 different kinds: (1) in-camp filming by Private Salazar, a Latino trooper who is filming 'the truth' of their tour as his pitch for getting into film school; (2) cross-filming by another member of the platoon; (3) scenes from a slow-moving documentary being made by a French TV company – who also then (4) produce news footage of a shooting incident at the checkpoint they have been observing (followed by [5] other TV stations' coverage of the incident); (6) streamed web images, from an insurgents' website watching the planting of an IED, unnoticed by near-by soldiers; (7) captured footage from security cameras at the US base; (8) official recordings of interrogations; (9) night-vision filming by Salazar of the raid, rape and murders; (10) clips from a distressed soldier's wife speaking via the internet to other women; (11) Skype internet exchanges between a trooper sergeant and his father; (12) a mujahideen film of the beheading of Salazar; and (13) an internet broadcast by an unnamed American woman, wildly condemning the soldiers as 'Nazi fucks' deserving death by torture. Very few scenes look authored directly for the film.

The opening caption declares the film a 're-imagining' of the actual rape and killings. This runs over into the voice-over of a Private Salazar, filming his buddies in their camp in Iraq, asking them about their lives, why they think they are there, what they think about the world. One of them, Corporal McCoy (a lawyer back home), tries to be a good guy throughout – to his colleagues' mockery. When Salazar insists he is 'telling it how it is', the lawyer responds: 'You know what the first casualty is going to be? The truth'. To camera, Salazar says, 'Don't expect some Hollywood narrative'.

Cut to a French television crew making a documentary about the American presence, to solemn music. There is a long sequence showing bored, tense soldiers man a checkpoint in glaring sunlight. A car goes through their checkpoint, as the film-makers ask: do these procedures work, and how can the soldiers know the differences between 'good' and 'bad' guys? Back to Salazar trying to interview another platoon-mate who is reading John O'Hara's *Appointment in Samarra*, finding his retelling of it boring, and cutting him short. Instead we see the other soldiers with soft porn. Cut to live filming outside, with local kids trying to con food off one of two new recruits, BB and Reno. The black sergeant warns him – 'Stay away from those midget Ali Babas, alright?' The sergeant is training his men that at any moment these football-playing boys will turn on them.

Back to the French filming at the checkpoint: a car doesn't stop, and is shot up. It turns out to have been a pregnant woman, who dies at the hospital. The French team try to interview her brother at her bedside. Cut to Arab news coverage of the death. Dissolve back to Salazar interviewing BB and Reno, who casually speak of 'sand niggers' and 'retards'. They pass off the checkpoint death as just 'waxing Hajis'.

Next day, in a moment of unsourced filming, we watch an officer informing them that their tour of duty is extended. Now there is anti-officer talk among the platoon, ending in the sergeant enforcing silence. Salazar now reads, to camera, O'Hara's story, obviously fascinated by it. Dissolve to an Arab website recording the unnoticed planting of IED. Next day again: Salazar captures his sergeant being killed by the IED, while saving a stupid soldier, BB. Cut to a security camera: BB and Reno wind themselves up for a revenge mission, then head for the house they are convinced must be hiding insurgents. Breaking in, they take away a local man. The French television crew turns up and films what they are doing.

Now the French crew are filming at the post: BB takes aside a passing girl and (although we do not see it) clearly sexually assaults her, under pretence of a search. To Salazar's filming: the platoon are playing poker, with pornographic cards. Reno and BB are aroused, planning to go back, calling the girl 'spoils of war'. The others cannot talk them out of it. A Soldier's Wives videologsite: McCoy's wife is talking desperately about a message he has sent home. Switch to night vision (Salazar has strapped a tiny camera to his helmet so he can capture what goes on): the raid, the rape and multiple murder. McCoy is forced outside, and gives up trying to stop them. Afterwards, back at their base, we watch on security camera BB threatening the others not to say a word. French television recounts the official story that the army puts out, that the murderers were Sunni insurgents ... or maybe Shia. The arrested man, in shock, tells what he found inside his house. Salazar is having psychological counselling: we see the grainy 'record' of the interview with an unsympathetic officer. McCoy talks over the Internet to his ex-military father at home, but the father warns him to silence: 'We don't want another Abu Ghraib'. Salazar is filming himself in the street when he is snatched by Muslim fighters (his camera, left running, is later recovered). Now there is news coverage of the discovery of his body, tortured and beheaded. We see the beheading video.

At the barracks, BB (wearing a bizarre pigeon helmet) mock-interviews a laid-back Reno about his memories of Salazar, and then about his own life story. Reno talks of his brother back home, a cruel but incompetent killer who got caught after offing a union official. He, Reno, is the exception: 'In any situation there's got to be that wild card'. The story now goes back home to America, via a face/voice-disguised video, asking for someone to tell the story and act. McCoy is interrogated, clearly with the intention of silencing him by proving him an unreliable witness. By contrast, we watch relaxed but unbelieving interviews with BB and Reno, who talk in the rhetorics of the popular press: 'We're keeping the Arab scum off your doorstep, keeping America safe', says Reno. Of the rape, he says she had the hots for him. He parrots official talk: 'If you prosecute guys like us, you're just aiding terrorists'. In response, an internet site shows a hysterical woman denouncing 'Nazi fucks' who did this, who should be tortured to death: 'You won't see the truth about My Lai in movies because that fascist orgy was even too much for fucking liberal Hollywood'.

Back home finally, McCoy is out with his wife and friends. They demand a story from Iraq. Unwillingly, he tells what happens, and breaks down: 'Everywhere you look it's just death, and suffering'. But no matter that the story is appalling, they applaud him as a hero – and the end-shot is a still photo of him posing with his wife. The film closes with a series of real shots of dead bodies from Iraq – men, women and children, with their faces 'redacted to avoid identification'.

To gain a proper understanding of this film, a number of issues need to be faced. The characters of the soldiers are very diverse, but not in the manner found in classic combat movies (as we will see). There is an irony in the charge thrown that de Palma 'stereotypes' them. Actually, much narrative time and work goes into differentiating between them (by class, race, attitude) and into showing the resultant tensions. There is here a complete breakdown of the distinction implied and created within other films in the cycle. Here, soldiers on patrol take with them the hatred, racism and misogyny that they display in barracks. Their back-home selves accompany them into their interactions with Iraqi people. And until it becomes an unavoidable embarrassment, officers are complicit in their behaviour. This seems to me to be the ground for the loathing expressed towards de Palma and his film. He steps outside the realm of acceptable debate, because he casts structured doubt on the innocence of American soldiers.

Only one other film shows anything like the decisiveness of de Palma's, and that is Marc Munden's *The Mark of Cain*. One of only two British productions in my set, this film centres around two Mancunians, Mark and Shane, friends since boyhood, in the army together in Basra, Iraq. They get caught up in the torture of Iraqi detainees, two of whom die. The story gets out when a girlfriend sees Shane's trophy photos on his phone. She is angry with him as he has been with another girl and calls the police. The army closes ranks against the two of them – 'loyalty is all you're left with, mate', says Gant, their bullying lance corporal, leaving them to face the music for attacks that were at his and officers' instigation. The film ends with Shane having committed suicide and Mark in a cell, badly beaten for telling what happened at his court-martial, to the horror of the army who have meantime promoted Gant as a 'good, popular soldier we can't afford to lose'. Coming out almost unnoticed in 2007, before the wave of popular sentiment about 'our heroes', *The Mark of Cain* avoided the vitriolic treatment awarded to de Palma's. But of course it was not American, nor about 'American soldiers'.

But most important is the contribution of those multiple kinds of filming. De Palma combines other people's partial accounts, editing them together with an array of startling transitions: image spins, in/out pixellation, smashed glass, closing jaws and so on. In one interview, de Palma was asked about his use of all the 'found footage':

Because I think it's important to let the audience know that even though this appears to be a documentary in many ways and real material, it's all fiction and you will believe it anyway. So all that stuff you're watching on television, just because it's on your screen in the news hour does not necessarily mean it's true. (Rahner 2007)

De Palma is aware of playing with the modalities of truth and persuasion. He is asking all through: what sources do we have? Which do you believe? What goes on in private and isn't revealed? And within that frame he shows us terrible but undeniable events, whose 'truth' has been largely hidden from us. In arguing this, I am writing in diametrical opposition to Garrett Stewart who argues – bizarrely – that *Redacted* 'barely aspires to a plot at all' (Stewart 2009:51). Stewart obviously cannot bear de Palma's film and calls on a style of film theorising to warrant his dislike. This style centres on film's visual techniques above all else and, with Stewart, requires film-makers to maintain a proper 'distance' (which he asserts is exemplified in *Apocalypse Now* [dir. Francis Ford Coppola, 1979]), but also, most oddly, to be transparent. So, the problem with *Redacted* is its calling its attention to its techniques, described as 'optical processing almost to the point of manic travesty'. Stewart's problem is that he sees, but cannot see past, the multiple modes of filming that de Palma uses – and he presumes that no-one else can, either.[5]

IMDb comments on the *Redacted* divide particularly fiercely. However, it is not their strength that I am interested in, but their terms of reference. It is clear that the film's admirers like what they see as deliberate artistry, and through that the unveiling of truths. They are unmoved by the hatred evinced towards it. One woman (telling people to 'get over it' because it is just 'free speech') writes: 'The thing we know for sure about de Palma is that there are no accidental or unintentional images, cuts, camera angles or words in his movies. What looks rough was intended to look rough. What looks like a careless frame was there to look careless'. Another calls it a 'thinking man's film', the very opposite of 'war-blind and ignorant Americans'. One (Turkish) poster points directly to the force of the visual motifs: '[T]he movie has an interesting appearance that the director preferred to use the online web cams and web sites etc to bring the stuff into our lives as in real life'. These become part of its persuasive force. For another again, the resultant 'messiness' does just the same – it makes you look differently, rather than being a simple voyeur. But just about all the positive comments begin by reminding themselves and their readers that the events on which the film were based, really happened. Hardly one of its critics does.

One hesitant reviewer defends the film on the most crucial charge: 'I don't think that *Redacted* is an anti-soldier movie at all in reality. Most of the soldiers are disenchanted with the war, just want to go home and want nothing to do with the rape and want nothing more than to see justice done, but are forced to stay quiet. We get to see some scenes where one soldier is being persuaded by his father, an army man, to keep quiet, and an attack on his story by military superiors when he attempts to tell them.' But this is to reduce the film to an accretion of parts – the whole escapes him.

Critics, on the other hand, do not see any value in the film's techniques at all. They step straight past these, to see only 'walking stereotypes' that 'poorly reflect how real American soldiers conduct themselves'. This is not open to debate.[6] Thus the film's aesthetic techniques become irrelevant, they are just 'plain bad film-making', 'poor execution': 'Just because *Redacted* is a "fake" documentary does not excuse it from the same criteria we give actual documentaries as well as all films in general'. And once again it turns on the issue of how we are entitled to think about 'American soldiers'. This transcends the politics of the war, as perfectly captured in this refusal of the film: 'I am not an advocate of the war in Iraq nor of our current administration (Bush) BUT I am a supporter of our troops, and I feel that this was a cheap shot against the vast number of soldiers that did not act like this'. It is conceptually inconceivable, even if true.

What *Redacted* reveals more generally is that, while soldiers' videos were to provide the distinctive look for fiction films of the Iraq war, they must not do this without large amounts of mediation. It is not simply a matter of cleaning out the unpleasant parts. Soldiers' self-filming had to become a new and special way for us to look at them, the means of accessing what I call an 'Iraq war experience'.

MODELLING AN 'IRAQ WAR EXPERIENCE'

I want to outline a model for addressing these films, with nine aspects. The rest of the book will, I hope, demonstrate its value. At the heart of these films, I suggest, is the construction of an American 'Iraq war experience', within which (1) soldiers are authenticated by being shown as ordinary. Being seen filming themselves in revealing ways (being crude, and so on) proves that a film is not sentimentalising them. But (2) the moment they step out of their bases, they become naïve innocents, stunned by the hostility they encounter. (3) Returning home to America, what they take back is the personal impact of that split, carried as stress and disconnection from civilian life. Next are three elements, constituting the 'Narrative account of motives'. Within this, (4) officers are presented as placemen, driving their men cynically into terrible situations, but primarily concerned with protecting the military's reputation. (5) The films therefore commonly show ordinary soldiers expressing confusion about the purposes of the war, sometimes directly challenging why they are there. (6) Often intruding without a diegetic role (for instance, on television screens), they (and we) catch glimpses of other forces in play – political, economic, bureaucratic – which are working behind their backs. Finally, there are three components to the ways soldiers may thus become 'moral heroes'. First, (7) soldiers are shown bonding with each other, giving this as their first loyalty. Officers, politicians, civilians all fail them. They are effectively alone, unwanted, sacrificial victims. They can therefore (8) be presented as struggling to hold on to values in the face of all that happens around them. And in extremis (9) special figures – perhaps representatives of minorities of one kind or another – will stand out, who can embody perfectly a new kind of soldier: the hero-victim.

Looking across all 23 films, Table 2 emerges. As I discuss each one in greater detail in the rest of the book, I hope the point and accuracy of my codings will become evident. A tick (✓) means that the film clearly and directly displays a feature. A dash (–) says that while it may be partly implied, it is not directly present, but nothing is present which conflicts at all with it. A cross (×) indicates the definite absence of the feature, and probably something in direct contradiction with it. These marks appear across each row in the same order as points (1) to (9) above.

What does this table show? It suggests, first, a core of films sharing common themes. Eight films have at least six ticks, with no crosses. Several others suggest, through the presence of dashes, that features might have been there, but are instead assumed as background. There are a small number with a significant proportion of crosses. It will emerge that this is for different reasons. Three are examined in Chapter 9, on Outliers. Others, upon close scrutiny, prove complicated. *Badland*, for instance, may withhold direct showing of an 'Iraq experience', but it will emerge that this is part of a narrative strategy designed to unsettle and disturb. Other important features will emerge as I explore individual films – in particular, the ways in which each film deploys particular narrative devices that, I will show, are rooted in their particular production circumstances, but which play crucial roles in securing this model in each case. However, the critical element in the model here is without question the address to 'what an American soldier is' and how each film handles this. This, I will argue in Chapter 4, is significantly new, and a significant ideological shift.

Table 2   Film presentations of America's 'Iraq Experience'

Title	'Iraq war' experience	Narrative account of motives	Moral 'heroes'
American Soldiers	– ✓ ✓	– ✓ –	✓ ✓ ✓
The Jacket	✗ – ✗	– ✗ –	✓ ✗ ✗
Home of the Brave	– ✓ ✓	– ✓ –	✓ ✓ ✓
The Situation	✗ ✗ ✓	✓ ✓ ✓	✗ ✓ ✗
GI Jesús	✓ ✓ ✓	✓ ✓ –	– ✓ ✓
The Marine	✓ ✗ ✓	✓ ✗ ✗	✗ – ✗
Badland	– ✗ ✓	✓ ✓ –	✓ ✓ –
Battle for Haditha	✓ ✓ ✓	✓ ✓ –	✓ ✓ ✓
Grace Is Gone	– – ✓	– ✓ ✓	– – ✓
In the Valley of Elah	✓ ✓ ✓	✓ ✓ ✓	✓ – ✓
The Kingdom	– – –	✓ ✓ ✓	– ✓ –
Lions for Lambs	– ✓ ✓	✓ ✓ ✓	✓ ✓
The Mark of Cain	✓ ✗ ✓	✓ ✓ ✓	✓ ✓ –
Redacted	✓ ✗ ✓	✓ – ✓	✓ ✗ ✗
Rendition	– – –	✓ ✓ ✓	– ✓ ✗
Day Zero	– – –	✓ ✓ ✓	– – ✓
Conspiracy	– ✓ ✓	✓ ✓ ✓	✓ ✓ ✓
The Lucky Ones	✓ ✓ ✓	– ✓ ✓	✓ ✓ ✓
Stop-Loss	✓ ✓ ✓	✓ ✓ ✓	✓ ✓ ✓
War, Inc.	– – –	✓ ✓ ✓	– – –
Body of Lies	– – –	✓ ✓ ✓	– ✓ –
The Objective	✗ ✗ ✗	✗ ✓ ✗	✓ ✓ –
The Hurt Locker	✓ ✓ –	✗ ✗ ✗	✓ ✓ ✗

4

From Doughboys to Grunts: the 'American soldier'

Running like a thread through the films, is the figure of the 'American soldier'. It is time to address this figure directly. What histories underlie and underpin it? What is tied up in it – and what is excluded by it? To tell this story, I am relying heavily on the other researchers' work, but there are aspects that I want to emphasise which have been neglected.

Its relevance relates to a question I posed at this book's outset: why make these films as fictions, when so much work goes in almost all cases into establishing their bases in fact? It means considering the most telling difference between fiction and documentary. Documentaries inevitably introduce the messiness of 'the real': the complexity of individuals, their back-stories, and their motivations. They draw on muddling intersections and conflicts of groups, interests and policies. Fictions create and control their own. Through the kinds of characters they create, through the motivations they depict and invoke, and the life-stories they hint at, they free fictions from the possible kinds of inspection and complaint which hit Michael Moore's *Fahrenheit 9/11*. Real figures may turn out to have feet of saints, or of clay. Fictional characters may be charged with being simplistic, stereotypes or caricatures. But they cannot easily 'lie'. And if a fiction film can add in some authenticating claims – ties to the real world, without professing to be literal transcriptions – there are additional benefits.

Fictions can work even better if they draw on representative types of character whom audiences are likely to feel they recognise. These can be of many kinds. There can be 'ordinary folks', whose looks and styles, whose pictures of the world and ways of behaving seem believable because we feel we have met them before. Then there are iconic, even mythic constructs that embody what we would *like* characters to be like. These are often embodied in successful star-images. Many war films use a combination of these two. The tasks of war are set and it is the job of the soldiers to find the means to fulfil them. Frequently, as many analysts have shown, this is done by having an iconic star-figure take on the task of welding a diverse group of soldiers into a unit. They do not mind being soldiers, but they do not yet know how to do so effectively. Their ordinariness is transcended by encountering and working under the exceptional star-figure, who guarantees that the qualities they offer are credible, right and effective.

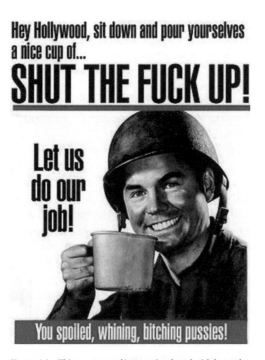

Figure 4.1   This un-sourced image circulated widely on the Internet up until 2010. A reference to a line in the comedy *Happy Gilmore* (dir. Dennis Dugan, 1996) is combined with a World War II poster encouraging rationing. The use of the smiling 'GI' image, representing plain, honest and committed soldiers, speaking in unapologetically offensive terms to a singular 'Hollywood' epitomises the way images of 'the American Soldier' can be deployed in political argument.

There are, of course, other types of character: loners, outsiders, rebels. There are troubled individuals looking for some kind of salvation. There are historic figures around whom stories unfold. The point is that fictionalisation allows an emphasis on their distinctive capacities, of whatever kinds, to make their difference. 'Figures' can assemble meanings, possibilities, wishes and hopes around them, and make them emotionally more satisfactory. I propose to look at the history of the 'American soldier' from this angle.

AMERICAN SOLDIERS IN WORLD WAR I

The story effectively begins with American entry into the World War I, in 1916. More than 3 million young men were drafted to the European war, and over 80,000 died. With many coming from areas of America which had for generations lost contact with their European past, they had little grasp of what the war was about. They quickly became known as the 'Doughboys'. The origins of the term have been debated.[1] In its early days the ascription was certainly sometimes mocking, but by the time of the Great War there is evidence that the term was now self-applied, 'from the ground up'. If there was a clear signification to the term, it was the implied *massification* of the soldiers, their loss of differentiation, along with a sense of a trudging and grudging participation in the horrors of the war.

This became a real issue when American soldiers showed the kinds of discontent that were found among British 'Tommies'. Two books (Hallas 2000; Keene 2003) well capture the discontents and 'low morale' (an expression representing how those in authority conceptualise and try to manage ordinary anger) experienced in particular by infantrymen. Hallas especially captures the meanings that the term had for soldiers. His collection of soldiers' letters and recollections shows their responses to all aspects of the war: from recruitment, through training and transport, struggles for food, reflections on military censorship, to their encounters with the French and the experience of fighting. Hallas displays the ways in which the soldiers became aware of themselves as a group, as a *kind* of soldier, with common experiences: 'It was an experience that would bind them together for all time' (Hallas 2000:195):

> The doughboy in France whenever possible avoids saluting. He could spot an officer a block away, no matter how crowded the walk; at the psychological moment he would turn to a shop window and gaze whatever was exposed.
>
> ...
>
> When the officer has passed, he would take up the stroll. (Hallas 2000:212–13)

As a small, shared act of resistance, this emphasised their shared 'ordinariness'.

The image of the 'Doughboy' lingered on in a series of minor films – all comedies. Bud Fisher (of 'Mutt and Jeff' fame) made an animated film *The Doughboy* in 1918. Another such animation, *The Doughboy* (dir. James D. Davis, 1926), and a Buster Keaton comedy, *Doughboys* (dir. Edward Sedgwick, 1930), followed. *Bosko the Doughboy* (dir. Hugh Harman, 1931) captures and repeats the spirit of these films: using stock comedy figures, it depicts soldiers as bewildered survivors hanging on to their lives and hopes in the face of a war that has been made to look mock-awful.[2] Things do not much change until after the entry into World War II. As late as 1941, Robert Clampett's animated *Meet John Doughboy*[3] updates the figure to its time, having Porky Pig displaying modern military gadgetry. Perhaps revealingly, the last two films to use the moniker are not about war at all, but are set at home. *Johnny Doughboy* (dir. John H. Auer, 1942) hardly connects with the military at all – it is the story of an aspiring actress whose double gets to play before an audience of GIs. The other is again a comedy featuring the well-known Three Stooges who find themselves up against Nazi spies in typical incompetent but ultimately effective manner: the film is entitled *No Dough Boys* (dir. Jules White, 1944). It is as if the term is being withdrawn and sequestered, to open the way for the new term: the GI.

The way through was charted in particular by one major film, which looked back to World War I and found in it the kind of heroism that would be sought for the coming conflict: Howard Hawks' *Sergeant York* (1941). Starring the fast-rising Gary Cooper, the film was based on the real story of Alvin York, the war's most-decorated soldier who was drafted despite his religious objections to fighting. Overcoming his internal conflict between duties to God and America, York went on to use his exceptional marksmanship to help win a seemingly lost battle. In the context of an America hesitating on the brink of joining World War II, York's story clearly resonated powerfully, and the film was seen as powerful recruiting material. Koppes and Black write: 'In 1940 [Jesse] Lasky again approached the ageing hero, telling him that a film about his life would be an inspiration to young men undergoing the same crises of conscience he had experienced' (1987:57). When the film was released, York marched down Broadway with an honour guard of World War I veterans for the premiere, and an eight-page recruitment pamphlet was given out to young men in the film's audiences.[4]

York's story attains its complexity from his initial unwillingness to fight. Necessity, rather than reflex patriotism, pushes him into battle. In World War II there was a figure who could be said to have embodied York without that blemish of questioning: Audie Murphy. Murphy became in his turn the most decorated soldier of World War II, having concealed his age so he could volunteer at 16. Winning a string of medals, Murphy was invited to Hollywood and became a major figure, including starring in a film of his own war-time exploits, *To Hell and Back* (dir. Jesse Hibbs, 1955). But – probably at Murphy's insistence – the film has an edge of grim realism to it, as soldiers are wounded, suffer and die. Although it was a huge box office success, it was not a picture of unmitigated patriotic heroism. Although Murphy bulks large as a hero, he never came to embody the *idea of heroism*.

Another figure who would serve far better to encapsulate what was needed to turn GIs into full American soldiers emerged: John Wayne. Wayne's story, told by many biographers but particularly brilliantly by Gary Wills (1997), runs far beyond his individual life, into the 'institution' he became.

JOHN WAYNE

Born Marion Morrison in 1907, and making a slow entry as a bit-part actor in Westerns from the end of the 1920s, Wayne made his breakthrough when picked by John Ford to star in *Stagecoach* (1939). Almost certainly because he wanted to guard his newly-achieved star status, Wayne managed to sidestep enlistment for the entire period of the war. Yet the military always welcomed him and even gave him awards for service. Wayne became synonymous with how the US military wanted to be seen, and his services as an actor for military parts were greatly sought. Wayne played the star-soldier in at least a dozen World War II-set films.

There can be no doubt about the impact that Wayne had on many American men. In 1997, the BBC broadcast a documentary on John Wayne in its *Reputations* series. The programme opens with on a clip from his *Sands of Iwo Jima* (dir. Allan Dwan, 1949), pulling back to show a cinema full of Marine recruits, four of whom offer brief verdicts on what Wayne means to them: 'When I watch a John Wayne movie, I get a sense of what it's like to be an American.' 'I love this movie. I've seen this movie about ten times already. One day I decided, hell, why not, join up.' 'John Wayne is an inspiration beyond belief. I've grown up my whole life just wanting to ... just the example of *Sands of Iwo Jima* is mind-boggling.' 'I think that John Wayne is an American hero, and that he presents and lives the values and the ideals of the Corps, and that he represents them very finely in this movie.' (BBC1 1997) It is for this very reason that we need to think of the significance of the oft-repeated tales of Vietnam vets laughing when they saw Wayne's characterisation of that war in *The Green Berets* (dir. Ray Kellogg, John Wayne & Mervyn LeRoy). This was a fallen god, not just a poor film.

This aspect is well captured in Lloyd Lewis' *The Tainted War* (1985).[5] This book analysed 19 narratives (a combination of novels, personal memoirs and oral histories) of the Vietnam war and claimed to find within them evidence of the war being assessed against failing 'old cultural maps', in particular deriving from World War II, seen as morally purposeful and cleanly fought. Lewis wrote:

> More than any other single factor in the Vietnam War literature, the media (especially motion pictures) served to initiate young American males into the mysteries of war, the purposes war is supposed to accomplish, and the role one is expected to adopt within that war. (Lewis 1985:22)

And no-one is seen to embody and solve these 'mysteries' more than Wayne. Tobey Herzog (1992:16–24) explores this in some detail in his 'innocence lost' account of the war, as does Katherine Kinney (2000), in her study of the 'harm done to America' by its involvement in Vietnam. Kinney identifies Wayne as a trope of disappointment in summarising the meaning of the war for America. It seems that both while he was alive and after his death in 1979, Wayne's very particular soldier persona became a measure of what was wrong. In Wayne's image, wars were fought on clear moral premises in which right was unarguably on America's side. Soldiers fight without fear or quarter, but without hatred; with respect for human dignity and for the differences between combatants and civilians, women and children.

SANDS OF IWO JIMA

One film best illustrates my argument: *Sands of Iwo Jima*. Produced by 'poverty row' Republic Studio in 1949, it was made in close collaboration with the Marines just as they were beginning to jostle for a presence in the US military high command (a campaign which led also to the eventual funding of the giant memorial statue in Washington).[6] The film tells the story of the build-up to the American assault on the island, largely via Wayne's story as Sergeant Stryker. Stryker is a tough dedicated soldier given the task of turning a squad of half-hearted soldiers into a fighting unit, while contending with his own personal despairs over the break-up of his family and loss of contact with his son. At the crux of the film is the re-enactment of the flag-planting immortalised in Joe Rosenthal's photograph.

The Iwo Jima photograph – argued by many to be the best known and most widely reproduced, reworked and parodied of all time – has been widely analysed.[7] Six unidentifiable men put their backs into planting a large US flag, which rears into a symbolically huge sky out of a war slag-heap. The visual power of the photograph is unarguable, and its reuse in hundreds of different forms ever since is direct testimony to this. One of the issues that confronted the image was the continuously-circulating rumour that the photograph, because it captured the planting of a second, larger flag, might have been staged.[8] Gary Wills argues that the issue became particularly important because the Marine Corps was very keen to raise its standing within the American military. Not having been the subject of any of the first wave of postwar combat films, they saw *Sands* as a vital opportunity, and were willing to invest more than $1 million in material support to Republic, upon an assurance that the film would be 'properly heroic'. Interestingly, Wayne may not have been Republic's first choice for the part of Stryker; that seems to have been Kirk Douglas. But the Marines wanted Wayne, and lobbied for him to have the role.[9] They also required, as a condition for their support, that the film emphasise the flag-planting as captured in the Rosenthal image. This required some reworking of the initial screenplay.

Wayne's image by this time was well-established. Here was a man who encapsulated a certain image of American masculinity. Built in 'the West', he was the perfect frontiersman. Straight-shooting and plain-speaking, he combined total courage, absolute ethical principles and overwhelming physical authority, along with old-fashioned courtesy towards women. Wayne physically commanded any scene he appeared in, and directors and cinematographers endlessly played to this. There was also his unquestioning patriotism. These provided a frame of associations for Stryker's characterisation. By the time the film was emerging in 1949, the story of Iwo Jima and its heroes was widely known. Republic worked hard to capitalise on that, using the surviving soldiers as part of their marketing campaign. Marling and Wetenhall (1991) give a full account of the nationwide tours to open the film, successful in that *Sands* went on to gross nearly $4 million in domestic box office. But although it was not yet the public issue it would become later, it was already known that Wayne had not fought in the war. His role in the film therefore had to be managed carefully.

Stryker is shown to have weaknesses. His family-life is broken. He has a drink problem. Yet these never impinge on his military abilities. The enemy is invisible in the film; we hardly see a Japanese soldier, and they are not discussed. The point is, rather, the making of real soldiers out of a half-motivated, half-disciplined mixed ethnic group. This is Wayne's/Stryker's task. The flag-planting scene comes after the mayhem of fighting for the island, with shellings, bombings, flame-throwings (many of them using actual news footage) and a slow progress up the heavily-defended slopes of Mount Suribachi. Stryker's unit receives the command to plant the famous flag, to signal that the mountain is captured. Here, the film faced its problem: the flag-planting was a real event. The identity of the six ordinary soldiers who had planted it was known. Not only was Wayne/Stryker not among them, but Wayne had not served at all. Stryker therefore has to die. He has completed his mission: the mix of ordinary soldiers, GI Joes, has become a disciplined unit. As they sit on the mountainside, one group – including cameo appearances of the three real survivors – sets out to plant the flag. The remainder pause for a smoke. One asks how the Sergeant feels. Stryker replies that he has never felt better in his life. And at that moment a sniper's bullet through the heart allows him to die a properly clean World War II death. No mess, no wounds, no blood: just, exit. As his troop gather round his body, they find an unfinished letter to his son, and – in a breaking voice – one of them reads it out. When it winds to a halt, he says: 'Guess he didn't have time to finish it. Well, I'll finish it for him'. But first there is the business of the flag.

The presence of the three original soldiers was made much of in the marketing campaign. But they only play a walk-on role. The *meanings* of the event had to be seen through the reactions of the fictional-ordinary characters. 'There she goes', calls out one soldier. And in a timed row, each to a musical chord, they turn to honour the moment with their eyes. The flag is planted exactly as in the photograph – even pausing on its way to the vertical at the precise position the photograph captured. And, to ensure that the planting is utterly 'clean' of any implications of being staged, here there is only the one flag-planting and no camera crews on hand to record it. Only the men's eyes do that, wearily but adoringly, before they turn back into the battle. Then the soldier whom Stryker has most brought on, almost replacing the son he had lost, takes over his command. 'Awright', he calls in a cracked voice, 'saddle up!' – evoking just for a moment Wayne's iconic expression in his Western roles. Wayne has returned from beyond his necessary death to provide the spirit and motive for ongoing military courage. To a stirring sonorous male voice choir singing the Marines' anthem 'The Halls of Montezuma', they move off into the smoke to complete the mission.

This well summarises the ways in which war films dealt with America's past and role. There is a careful stage-management of the relationship between the real and the fictional. Authentication is offered by the presence of the three real soldiers. As in so many World War II films, the ordinary soldiers are a mix of various parts of America, occasionally 'bravely' including a black or Hispanic soldier. The hero has to be above that, and to lift them above it, too. No-one embodied this ability more than Wayne. Marling and Wetenhall suggest that there is a precision to the image which Wayne embodies:

> The emphasis on Stryker's unheroic professionalism – the training, the drill, the routine – may stem from the close advisory relationship between Republic and the Marine Corps. Wayne's character ... anticipates an emerging trend in Pentagon thinking: in the 1950s, the Defense Department came to believe that national security was best ensured by the creation of a professional military elite, untouched by the passions and politics of civilian life. Whether or not such ideas were current in Hollywood in 1949, the Marine decision to support production of *Sands of Iwo Jima* was predicated on a script in which John M. Stryker exemplifies the new, post-war warrior (Marling & Wetenhall 1991:136).

Thus, there is more to this than simply a story of a very successful movie star. The American military, by the time of World War II, were intensely aware that they *needed* figures like Wayne. Why?

SAMUEL STOUFFER AND *THE AMERICAN SOLDIER*

As America inched towards entry into the war, one of the notable acts of the American high command was the establishment of a

Research Bureau within its 'Morale Division', under the directorship of sociologist Samuel Stouffer.[10] This was just one part of a much wider recruitment of appropriate academics into other fields, perhaps most notably communications, and propaganda analysis.[11] Stouffer, a brilliant research designer and analyst, led a team whose brief was to explore soldiers' understanding of the war and, in particular, their motivation to fight. Working within the emergent paradigm of American sociology which emphasised prediction, and thereby intervention and management, of social processes (within a broader theoretical frame emphasising the need to sustain 'balance' and remove conflict), Stouffer's style of research had several key facets. He emphasised the need to keep research tightly focused. He put the concept of 'attitudes' at the heart of his programme. And he developed a concept which allowed a subtle depoliticisation of discontent: the concept of 'relative deprivation'. 'Relative deprivation' suggests that people estimate their own status and position by measuring themselves against surrounding reference groups. So, notions of absolute inequality, of hierarchy, power and ideology, become replaced by close examination of (and, of course, attempts to influence) those whom people compare themselves with. Here is how Stouffer describes in retrospect one of their key studies:

> For the benefit of those who think (a) that behaviour is unpredictable and (b) that complex attitudes cannot be measured, may I offer one illustration? Before D-Day we surveyed the attitudes of men in 108 rifle companies of four divisions in England. All these companies landed in Normandy on D-Day or within the next four days. From the daily morning reports of these companies in the first two months in France it was possible account for each man among those making the invasion. Then we could compute for each company a nonbattle casualty rate – the number of nonbattle casualties (many, if not most of which were psychiatric or psychosomatic cases) divided by the average daily strength. What did we find? We found that, if in a given regiment with nine rifle companies, we picked those companies with the worst attitudes before D-Day, these three companies were destined to have a 60 per cent higher nonbattle casualty rate in France, on the average, than the three companies in the same regiment with the best attitudes. (Stouffer 1962:8)

'Attitude' here is made to seem a neutral measure of will-to-fight. A different picture emerges through the cracks as Stouffer reports another aspect of their research: investigations of enlisted men's 'attitudes' towards their officers, in the US and on the war fronts. This was a concern throughout the war, and became a sufficiently hot potato to lead to the creation of a Board of Investigation under General Doolittle in 1946, after soldiers' complaints about a virtual caste system affecting food and drink, clothing, accommodation and recreational facilities became a topic of debate at home. Stouffer reproduces some of the enlisted men's comments. One, a not atypical one, reads thus:

> It is said that the American soldier is fighting for freedom and justice and equality. Somehow the army represents the very things we are fighting against. Such as: Everything is special for the officer (as if their bodies are more genteel or fragile than ours); a nurse is frowned upon if she associates with an enlisted man; even the Non Coms are urged to stay in a station above the 'common herd'. Better establish a little justice and equality. (quoted in Stouffer 1962:33–4)

This is not the language of relative deprivation. This is a soldier spotting contradictions in an overarching political ideology. But that is not Stouffer's reading, and he was even keen to say that his Bureau could have solved the problem before it became a public issue. That last is highly debatable. In a droll history of official American psychology, Ellen Marken has reconsidered the role of specialists like Stouffer. She notes the repeated efforts by the military authorities to counteract what their researchers discovered: that perhaps as many as 80 per cent of soldiers didn't know or indeed care about what they were fighting for. A series of special films, the 'Why We Fight' series (1943–45), was made by Frank Capra to try to alleviate this, but again the Research Bureau's enquiries showed that while they increased *knowledge* about war plans,[12] they failed to raise 'morale'.

Irrationality, however, was only the beginning of the bad news. To all appearances, US soldiers were motivated by the same primitive feelings and loyalties, the same absence of conscious and reasonable motivation, and the same ominous emotional attachments to authority figures that had been identified as such alarming traits in the German and Japanese national characters. The influence of the soldier's immediate group and the calibre of his immediate leaders were found to be the most salient factors in morale. From this, an unflattering portrait of the ordinary soldier gradually materialised. He was preoccupied with physical discomforts, displayed all sorts of aggression and worried most about moving up the chain of command, making more money and staying out of combat. This was not exactly the democratic warrior the experts hoped to find.[13]

It's easy to see why Stouffer might have found his interventionist proposals barely palatable. To a military elite well-rooted in American financial and political hierarchies, this picture of soldiers looked just fine – as long as they still fought. Better, perhaps, to pander a bit to the soldiers' desire for close-up 'authority figures'. Intended or not, planned or accidental, the emergence of a figure like John Wayne was just the ticket, and he was loved by the American military with no questions asked about his war record.

'WAYNE' AFTER WAYNE

Long before his death in 1979, Wayne had entered the realm of legend. Streets were named after him, children had their futures mapped by being called after him (some of these becoming troublingly notable: John Wayne Bobbitt (of the snipped penis), Fox (a controversial Congressman) and Gacy (the serial killer) being obvious examples).

Alongside these, however, went many metaphorical references, showing the extent to which Wayne had become iconic, signified most obviously in phrases such as 'we weren't John Waynes', 'doing a John Wayne', 'with a dash of John Wayne', or instructions like 'don't John Wayne it'. What these reveal is a series of conflicts over his meanings, whose dominant version is of Wayne as plain-speaking, no-nonsense, clear-headed and competent, with a gritty face towards pain or difficulty, utterly moral, a 'perfect American' – to which is counterposed a critical stance on him as bull-headed, unthinking and hyper-patriotic, a badly cleaned-up myth of how America likes to see itself. An example captures the tensions inside this well. The Cleveland *Plain Dealer* commented on a proposed law to exempt people who use guns in 'self-defence' from prosecution: 'Supporters of the proposal have given it a name that would make John Wayne proud: the "stand your ground" law.' (Martin & Johnston 2007) It is a nice example of Wayne's image as a battleground – to appeal to his name is to appeal to a set of ideas, here, about (over-)simplicity covering up a very questionable purpose.

No irony appeared to attach to Wayne himself, however. So, when in 1950 he won a place in the Hollywood Walk of Fame, no-one appears to have commented on any paradox in the casting of his commemorative block from sand from Iwo Jima; it seemed as if the cinematic version of the events had altogether superseded the real history. 'From now on, the man who evaded World War II service would be the symbolic man who *won* World War II' (Wills 1997:156).

For a long time, 'John Wayne' ruled. But this was at a price. 'Wayne' could increasingly become tied to the fortunes of those who appeared to use and profit from his image. And as we come into the period of the Iraq wars, we can see this quite clearly. A study of US newspapers across the period 1998–2008 reveals a curious pattern.[14] Post-9/11, Graph 1 reveals a rise in mentions of his name, reaching its high point in 2004. This continues high until 2006, but then sharply diminishes. To see the extent and significance of this trend, remember that there is a continuous 'background noise' of mentions of 'John Wayne' by virtue of references to the airport, streets, people and other things named after him. Allowing for these, suggests that metaphorical uses of his name shift dramatically across the period.

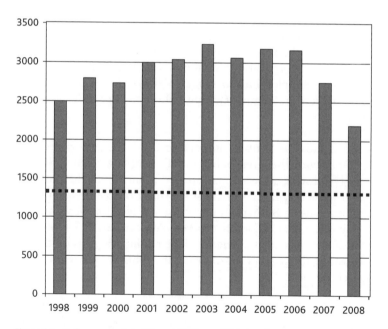

Figure 4.2   References to 'John Wayne' (US Press, 1998–2008). Figures in this graph were obtained by searching the Nexis Press database for all US Press, using the search expression 'John Wayne'. The broken line is intended to indicate the likely level of 'background noise' generated by references to things such as John Wayne Airport, or individuals named after the actor.

The start of the change is the death of Ronald Reagan in 2004. Reagan, himself a former actor in Westerns, had been widely seen as trying to recruit to his image elements of a Wayne-like machismo, as these examples from obituaries indicate:

In 1983, former Sen. George McGovern [D-S.D.] denounced Reagan as 'the most reckless and dangerous president since the end of World War II' and predicted 'we are drifting toward war and I mean nuclear war.' 'I don't think [Reagan] understands diplomacy at all,' McGovern said. 'He's a shoot-from-the-hip, macho John Wayne type. His experience with war is limited to Hollywood'. (Kondracke 2004)

Reagan played a patriotic, John Wayne-style role that only he, the Great Communicator, could have managed. And most Americans loved him for it, handing him 44 states in his 1980 campaign and 49 four years later. Or rather, they loved the image. (Melton 2004)

There is in these a great deal of reflection on the operation of images, with the implicit question what those images might be withholding, or hiding. Perhaps most importantly, these reassessments were spilling onto George Bush, and his political and military adventures. Take one example: the *San Francisco Chronicle* used a popular public lecture by linguist George Lakoff to capture part of this mood:

Lakoff advises political liberals to think metaphorically, not simply with their reasoning minds, and come out swinging. So Hendricks, a lawyer, has created a line about the president and John Wayne. 'There are some smart people in Washington who are using Bush as a puppet John Wayne,' he ventured at a club meeting after Lakoff's speech. 'We can say, as Lakoff, that Bush has weakened the nation. Their John Wayne is destroyed. Without the perception of strength, John Wayne is nothing.' (DelVecchio 2004)

From 2004 onward, an equation of Bush with a fake use of Wayne gathered force. There is a repeated use of phrasings such as these: 'Eschewing Bush-esque John Wayne-isms in true antihero form ... While the John Wayne impulse is appealing, we have to be careful'. The Wayne–Bush equation was now damaging to all parties. Wayne appears more as a bloated, manipulable icon. Bush looks like a thin silhouette hiding behind him. Even some rightwing commentators had now to acknowledge that a reference to Wayne no longer constituted a guaranteed shared appeal:

> Jim Hubbard, director of the conservative, Dallas-based American Renaissance Film Festival, has not yet seen all of the new films but is afraid they will represent a singular, liberal point of view. 'A lot of them deal with the tragedy of war and, for lack of a better term, moral relativism. Where's the John Wayne movie?' he asks. 'I have no problem with any of these films coming out, but there should be films from every perspective. In the Vietnam War, there was at least one film that was taking the side of the American as hero: *The Green Berets*. It was a propaganda film, and I'm not saying we should return to the '40s and '50s where everything is glorious. But there is no balance'. (Darling 2007)

Wayne = 'propaganda': a revealing shift. But the people who might be suffering the most as a result are – many now argued – the soldiers, who were suffering precisely because of this exaggerated play of images:

> The word Hero is overused these days, at a time when the military is back in favor and many hesitate to criticize foreign policy for fear of being accused of not supporting the troops. But those serving in the military – all of them volunteers, remember – aren't all necessarily heroes in the John Wayne sense of the word. They all deserve respect for doing a difficult job, a job most of their fellow citizens are happy to leave to somebody else. (*Arkansas Democrat-Gazette* 2004)

Wayne was OK for films, but as a political image he was becoming too tainted. And the remarkable thing is the virtual absence of any appeals to 'Wayne' in or around the Iraq War movies.

FROM THE GREEN BERETS TO RAMBO

The first major challenge and change to the Wayne image came in the late 1960s – precisely as Wayne himself was stumbling into his inept *The Green Berets* – with the release of *The Dirty Dozen* (dir. Robert Aldrich, 1967). Here, the soldiers are not ordinary and do not want to fight – but have to be made to. They are transformed against their will into a deadly fighting force by the tough-as-nails

Major Reisman (Lee Marvin), himself an anti-authority maverick. Unrelentingly disciplinarian, he binds them to each other. This was a challenge to the notion that a figure like Wayne could by force of personality alone reach and transform the ordinary guys. Now they had to be threatened and manipulated into military action. But the characters of the condemned men also had some 'disturbing' features: the black soldier (Robert Jefferson, played by Jim Brown) who has been condemned to death for defending himself against a racist officer ... the religious nutter (Archer Maggott, played by Telly Savalas) who will ultimately compromise their mission and have to be shot by another soldier ... the ethnic soldier (Joseph Wladislaw, played by Charles Bronson) facing death for shooting a deserting senior officer. *The Dirty Dozen* showed the significance of class and ethnic differences and experiences among soldiers. That was a dangerous can of worms to open. But no individual 'figure' emerged from the film, and its successors (for example, *Kelly's Heroes* [dir. Brian G. Hutton, 1970]) were pale comparisons.

It took a different strand to begin to form a lasting alternative to Wayne's charisma: the Green Berets. And they would do this in the teeth of Wayne's awful eponymous film about them. In a summary essay, Alasdair Spark (1984) has traced the evolution of the mythology of the Green Beret. He outlines its origins in the early 1960s rescue of the corps from near-extinction by John F. Kennedy, who saw in them the potential embodiment of his 'noble' military/ideological war on communism. Across the 1960s, they were promoted and fictionalised by Robin Moore's novel *The Green Berets*, which lovingly retails the corps' view of itself, then by John Wayne's rather different film of the novel. While in Moore's account, Green Berets were a multi-skilled, ideologically-trained elite who knew and even admired their enemy, but ignored all rules to 'do the job', under pressure from the military the film carefully legalises them. The Vietcong become simple thugs, the Green Berets only taking action when the local population is threatened. And where in the book the local South Vietnamese are corrupt, in the film that corruption has been transferred to the North Vietnamese.

In the 1970s, as the Corps itself declined, partly through dilution, partly through its own failures, so Spark shows the mythic figure transferred to a separated sphere of popular culture. In a series of novels and films the myth now centred on returning vets, who use their deadly survival skills but also display their outsider/ elite attitudes by inflicting vengeance on an uncaring America for any refusal to acknowledge their sacrifices. But it was these very attitudes which produced the next version of the myth, in the figure of John Rambo. Sylvester Stallone's hero appeared in four films (*First Blood* [dir. Ted Kotcheff, 1982]; *Rambo: First Blood Part II* [dir. George P. Cosmatos, 1985]; *Rambo: First Blood Part III* [dir. Peter MacDonald, 1988]; *Rambo* [dir. Sylvester Stallone, 2008]). A great deal has been said about these by film scholars and I have little to add to their accounts. Rambo as an individual embodied sullen determined resistance to what he saw as a great betrayal of America by weak politicians and generals. Using just brute force, he would take on what they were too cowardly to do. In the first film he is just the outsider, rejected by the country he has just served and using his honed skills to exact revenge on those who maltreat him. Finally captured after being reached by the only person who understands him, his former commander, he faces a future of convict labour. At the start of the second film, when he meets his old mentor prior to being sent on his mission to rescue putative MIAs, his muttered 'Do we get to win this time?' became emblematic of a bitter rejection of all that he had been told the war was about. The duplicity, cover-ups and incompetence he subsequently has to battle against, and of course the viciousness the film attributes to the North Vietnamese who capture and torture him, all conspire to make the film a perfect expression of all the wish-fulfilling loathing which many disgruntled Americans were feeling. Rambo fed powerfully into the rising conspiracy theories about missing-in-action US servicemen who must be imprisoned in post-war Vietnam. Denied and dismissed by officers and politicians alike; Rambo deploys all the skills and loner instincts of the mythic Green Beret to go alone, endure the pain, and enact the rescue. The image resonated strongly. Spark brilliantly shows how the two films which marked the completion of the rise of Vietnam War to the 'Big Picture' (large scenarios, and larger-than-life characters) – *The Deerhunter* (dir. Michael Cimino, 1978) and *Apocalypse Now* – are both premised on embodying in a central character (Michael in the former, Kurtz, self-destructively, in the latter) of all the qualities and attributes assembled in the mythic Green Beret. The evolution is 'completed', he argues, with the appearance of the TV series *The A-Team* (by Stephen J. Cannell Productions & Universal TV, originally shown 1983–7) in which, weekly, the four on-the-run ex-special forces servicemen use their exceptional skills to undertake a 'mission', defeat corruption and help the innocent.[15] Spark's argument is that the figure of the Green Beret gradually lost its hold. Beginning as an embodiment of confident ideological commitment, ultimately it declined to become a figure of cheerful cartoon-ish popular entertainment.

Somehow, though, 'Rambo' lived on. In a striking essay on the Rambo mythology, Gregory Waller (1988) captures well some of the features of *Rambo II* (1985) and Stallone's character within it. Surly, defiant, and refusing any markers of military discipline, his body bared but winning by animal cunning, Rambo single-handedly defeats all his enemies – but there is no real resolution, and he cannot return to America, because he knows himself to be unloved. The implication, of course, was that this is a pyrrhic victory. Rambo is not just an outsider; now, he is outside. Waller captures the amount of cultural noise that greeted the Stallone film. People wondered endlessly what this all meant. The huge popularity of the film, in the face of overwhelming critical rejection, scared cultural observers. *Newsweek*, for instance, put Rambo on its cover, for a major discussion in December 1985 (see Schechter & Semeiks 1991). It placed Rambo in line of descent from the original frontiersmen. His figure came veiled in feelings of myth. It is a myth, however, which looks backward, to what might have been but cannot ever be.

Stallone's Rambo did not spring fully-formed from nothing. In a prescient essay written before his first film emerged, Auster and Quart (1981) examined the cycle of Vietnam films up to 1981. They identify two competing heroic images. The 'Wounded Hero' was to be found in now-forgotten films such as *Heroes* (dir. Jeremy Kagan), *Tracks* (dir. Harry Jaglom), and *Rolling Thunder* (dir. John Flyn), all made in 1977, and indirectly in films like *Taxi Driver* (dir. Martin Scorsese, 1976). As they say, this image not only reflects the wide public 'disillusionment and growing apocalyptic rage and radicalization that created home-grown terrorists', it also 'mirrors the public's anxiety about what the vets would do once they got home' (Auster & Quart 1981:61).[16] The other more obviously mythologised strand saw in the Vietnam vet a figure of primal power, a 'proletarian Nietzschean who believes he can will reality in any form he desires' (Auster & Quart 1981:62). Stallone showed a way of merging these two, in his exaggerated body.

Rambo emerged from a clutch of competing ways of conceiving the 'American soldier' post-Vietnam. A good summary of these is given by Eben Muse (1993), who asks how American film dealt with the echoes of the rapes and massacre by American soldiers led by Lieutenant Calley at My Lai.[17] He shows how responses shifted and evolved from the earliest films such as *Glory Boy* (dir. Edward Sherin, 1971) and *The Visitors* (dir. Elia Kazan, 1972) in which veterans are seen as made weak, and unable to protect their families, through the mythic images of *The Deerhunter* where evil is transferred to the enemy in for example the notorious Russian roulette sequence, to the turn to different kinds of realism in *Platoon* (dir. Oliver Stone, 1986) and *Full Metal Jacket* (dir. Stanley Kubrick, 1987). But the one image to survive was Rambo, who just wants to return to Vietnam to finish the war:

> Nowhere in this Vietnam does the spectre of Calley appear. Rambo does not commit atrocities or kill indiscriminately; he does what he has to do to win. The fact that achieving this victory requires that he decimate a peaceful village is immaterial. He had to light the fires and fire the explosives, after all, because the Vietnamese were after him. The climactic scene between Rambo and the Russian commander is nothing less than a wild west shoot-out with helicopters instead of guns. His ethos assumes that the end will justify the means, and in Rambo's universe it does. (Muse 1993:91)

'Rambo' became, like 'Wayne', a transposable figure, if not on the same scale. But his qualities were always far more questionable than 'Wayne's'. 'Rambo' was associated with fanatical attitudes, fascination with weapons, tendencies to excessive violence and being out of control. Mildly crazed people could be dubbed 'Rambo wannabees' or described as 'doing a Rambo'. From early on, he became associated with the figure of Ronald Reagan. Susan Jeffords' study of the political resonances of 1980s Hollywood 'hard body' films is important here. Jeffords (1994) argues that a series of films and film franchises across the decade – notably the *Rambo*, *Die Hard* (1988, 1990, 1995, 2007), *Lethal Weapon* (1987, 1989, 1992, 1998) and *Back to the Future* (1985, 1989, 1990) series – closely play out the ideological drive of Reaganism, in its battle against the legacy of the 'soft and weak' Jimmy Carter. The films were important, she argues, because they helped to resolve the emotional anxieties of 'the American audience', after America's defeat in Vietnam. This explains the films' emphases on the need for bodily discipline to overcome betrayals, on the role of a trusted yet vulnerable 'father' and on imaginatively rewriting the past, all helping to defray the sense of loss and betrayal.

Jeffords does offer some acute readings of aspects of the films, but in a way that brooks no ambiguities. Under the aegis of the psychoanalytic turn in feminist film studies, 'Hollywood' becomes a virtual branch of Washington, producing a perfectly coordinated 'masculine political imaginary' for, first, Reagan and then George Bush Sr. Small, missable points in a film become bearers of this. So, the fact that, in the first *Back* film, Marty McFly's father's death occurs in 1973, marks this date as highly symbolic: 'That is the year, the film seems to be saying, in which the nation lost its direction' (Jeffords 1994:67). Characters become their political 'equivalents': 'who is Doc Brown other than Ronald Reagan himself?' (Jeffords 1994:78). This exaggerated parallelism with its attendant use of heavy and timeless psychological theory threatens her more valuable lesson: that in this period a new figure was produced which became usable within the wider political debates of the period.

'Rambo' too has risen and fallen as a point of reference for debates. Graph 2 shows that again press mentions rose significantly after 2001 (indeed were already rising), but decline again after 2004. Again as with 'Wayne', and possibly more intensely, there is background noise within these numbers: Rambo street names, sports star Ken-Yon Rambo, playwright David Rambo, Judge Sylvia Rambo, an apple variety with the name and a baboon named after Stallone's character. Recalibrating to discount these, the changes would be markedly more dramatic. (The rise up to 2008 arises almost entirely from talk about the last Rambo film, alongside in the same year the gently-mocking *Son of Rambow* [dir. Garth Jennings, 2007].)

As the new millennium progressed, the world appeared to come close to his fantastical figure. 'Ramboism' was increasingly traded as an accusation – in all directions. John Kerry, Bush's Democratic opponent, whose Vietnam record was feted, was accused of seeming a bit too much like a 'real-life Rambo' by one columnist (Clark 2004). Michael Moore was accused of *wanting* Bush to react like a 'Rambo', when he featured in *Fahrenheit 9/11* the bemused Bush hearing about 9/11 while reading to young children (Anon 2004). But the incident that crystallises how 'Rambo' could shift to being a figure of deceit was the Jessica Lynch case. Lynch was injured in a crash, and was helped by Iraqi doctors. But American Special Forces staged a 'rescue', while a story was planted by White House officials that she had been taken as a hostage after a gun battle and was possibly being tortured. As the lie unravelled, so commentary began to make the 'Rambo' association, as here: 'The myth of Jessica Lynch as "Rambo Warrior" says more about Americans' desire for happy endings than it does about the young soldier' (Anon 2003). And when the news management went to work again after

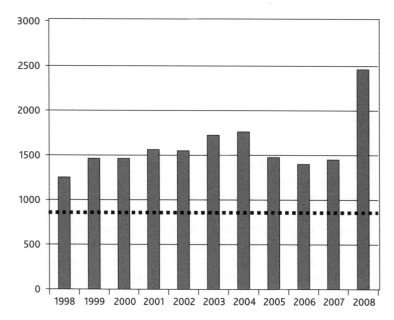

Figure 4.3   References to 'Rambo' (US Press, 1998–2008). Figures in this graph were obtained by searching the Nexis Press database for all US Press, using the search expression 'Rambo'. The broken line is intended to indicate the likely level of 'background noise' generated by references to things such as Rambo apples, or individuals happening to share the name 'Rambo'.

Pat Tillman, a football star who signed up in a burst of patriotism, died from friendly fire, the link was extended:

> Pat Tillman's case is itself a replay of the fake 'Rambo' escapades ascribed to Pfc. Jessica Lynch a year earlier, just when Operation Iraqi Freedom showed the first tentative signs of trouble and the Pentagon needed a feel-good distraction. As if to echo Mary Tillman, Ms Lynch told *Time* magazine this year, 'I was used as a symbol'. (Rich 2005)

The main result was a judgement that 'Bushism' amounted to 'Ramboism' (out-of-control aggression driven by fantasies), which was bad judgement, bad politics, bad for America's image, and particularly for its soldiers:

> The prisoner abuses are a stain on the dedicated, dangerous work done by thousands of American soldiers and Marines

who have served in Iraq and Afghanistan and continue to serve there. Most are not involved in interrogation and in their interaction with locals treat civilians with respect. Every war has its Rambos, people who choose to throw their weight, or their ammo, around with abandon. What happens on a battlefield can be hard to control. Not so an interrogation room, or a prison. The environment is contained and rules can be enforced... (Fitzpatrick 2005)

'Rambo' was becoming too risky an image for 'America's' good. And it is the specific nature of the Iraq conflict which makes it so, as this review of a book by an ex-soldier captured:

Jonathan Cote's years in the 82nd Airborne opened cracks in his seemingly charmed life. He came home restless, with memories of mangled bodies filling sleepless nights. Cote soon returned to an imperfect war in an imperfect way – as a mercenary. Some of the hired guns are like Cote, who – with his military discipline – stay within blurry lines of conduct and conscience. Others, like the worst of the Blackwater mercenaries, were Rambos whose consequence-free killing of civilians damaged America's cause. (Esmonde 2008)

GRUNTS

There is one other category whose provenance is at once simplest and most deceptive: the Grunt. Born in Vietnam, the term originally marked the effort infantrymen made in getting up from the ground with a heavy pack (Longley 2008). But it quickly gathered other meanings. The key was that these were ordinary soldiers, whose stories may be worth telling, but who do not have ideas or commitments beyond their situation. As one report puts it, 'To the uninformed, the term "intellectual grunt" may seem to be an oxymoron' (Blanton 2007). This was actually far from the truth. As Joel Geier explains, foot soldiers in Vietnam quite quickly became aware of their role as sacrificial victims:

At this time, college education was universal in the middle class and making strong inroads in the better-off sections of the working class. Yet, in 1965 and 1966, college graduates were only 2 per cent of the hundreds of thousands of draftees. In the elite colleges, the class discrepancy was even more glaring. The upper class did none of the fighting. Of the 1,200 Harvard graduates in 1970, only two went to Vietnam, while working-class high schools routinely sent 20 per cent, 30 per cent of their graduates and more to Vietnam. College students who were not made officers were usually assigned to noncombat support and service units. High school dropouts were three times more likely to be sent to combat units that did the fighting and took the casualties. Combat infantry soldiers, 'the grunts', were entirely working class. They included a disproportionate number of Black working-class troops. Blacks, who formed 12 per cent of the troops, were often 25 per cent or more of the combat units. (Geier 2000)[18]

Geier outlines their growing realisation of their position, and the ways they began to organise, using GI newspapers, leaflets, and the like. A number of mass revolts took place, alongside the more individualised fraggings of officers.[19] These revolts were among the major reasons for America's moves to seek a peace deal.

The word 'Grunt' carried forward from Vietnam to Iraq, but conveys little of this sense. It certainly indicates that these are the ones who carry the load of combat, who do the 'grunt work'. This decontextualisation of the soldiers moves uneasily between being description and recommendation, as in this article by a former Marine captain discussing soldiers' views of the Iraq war:

There was a running joke in my Marine units in Afghanistan and Iraq. Each grunt thought he was the best, the platoon above him was good, the company above that was mediocre and the overarching battalion was actively trying to get him killed. So it is with most organizations. People near the bottom wear blinders, and their diligent attention to the task at hand is precisely what makes them less qualified to assess the bigger picture. (Fick 2006)

Fick goes on to discuss a series of opinion polls which appear to reveal a confused state of mind among ordinary soldiers – wanting out within a year, but saying the American cause is good. The solution?

Consider this poll finding: 85 per cent of the troops who believe that the US should exit Iraq in the coming year also said that the US mission there is mainly 'to retaliate for Saddam's role in the 9/11 attacks.' How can we reconcile the so-called wisdom of the former with the demonstrable falsehood of the latter?

In short, we can't. Asking young soldiers and Marines about national strategy is almost as fruitless as asking senior political leaders about platoon-level tactics.

'Grunts' should not have views. That is part of the currency of the term. But of course in reality they do: contradictory, altering, and to a considerable extent disorganised. And among the things they take with them are the prejudices circulating at home. Matthew Harwood (2008), in the British *Guardian*, caught one strand of this, writing about the role of the American religious evangelicals, whose 'interventions' led to some soldiers abusing the Qur'an, giving out leaflets advising Iraqis that they were 'bound for hell', and treating the American invasion as an 'opportunity for converting the heathen'.[20]

After Vietnam, then, the 'Grunt' became a moveable feast within popular culture. In most versions, he is a soldier just desperate to survive. Fighting wars he (or she)[21] does not believe in, invading space, alien worlds,[22] even taking alien form,[23] the 'Grunt' becomes a virtual mercenary. And this is important since, unlike Vietnam, for Iraq there has been no draft. The American army in Iraq is a volunteer army, aided by privatised mercenary forces. It is vital to our understanding of these films to see that the images of 'the American Soldier' were in meltdown. Yet they were somehow supposed to remain heroes. I return to how this was done, in Chapter 10.

5
Understanding film 'failures'

With the one partial exception of *The Hurt Locker* (on which, see the final Chapter), all 23 films achieved weak box office at best. Accordingly, on this one important financial measure, virtually all of them must be judged 'failures'. But that is just the start of a more complicated story. Begin with the fact that commentators were waiting for them to fail, endlessly discussed it when it happened and greeted each new one with the question: will this one do any better? To which they frequently added: will it *deserve* to? They even discussed each others' comments and explanations on this in considerable detail. Take this example:

> After the well-reviewed *Stop-Loss* failed to pack 'em in opening weekend, a studio source told *Deadline Hollywood Daily*'s Nikki Finke: 'No one wants to see Iraq war movies ... It's a shame because it's a good movie that's just ahead of its time.' *Stop-Loss* was far from 'ahead of it's time', and thankfully, through emerging new media, the public was clued in by talk radio and Internet blogs to the fact that *Stop-Loss* was yet another anti-war screed where the filmmakers take their war bitterness out on our troops by portraying them as drunks, crazies, and wife-beaters. The public was also clued in that by any reasonable artistic standard *Stop-Loss* was a melodramatic mess filled with contrivances only awarded positive reviews because its politics were correct. In March of 2008, *Stop-Loss* was about to open, but the *Washington Post* had already its obituary written: 'After five years of conflict in Iraq, Hollywood seems to have learned a sobering lesson: The only things less popular than the war itself are dramatic films and television shows about the conflict.' A spate of Iraq-themed movies and TV shows haven't just failed at the box office. They've usually failed spectacularly, despite big stars, big budgets and serious intentions. The underwhelming reception from the public raises a question: Are audiences turned off by the war, or are they simply voting against the way filmmakers have depicted it? (Nolte 2008)

This article, like the many others, is intensely aware of the advance debates. It does, of course, appeal to the idea of 'the public' as anti-left arbiters. But it does not dispute that the war is in itself unpopular. There is conservative delight in the films' failure, but still that sense of some puzzlement – which is shared by more liberal sources. Eugene Novikov, in the online portal *Cinematical*, reviewed a long list of films – in fact, making a case that the box office of some of the films (notably *The Kingdom*) were not as bad as made out. Even *Redacted*, he reflects, whose box office was terminally bad, probably did not set out expecting major returns:

> [T]hink about it: how do you market a movie about the rape of an Iraqi girl by American soldiers? A movie that basically sets out to lecture, shame and outrage the audience? Maybe it could have fared a little bit better, but I don't think it was ever going to be any sort of hit. The vast majority of moviegoers simply don't go to the movies to see what *Redacted* had to offer, regardless of whether its message was liberal, conservative, communist or neutral. (Novikov 2008)

Novikov thus ends his considerations with a thought and a question, to himself and those around him:

> There's nothing special, in other words, about the Iraq War as a subject. Looks to me like audiences have pretty much behaved like they normally do. Most of these movies are freakin' *depressing*. And depressing movies are often a hard sell. But riddle me this, *Cinematical* readers: are you among the hundreds of millions of Americans who avoid Iraq War movies like the plague? And if so, why? (Novikov 2008)

The issue of failure also, inevitably, became linked to the summoning back of Vietnam, and Hollywood's failure to comment while the war continued. Was failure now a sign that it is not possible to make successful movies while America is still militarily engaged? Two human rights commentators addressed this head-on:

> Much has been made of the fact that each of the commercial films dealing with the Iraq war or the 'war on terror', such as *Redacted* (2007), *Lions for Lambs* (2007), and *In the Valley of Elah* (2007), have fared poorly at the box office and left audiences numb to the violence. Perhaps this is no surprise. The Vietnam

War spawned some of cinema's most potent anti-war movies. However, what is noteworthy is that the most successful films were made nearly a generation after the US withdrawal in 1975 (Betsalel & Gibney 2008:522)

This need to make sense of failure shows up too in more academic spheres, in an interesting essay by Susan Carruthers (2008). Writing in a tone of puzzled concern, Carruthers begins by identifying the failure as a specific kind of refusal. It is not that the war is popular, it is that people do not seem to want to know anything about it. She points out, among other things, how awkwardly this refusal sits with the popular left arguments about the 'political-military-industrial complex', which its advocates see as selling wars to the American population as a form of entertainment. In this case, people do not even seem to want to be entertained. Writing as someone clearly hostile to the Bush war, she identifies an 'anaemic' strand in the anti-war movement that does not know how to communicate with ordinary people – and even lacks the academic tools to investigate viewers' responses with any subtlety.[1]

The issue of 'failure' was clearly a complex discursive topic. For conservatives, a film doing badly was almost as good as a favourable public opinion poll. For liberals, it could be a ground for recommending the film precisely *because* it did not court popularity.[2] A film doing reasonably well – as *The Hurt Locker* eventually did – required special explanations. The idea of 'failure', in other words, is not some self-evident measure. We need to approach it carefully.

In fact, even in pure financial terms, identifying outright failures in Hollywood is notoriously difficult. The mantra that nine out of ten movies lose money only holds true if we neglect rental and sell-through video and DVD, television, cable, airline and other downstream earnings. Where studios are involved, films are not generally seen as individual releases, but as annual slates, spreading risks, filling the schedule appropriately. Hollywood accounting is also famously opaque, as court cases have sometimes brought to light (see, for instance, Pfeiffer et al. 1997). The rough rule, that box office earnings need to be two and a half times the negative costs before a film enters clear profit, is just that: rough. It takes no account, for instance, of laid-off risk, ancillary earnings from merchandise, and the like. *The Lord of the Rings* trilogy (dir. Peter Jackson, 2001–03) is a great example; if reports are to be believed, virtually the entire negative costs were offset before release by licensing deals (see Gilsdorf 2003).

However, if identifying definite failures is hard, explaining them is even tougher.[3] The most popular explanation is studio failure to control directors' pretensions. A good expression of this is James Parish's gleeful semi-insider book *Fiasco: A History of Hollywood's Iconic Flops*. For Parish, 'flop' combines budgetary and artistic dimensions. Told through the history of 14 movies, from *Cleopatra* (dir. Joseph L. Mankiewicz, 1963) to *Town & Country* (dir. Peter Chelsom, 2001), his explanation speaks almost exclusively of artistic excess and management failure, of 'undisciplined' directors or stars 'blinded by vanity', given too much rope to become 'outrageously expensive', producing 'runaway film-making' (these phrases, Parish 2006:6–10). The problem with this is that, while on occasion true, it is just as true of some astonishing successes – the most obvious being James Cameron's (1997) *Titanic* (self-indulgent, wildly over budget, and so on). The second problem in Parish's account lies in his account of the audience, seen just as Jo/anna Public who are put off by the pretentiousness of indulged films, where all they want is 'entertainment'. And, of course, again *Titanic* provides a very good test-case. Not only was it the outcome of very evident directorial excess, but it also importantly tapped into the much-sought repeat-viewing syndrome, in which seriously adoring audiences will pay to see a film many times over. And that adoration, as Massey and Hammond (1999) among others have shown, is about much more than entertainment. Reducing audiences to thrill-seekers is lazy thinking – an error repeated in Tom Shone's (2005) *Blockbuster: How the* Jaws *and* Jedi *Generation Turned Hollywood into a Boom-town*.

One much-cited study does purport to offer a wider theory about 'success' and 'failure', across the range from books, to music, to film. Chris Anderson's (2006) *The Long Tail: Why the Future of Business is Selling Less of More* is in the tradition of American books that propose a Big Idea.[4] Anderson's Idea is that over the past 20 to 30 years we have been moving inexorably from a cultural system based on limited supply, to one based on endless choice, and that digitisation and the internet are providing the technological means to complete this process. As a result, there are no longer any absolute failures, since everything has the potential to find its niche, and diminished costs through online buying and selling mean that products can succeed on small, slow sales. These, coupled with the rise of what he calls 'producerism' – that is, the ability of consumers to cross over and make their own – are moving us towards a 'democratised culture' and a 'consumer paradise' of abundance.

Dressed up with graphs and anecdotes, this is essentially a non-fiction version of Samuel Smiles, with garage music-makers and dot.com entrepreneurs as the new heroes. Entirely missing from Anderson's explanatory universe are such key issues as problems of borrowing and rates of amortisation of capital, the ratios of successful to unsuccessful start-ups among new technology businesses and the tendencies of the major cultural producers to acquire the success stories. To think usefully about 'failure', we need to get past this absurd Big Idea but hang on to a few of its components. It is evident that, for instance, cheapening digital film-making has opened spaces through which new producers have sought visibility – and a few have broken through. It is also true, as Janet Wasko and Paul McDonald (2008) among others have shown, that the rise of new technologies like DVD has shifted the bases of decision-making about the viability of many projects. Wasko pointedly challenges the illusion that Hollywood is a particularly risky business, because 'theaters are only the beginning of a chain of windows or markets' (Wasko & McDonald 2008:222). McDonald meanwhile puts figures on the importance of DVD, in particular, to the studios (who, as Frederick Wasser [2001] has showed, were much more ambivalent about the emergence of video): 'Approximately 80 per cent, or US$8.7 billion, of consumer spending on sell-through video returned to distributors as revenues, compared to 25 per cent (US$2.2 billion) from video rental and 47 per cent (US$4.4 billion) through the box office' (Wasko & McDonald 2008:152). The implications of this kind and scale of development are still being worked through. But again, the risk is not noticing the problems which arise from the rate of amortisation of capital – that is, how long it takes for a full return on investment (most often funded by interest-bearing loans) to be achieved. And, of course, dependence on DVD sales becomes really troublesome when sales decline, as they have since 2005 (Belson 2006) – or virtually collapse, as they did in 2009 (Wilkerson 2009).

From another angle altogether, Jeffrey Sconce (2007) has written on the longstanding critical tendency to condemn cinema as a failure *tout court* – and then to delight in that failure; to hear of a new film, listen intently to the gossip on its production difficulties, and then to go, perversely, in hope of watching its makers make fools of themselves. This 'inverted cinephilia' – loving the idea of cinema, hating what it is – is, as Sconce deliciously indicates, predicated on a dislike of the audiences who do go and enjoy such 'junk'. Sconce sees cinema as particularly blessed/cursed with this sort of pessimistic critique. But even here, although he does touch on the perverse pleasures of watching films like *Heaven's Gate* (dir. Michael Cimino, 1980) and *Waterworld* (dir. Kevin Reynolds, 1995) sinking to disaster, Sconce is still primarily focused on the issue of the wrong films succeeding.

The lesson I take from this is that judgements about success and failure are essentially rhetorical, but that these rhetorics are part of the very arena we need to explore. And certainly, box office failure cannot be equated with simple rejection of a film's narrative and argument. People go to see, or stay away from, films for an indeterminately long list of reasons – and among those can be their awareness of the very debates about whether they will go or not. Tom Poe (2001) has explored the reception of Stanley Kramer's (1959) *On The Beach*. The film dramatised Nevil Shute's novel of a post-nuclear conflict world, with the last survivors waiting for the clouds of radioactivity to reach them in Australia. It scared the US authorities. Poe's research revealed the distinct concerns of the Eisenhower administration (it threatened their 'Protect and Survive' doctrines), the FBI (was Kramer a communist?), the Production Code Administration (how could this film possibly fit their guidelines?), and the Catholic Church and its cultural enforcement arm the Legion of Decency. These last worried at the pessimism of the film, but focused on the script's inclusion of suicide pills, given out so that people should not suffer lingering deaths.

Poe begins from a puzzle about responses in some cinemas:

> Robert Hatch, film critic of *The Nation*, admitted to being perplexed by audiences' positive reaction to Kramer's dark and pessimistic film. 'As the last flicker of life disappeared off the face of the earth', he wrote, 'the audience applauded. That is unusual movie-house behaviour, and I wondered what they were applauding. Had they "enjoyed" the picture or were they glad to be alive?' (Poe 2001:91)

Poe records that the film did not perform well at the box office. But that did not diminish its enemies' fears, because of the debates which it had initiated. Poe's final comment – inevitably somewhat speculative, but surely insightful – is this:

> The film had an unanticipated impact, however. The public discourse it generated resulted in its having a secondary audience beyond its actual spectators. This secondary audience, who viewed

the film as a cultural event rather than as a text, was made up of countless numbers of people who read news reports, columns and letters to the editor arguing its merits. Attendance is only one indicator of a film's social impact, and this form of spectatorship has to be considered as a broader activity than film-going. As an 'event', a film may have more impact on the production of culture than as a 'text'. In that regard, *On The Beach* seems to have been very successful in winning the rhetorical debate that surrounded it. News reports of Government actions against it appear to have enhanced rather than damaged its credibility. Despite the 'official' civil defence statements press statements opposing the film, letters to the editor ran highly in its favour and questioned the government's intentions. Ironically, public opinion polls of the time suggested that most Americans found the film realistic and accurate in its depiction of the real threat of nuclear war, and that is why they stayed away from watching it. (Poe 2001:99)

The fit between this and the Iraq war movie cycle may not be perfect, but the general lessons surely hold. We cannot take at face-value the 'failure' of these films. The talk (predictions, fears, hopes, puzzles) about their failure is one feature of the highly constrained circumstances under which the films were made. *For that very reason* budgets would be weighed differently; they would be marketed with special care; some might not come out through standard cinema routes, but would especially target those arenas and populations who might most readily respond positively. But also, the films themselves are most likely to show the signs of addressing expected challenges. They could come out fighting, or ducking and diving – but they would certainly come out ready-armed. In particular, therefore, we need to look at the ways in which films could be determined to mount an anti-war argument while not falling into any of the elephant traps which time, circumstances, and political forces had laid for them. That is not easy. It is like expecting a dancer to perform gracefully while crossing a mine-field.

AMERICAN SOLDIERS: A DAY IN IRAQ

Take, then, a film which many adjudged a complete failure. With a low cumulative rating on IMDb (2.5 stars out of 10), *American Soldiers* has been called 'the worst war movie ever made'. Directed by Sidney J. Furie, and produced and distributed by oddly-named Canadian-based Peace Arch Entertainment Group, the film tracks a patrol of US soldiers through an unnamed Iraqi city on one day in 2004. It shows their actions, their responses to being under attack, their thoughts about the situation they find themselves in, and their responses to their superiors – who seem to do very little to support them. It tracks across a time-coded day from 6.35 a.m., and shows events in brief edited snatches, fading to black between sections. The film begins with them going on patrol. An intertitle announces: 'During the month of April 2004 American casualties were at their highest levels since the war had officially ended. This is the story of one of those days.' In the course of the day, they experience up to 20 attacks, including repeated machine-gun and grenade assaults, yet – while sustaining losses – fight on to 'win home'. Along the way, they help civilians after a suicide bombing, save a hospital from an insurgent attack, rescue prisoners from CIA torture – and discourse endlessly about why they are there, and hated. This early exchange is typical: 'Sergeant, why the fuck are these guys so pissed off with us?' 'Just cos we're here. How would you feel if they were in Miami? Nobody likes being occupied, it's like living with your parents.' Finally making it back to base, they mourn their losses, and the film closes with a quote from General Zimmi saying that serving soldiers are 'the US's greatest treasure, not to be used lightly and without good cause'.

The film is strangely composite, a mix of all the main images of the 'American soldier'. Like Wayne, first, the soldiers are resolute, disciplined, and courteous to women (one apologises to an Iraqi nurse for blowing away insurgents in her hospital, and wonders about returning later to take her out to a dance). There are occasional touches of *The Dirty Dozen*, as their back-stories reveal grubby pasts (notably, the terminally wounded sergeant who tells his troop that he is glad he met his judge. Who? The judge who said he could choose to 'serve my sentence or serve my country'). There is more than a bit of Rambo when, having run low on ammunition, they pretend to be dead until their triumphant attackers come close enough to be engaged in hand-to-hand combat, with curved Rambo-style knives. (Just before this, one character remarks on the way their muscles 'remember' their training.) There's definitely Grunt-stuff, too, in their endless homoerotic teasing of each other, equivalising weapons with cocks and balls, calling each other 'wet pussies', yet then *caring* – weeping at their sergeant's death, for instance. And there is hardly an officer among them. The highest rank is sergeant and, of the two of these, one is dead within the first 20 minutes while the second is critically injured, forcing a corporal to act up. When they do meet a lieutenant, he ends up virtually taking orders from the Corporal. But there are no star-heroes anywhere, either presented or implied.

Figure 5.1 Still from *American Soldiers: A Day in Iraq*. The one 'Abu Ghraib moment' in the cycle of films. While real evidence of abuses became strangely absent from the film cycle, in the very first, *American Soldiers*, the patrol at its centre finds itself delivering prisoners to a CIA-controlled torture centre. Horrified at this challenge to their sense of what being soldiers is about, they break orders, threaten to shoot the guards and exit again with their prisoners. This scene immediately follows one in which a prisoner has denounced the Americans for killing all his family, turning him into their enemy 'until I die'.

Yet through all this is their devotion to 'America'. They may question the war and what it's for. They may be furious when Base fails to supply any tactical support when they are under fire. They may want more than anything to be at home again. But these never detract from their utter devotion to 'our country'. These soldiers are a military man's wet dream. So, against what measures was it judged to be a failure? With no cinema release, it produced no box office figures. Small hints in citizen reviews suggest it circulated quite widely among soldiers and their families. The major visible debates appear to be over three things: the acting; its accuracy; and (differently) its realism. A look at the User Comments section of the film's IMDb page discloses some striking features. It is clear that it took time for those who might have enjoyed the film to find the courage to speak. The first 20 comments are uniformly extremely hostile and dismissive. Only gradually do voices appear saying 'Not as bad as I first thought', 'Actually quite enjoyable/reasonable', until ultimately a few are prepared to say 'This was a really good movie in my judgement'. Of course there can be an element of contrariness, with later reviewers being determined to speak the unspeakable. But to play that game well, they still have to find good reasons. In the face of critics dismissing the film for inaccuracies, impossibilities, and bad production values, what is attended to by IMDb's most positive commentators? What grounds of defence/uplift are found?

The strongest share certain characteristics. The film is less pro- or anti-war, than so close-up as to be repulsive: 'This film took me there and convinced me this is as close as I want to get to it. If I had a child there on either side I would be sick.' The fact that it puts political ideas into the soldiers' mouths is welcomed, but helped by the film's provenance: 'Made by Canadians who can't be intimidated by our President and his Vice, this film tells it like it is.' Another sees the film's precarious position: 'Better movie than the military haters would have one believe. ... If one is a Democrat one will love this movie. Many Michael Moore moments including the death of American soldiers and torture scenes.' This coupling of military-loving with Democrats/Michael Moore is tense and unresolved. A third, while acknowledging the film's limitations, made a virtue out of the actors' anonymity: 'I am glad there were no "name" actors. As a result, stardom did not get in the way of warming up to the characters. You really wanted them to succeed and cared about them.' There was in effect a reduced line between their fictional character status and their real-world analogues. This meant that the very nature of the film made acting desperately difficult. Being attacked every few minutes leaves little time for that. But if you want to convey the extremity of their experience, all you can do is show their determined reactions. One reviewer makes this point explicitly:

> The acting is good, based on the fact that all of these actors have not had much acting experience (the most experienced actor acted in only four movies). Some people might find them as amateurs, but this, in my opinion, really brings out the realism of the char-acteristics of the American soldiers.

This same comment uplifts the very mix of elements I noted above, to a valued achievement:

> Where most of the war films are over-dramatized and use the most overrated war-is-hell clichés, *American Soldiers* shows almost every aspect of a soldier's life from the excitement of your first

confirmed kill to losing your comrade/best friend to just joking and Moshe-pitting around with your army buddies.

That same sense of a *deliberate composite* is welcomed by another:

> In my opinion, this movie is a 'must see'. In this movie we see 'a day in the life' of American Soldiers fighting, killing and dying in the absurd situation the leaders of this country forced upon them in Iraq. You get a sense of the bravery and skill of the regular soldier and a taste of what the reserves who never expected to be there are feeling. This story tries to show us as much as possible about what's happening over there as they can in the limited space of the movie.

Messy melange here turns into a 'day in the life' summary. Another tells of showing the film to an Iraq veteran who found himself 'reliving his experiences' through the film. That takes it past the limitations of budget and script:

> I guess what I am saying is look past the budget part and take in the whole message. Our boys are in hell! Real life hell! Their friends are dying around them daily, they are in a country where they are hated! I guess that's why I like the part where the US soldiers rescue the prisoners, shows the side the news never covers. I ramble on, but I like the movie, one of the best I have seen.

Defenders of the film are making a virtue out of its very limitations, even amateurishness. This allows it to be 'truthful' (a key and important word in defenders' lexicon, along with 'realism' and 'courage') in a way that anything more obviously manufactured could not be. Significantly, the film's provenance (Canadian, as against heavily compromised American films; low budget as against spectacle-driven) is among the grounds of defence.

CONCLUSION

So what does it mean to judge films like this 'failures'? Even on the minimalist criterion of return on investment, many of them will have broken even by the time DVD rentals and sales are included. And defenders can always be found, with articulate grounds and criteria. But these are not the point. The charge of 'failure' is a form of political point-scoring. To dub a film a 'failure' is a rhetorical move, a way of asking people to ignore it. And many of these films are what I will call Statement Films – made to challenge, intended to disturb – so that the sheer venom unleashed on them is almost a mark of their effectiveness. Being grit under the fingernails of opponents can itself be an ambition. What is remarkable, as we will see in Chapter 8, is the dubbing of the entire cycle as worse than failures, a 'toxic genre'.

6
Bringing the war home

There is a curious story behind *In the Valley of Elah*. The script was developed by journalist Mark Boal from a story he researched for *Playboy* (2004). The case, as already noted, was of Richard T. Davis, son of a military family, reported as having gone AWOL after returning from Iraq. His father, not believing it, set out to investigate and struggled to eventually uncover the truth, that his son was murdered by other members of his platoon. The film follows Davis' story very closely, even including the account of his learning to torture wounded Iraqis. But in one critical respect Boal's script does not follow his journalism. In a concluding section to the article, Boal discusses theories as to why Davis was murdered:

> On the last day of November an e-mail was posted on a conservative open-forum Internet site. [...] The writer said he had heard at Fort Benning a 'soldier stating that the reason your cousin was murdered was because he had some information on the suspected individuals who were involved in raping a young girl in Iraq and that your cousin was going to report them.' The author of the e-mail, who remains anonymous, went on: 'It sounded sensible to me, because I doubt that your cousin was killed over something as stupid as insulting a stripper in a nightclub.' [...] [T]he rape theory had been circulating in the platoon for some time, long before Lanny heard about the anonymous e-mail. One soldier says, 'Even before we heard Richard's dad talk about that, me and some of my friends were saying that it might have been over an Iraqi girl.' [...] But when Pruitt, Davis's team buddy, is asked about the theory that Davis had witnessed a rape involving Martinez and Navarrete and was killed because he planned to report it, his answer leaves no ambiguities. Sitting on his bunk at Fort Benning, disassembling his SAW, Pruitt says, 'Even if he did see something extravagant like that, I don't think he would've cared too much about it. Not Richard.'

Boal acknowledges that this rumour is unproved, but it is nonetheless striking that this disappears completely from the film. What comes in its place? The film offers an unequivocal alternative construction of the events. The scene in which this comes together is the one in which, finally, one of Mike's buddies tells the story. Brilliantly acted and filmed, it shows the soldier as having lost all emotional resonance. He becomes an exemplar of ordinary soldiers, basically good men, but stressed beyond their limits by the war. Their murderous behaviour, their torturing of prisoners becomes explicable, even excusable, because they must be suffering from that syndrome known as post-traumatic stress disorder, or PTSD.

WHAT IS PTSD?

There is a wide perception that PTSD is just a new name for a long-recognised condition, simply naming the harm resulting from major stresses such as war. On this basis, there is nothing anachronistic about IMDb's summary of the 1977 film *Heroes*: 'A Vietnam veteran suffering from post traumatic stress disorder breaks out of a VA [Veteran's Affairs] hospital and goes on a road trip with a sympathetic traveler to find out what became of the other men in his unit'. In fact, PTSD only emerged as a defined category in 1980, as part of a major reformulation embodied in the American Psychiatric Association's defining document, the *Diagnostic and Statistical Manual of Mental Disorders, Version III*. DSM–III, as it is universally known, represented a defeat for older psychoanalytic ways of conceiving mental illness (in which mental distress might arise from interconnected parts of a person's previous life), and victory for one centred on isolating, naming, describing and treating distinct dysfunctions. A clear scientific status could now be asserted.[1] So what precisely is the purpose of this and other versions of DSM? These are used not only by therapists but also by, among others, the military in determining fitness to fight, and by insurance companies, lawyers and judges in deciding compensation claims. They are, in other words, the basis of an entire official medical regime in the US. DSM–I in 1952 had proposed the concept 'gross stress reaction', but emphasised expected speedy recovery. 1968's DSM–II dropped this, almost unnoticed, because at that point military psychiatry was not very influential. Its reformulation as PTSD in 1980 was crucial.

In the last few years, a rising tide of unease over the PTSD's status and uses has emerged, particularly in the US. One strand of this unease comes from people close to its research community.

Frequently the rates of incidence of PTSD are confidently stated, at around 8 per cent for the overall population of the US, but higher for the military. Yet different diagnostic tools produce radically divergent results, in extreme cases producing up to 300 per cent variation. Studies which have looked at the relations between actual combat experience and resultant rates of diagnosed PTSD have found faulty relationships, with more apparently among those with less combat experience. This has reinforced worries about the unusual nature of this 'disorder' – uniquely defined by what is supposed to *cause* it, and therefore wholly dependent on there being a consistent meaning attached to the originating 'trauma'. But this consistency is missing. It has therefore become essential to stress that 'being upset', even badly, does not qualify as PTSD. Beyond these broadly diagnostic concerns, related worries have been expressed about the consequences of PTSD depending so heavily on self-referral and self-report. When continued financial support can depend on a soldier not getting better, is it any surprise that many soldiers suddenly 'remember' more and more troubling traumatic incidents well after the event?

Then, there have been concerns expressed about the efficacy of the supposed therapies. In extremis, one researcher declared that he had never known any sufferer walk away cured because of their treatment – although many 'got better' on their own.[2] Relatedly, there have been worries that because PTSD is defined as a psychological syndrome, it may be missing cases where there are actual brain injuries from proximity to explosions, for instance. Finally, there have been queries about the sheer range of kinds of condition it is supposed to cover, making it too convenient as an explanation. Consider this list of possible occasioning factors: 'Violent attacks on the person. Rape. Sustained verbally aggressive attacks. Sudden illness events like a heart attack. Traffic accidents. Industrial injuries. Witnessing sudden violent death, as in train crashes, bombings and war-zone incidents. Panic attacks where the person thinks he is dying. In fact, any event that triggers a strong fear (phobic) response can lead to PTSD. Children have even developed PTSD symptoms from watching horror films on TV' (Human Givens Institute n.d.). That last factor in particular speaks volumes for the exceptional nature of this category. There is good reason to doubt the clinical coherence of this label. It shifts uneasily between being a medical category, a legal manoeuvre and a fictional explanatory device.

These kinds of insider critique have been thrust aside vigorously by the PTSD industry. Powerful alliances have been formed since

1980, none more so than that between the military authorities, the Veterans Association, hospitals that are heavily funded for PTSD-related initiatives, the Department of Veteran Affairs, politicians smelling votes in military-related initiatives, an uncritical media and a much-benefited research community. It is this very sense of a psychiatric industry that is the subject of an essay by two sociologists of science.[3] Mayes and Horwitz (2005) brilliantly analyse the concatenation of forces that led to the production of DSM–III. They show the effects of, among other factors: the rising interest of the pharmaceutical companies in securing a market for their products; the worries of insurance companies at the open-ended costs associated with psychoanalytic therapies; a determination by a coterie of medical experts to make medicine more 'scientific'; and, of course, the political acceptability of this new approach: 'During the 1980s, a period when President Reagan and Congress slashed funding for community mental health services and Social Security disability benefits for the mentally disabled, the National Institute for Mental Health's budget grew 84 per cent, to $484 million annually' (Mayes & Horwitz 2005:264). Mayes and Horwitz explore in detail the debates over the status of homosexuality (which gay activists were demanding to be taken off the list of medical 'disorders') and of neurosis (a condition without a clear aetiology, but one crucial to many psychiatric interventions). But within this, PTSD stood out as a striking exception. Where the mantra for all other disorders was to produce tight empirical descriptions of symptoms, to stay away from causal ascriptions and to prove their distinctiveness, in the case of PTSD every one of these rules was bent, if not broken.

Wilbur Scott (1990) fills out the processes whereby PTSD entered the canon.[4] Its roots were in the tide of hostility to the Vietnam War, which emerged in the late 1960s. A loose collection of therapists, Vietnam veterans and anti-war activists began to worry about the war's impact on returning soldiers, and realised too late their loss of that diagnostic definition in 1968. This had implications for their access to facilities and treatment. Scott traces the increasingly effective campaigning across the 1970s, resulting in the inclusion of several of their number in DSM–III's drafting working party. Realising that to win they needed wider support, an initial definition of 'combat disorders' was expanded to include the concerns of other fields, to become PTSD. PTSD took on a life of its own, with the added distinction of being, as Allan Horwitz (2009) points out, the only mental disorder whose diagnosis is by and large welcomed. PTSD posited that *any ordinary person* experiencing traumas could be expected to experience some kind of breakdown. Post-battle suffering was therefore the norm, not the exception. The subsequent redefinition of PTSD's symptoms, in DSM–IV in 1994, added 60 per cent to those meeting its criteria and led to studies after 9/11 that found levels as high as 50 per cent among people who simply watched the news on television.

PTSD has become far more than a diagnostic label. It packages soldiers' responses to war as bundles of symptoms within the individual. Essentially depoliticised, it cuts away the possibility of discussing the very thing which was at the heart of the Vietnam war: soldiers' increasing discontent with the war. It is a terrible irony that Wilbur Scott's history of the struggles that led to the appellation begins with a young New York therapist being laughed at when she recounts the story of one paranoid patient convinced that he is being hunted down by former colleagues, because he knows a story of their atrocities. Her colleagues dismissed the story, which involved a place called ... My Lai.

We get a good idea of PTSD's peculiar status from Rosen (2006). The various essays in this book show the accumulated uncertainty over the condition. It is noticed how political its origins were, and it is recognised how easily it has been used and manipulated. As Rosen says in his Introduction, 'It is the rare moment when most every assumption and theoretical underpinning of a psychiatric disorder comes under attack, or is found to lack empirical support. Yet, this is the situation faced by PTSD' (Rosen 2006:xi). Yet in all this, there is no hint of anyone deserting the paradigm. Again and again, people speak – even as they acknowledge the problems – about 'the disorder', as if it remains a meaningful entity. Let me be very clear what my critique is saying. It is *not* denying the many kinds of distress, or accusing psychologists of collaborating with malingerers, as some defenders of the PTSD label suggest. In his book on the controversy, Chris Brewin (2003) makes just such an assumption. Brewin offers an apparently very balanced evaluation of the experimental status of PTSD, presenting his argument as a running debate between proponents and sceptics. But he assumes that scepticism has essentially to do with concerns about over-diagnosis, and patients passing off ordinary stresses as severe conditions. So, in his closing remarks, he considers sceptics' responses to people claiming asylum because of trauma after torture. Brewin speaks for the defence, citing recent research showing that people who at different interviews give inconsistent stories about their torture may be telling the truth – because of the ways traumas can be suppressed. They can still be legitimate asylum-seekers:

> This is a good example of how decisions affecting victims' lives are sometimes made on the basis of inaccurate scientific knowledge, and of how people with PTSD may be at greater risk of injustice. A sceptical attitude may correctly identify some malingerers, victims of inappropriate therapy, and undeserving asylum seekers, but runs the risk of overlooking, minimising and frequently exacerbating much genuine suffering. (Brewin 2003:224)

The problem here is Brewin's assumption that immigration officials conducting interviews are kindly folk who just need to be better informed by psychological science, rather than seeing their interviews as usually somewhere between bureaucratic and bullying. Therefore, adding a requirement that desperate people have to show that they meet some diagnostic criteria itself worsens their situation. The critique of PTSD I am offering is not in any sense trying to deny suffering, but to say that suffering is intensely political and cultural as well as individual, and that the PTSD industry is part and parcel of a depoliticising tendency, which needs people to be victims before they can be said to need help. And of course an entire well-lubricated industry hangs on it. What remains unexplored and unacknowledged is the powerful discursive role PTSD plays: the way it *theorises* soldiers' experiences; the way it *depoliticises* their reactions to war. Whether ignorant of or ignoring the crisis in medical research circles, film-makers who present it risk offering a narrative warranty to bogus science.

THE POLITICS OF COMING HOME

My argument is that PTSD has become a convenient label for bundling together problems and behaviours in a manner which prevents their exploration. PTSD *sounds* like a problem of the individual soldier. We (back home) can only imagine what it is like over there, for these men cut off from ordinary life. Combat exhaustion, fears of attack, continuous stress: these will impact differentially on individuals. Some will crack, and we must sympathise – and of course the military authorities should be providing support and facilities to enable those soldiers to recover. But whatever they do, while suffering this condition, is not their fault. Let me be clear: I am not saying that it *is* their 'fault'. Rather, I want to return to Samuel Stouffer's studies of soldiers in World War II. As we saw, Stouffer studied the differential levels of non-combatant losses (that is, soldiers suffering injuries and deaths other than in the course of battle) in army units. Stouffer found that where soldiers were convinced of the purposes and morality of the war, they were less likely to harm themselves or other Allied soldiers. The safe explanation is to talk in terms of 'morale', a concept which should make us very suspicious. Essentially, 'morale' is a term for people's willingness to commit to official organisational purposes. It presumes that soldiers, once in an army, are effectively detached from who they were, where they came from, what they believed, and how they saw the world. And as 'total institutions' (Goffman's [1961] valuable concept), military organisations work very hard to try to effect this separation.

But Stouffer's results arguably point in another direction. They suggest that a crucial variable is soldiers' beliefs about the worth and validity of a war, and their perceptions of their enemy. It concerns their political convictions – something which military authorities tend simultaneously to deny (soldiers have to learn simply to follow orders and do their duty) and acknowledge (when officers speak to them and politicians visit them, and the like). Stouffer's findings suggest that where they do not believe in a war, soldiers' behaviour will become erratic. Some will turn to forms of self-destruction, others to shapeless hatred of those who threaten them. Occasionally, they may refuse and revolt.

It is 'coming home' movies which address this most directly. Post-World War I, and in response to a growing recognition of the waste and pointlessness of that war, a number of films homed in on the issue of 'shell shock', and the ghastly official killings of soldiers who failed to fight or fled battles. Few films addressed this at the time, but the 1960s saw a revisiting of these issues, after Stanley Kubrick's *Paths of Glory* (1957) had opened the way, showing the infamous executions of World War I soldiers for cowardice. After World War II a few movies had dealt with the difficult transitions back to civilian life. *The Best Years of our Lives* (dir. William Wyler, 1946), most notably, showed one of the three central characters, Fred Derry, having intense flashbacks and struggling to adjust. But it ends optimistically with civilians recognising the returnees' sacrifices and heroism, who in turn find ways to readapt. With Vietnam, the situation was different. Most famously, *Coming Home* (dir. Hal Ashby, 1978) centres on two characters who are both physically and emotionally disabled by the war. One turns to opposing the war, the other to suicide. As Jeremy Devine (1995) well captures in his long discussion of the film, the ending of the film in effect offers us these as two possible responses to the horror and guilt associated with the war.[5]

If the Vietnam movies edge around the topic of guilt, that is surely because of the emergence of what Jeffrey Kimball (2008) calls the 'stab-in-the-back' legend: that America only lost the war because of weakness and treachery at home, from pussy-footing politicians to anti-war activists. Kimball documents the ways in which what began as a marginal conspiracy-theory attitude moved into the centre of politics as Republicans sought to recapture the ideological initiative. A requisite for this was, he argues, recreating a frame within which the rebellious attitudes of US soldiers in Vietnam were completely hidden, and which showed them still receiving overwhelming support. To this end, I would argue, some unifying rhetoric had to be found that could handle the anger over the treatment of veterans. PTSD is a major strand of this. With Iraq, the PTSD theme comes to predominate. PTSD has become a vital juncture between 'caring' politicians and military leaders and civilian critics.

One notable example of this can be found in Garry Trudeau's long-running newspaper strip *Doonesbury*. Trudeau, a liberal, has long taken swipes at George Bush, the Republicans and the war, to the point where Senator John McCain, later Republican Presidential candidate, denounced him from the floor of the US Senate in 1995. At the time, Trudeau took this as a badge of honour and quoted McCain's attack on one of his book covers. But when Trudeau had one of his main characters, the conservative BD, sign up for Iraq, get wounded, and come back traumatised, they were reconciled. Trudeau takes BD through every conventional step of 'recovery' from PTSD, including the now-required help from an older Vietnam vet. In appreciation, McCain wrote a forward to the book edition of the strips.[6] PTSD has thus provided a common ground where pro- and anti-war speakers can meet, to care about the soldiers.

HOME OF THE BRAVE

The idea of PTSD is at work at different levels in many of my 23 films, but four films particularly address it. The most obvious is *Home of the Brave*, arguably one of the most mainstream of the Iraq war movies. Produced by MGM, and written and directed by Irwin Winkler (an experienced producer and, to a lesser degree, director), the film opens with some 'Iraq war experience'. First, we watch the planting and explosion of a roadside IED. Then, we meet the cast – two black and two white, three men and one woman, from across the class spectrum – who are to be part of a medical mercy mission to Baghdad after the explosion, explained by their cynical officer as 'some good hearts-and-minds shit'. En route, they get trapped in an ambush. One of them (Jessica Biel as PE instructor Vanessa Price) loses a hand. The others are a black army surgeon (Samuel L. Jackson as Will Marsh) stressed out by the injuries he has to treat, specialist Tommy Yates (Brian Presley) who loses his main buddy in the ambush, and a black soldier Jamal Aiken (Curtis Jackson) who shoots a woman and cannot decide if she was innocent or not. The ambush and battle sequences are long and seen from their perspective – they appear deeply unprepared for it. All are damaged in different ways.

The rest of the film follows their return to America, and their inability to cope there. We see the poverty of the resources to help them. A useless therapy group does introduce one standard figure of these stories, the Vietnam vet, who ultimately proves especially insightful. The only people who understand their situation are each other, and this is reinforced by the trope that they all live in the same town. Attending the burial of their killed comrade reminds them of each other, and reveals the wounds they all carry. Marsh finds neighbours assume they can just welcome him back, hold barbecues and praise him – while his son has turned anti-war (wearing a teeshirt saying 'Buck Fush'). Ultimately, Marsh finds help from a therapist to tell his story (which we listen to with flashbacks),[7] leading to his pronouncement that he 'can't feel anything' (one of the diagnostic markers, of course, for PTSD). Yates takes a menial job selling tickets in a local cinema. Meeting Price, he tells her: 'I work in this fucking movie theater selling tickets to these stupid movies, but I'll never go to see any of them, it all just seems so unimportant, you know?' The final 'you know?' is important – only someone like her can understand him. Jamal, meanwhile, takes his former girlfriend 'hostage' and is killed during Yates' attempt to coax him out (another sign that civilians cannot understand a man like this). Price finds a new man who knows how to listen to her, and can tell her she is still beautiful. Tommy returns to Iraq, and the film ends on his voice-over telling his parents why he has done this. His country is in this war, even if they went in for the wrong reasons, and there are soldiers over there, fighting and dying, and he cannot walk away from them. This is the call of loyalty to your buddies, the military becomes its own motivation. The film closes on a quote from Machiavelli: 'Wars begin where you will but they do not end where you please'.

That tag-quote marks that these are not four individuals, but representative sufferers. This is a film about America divided against itself. The people back home do not understand what has happened to its soldiers, and what they come back with. 'Ordinary life' is thus impossible. Once again, this film is not just about the American experience, it is about people who went naive and came home 'experienced'. Interestingly, the DVD cover reveals the whole thrust of the narrative, even revealing its outcomes. What it therefore offers us is the experience of seeing how the characters go through it.[8] This feels like a by-the-book film, with good intentions written all over its sleeve. This was picked up on by some who disliked the film, as in this comment from an IMDb user on Yates' remark at the cinema:

Screenwriter Mark Friedman works in that little piece of commentary to congratulate both himself and the viewer; the film you're watching is not like all those other 'stupid movies', you see. It's important. The problem is that Home of the Brave is an execrable film, so poorly made and obvious that it is impossible to take seriously, no matter how earnest and noble the intentions.

The film is easily dismissed for its 'corny, cliché-ridden platitudes'. Defenders of the film knew they were swimming against a tide, and did so in revealing ways. They defended the *enactment of PTSD* as a 'thing-in-itself', as here, also from IMDb:

The striking thing is that this film focuses on the emotional impact on the returning soldiers, and the people around them. The dialogs are raw, truthful and at times politically provocative. The portrayal of post traumatic stress disorder is subtle but palpable, and Jessica Biel's performance of a tough woman to hide her pains of losing her hand is astonishingly well acted. I do not see this as an anti-war vehicle.

What differentiates approvers and disapprovers more than anything is that while the latter find only clichés, manipulated situations and cheesy production values, the former agree to step inside the 'experience' of bewildered soldiers and feel pain with them. But in doing so, they separate the question of being a soldier from politics, and from military reality.

THE LUCKY ONES

The Lucky Ones is a little different. The product of a combination of independent companies, led by Lionsgate (most famous for *Crash*, 2004), it tells the story of three injured soldiers returning to the US, forced to journey across it together because their flights are cancelled: Latino TK Poole (Michael Peña); Fred Cheaver (Tim Robbins), an older middle-class reservist; and Southerner Colee Dunn (Rachel McAdams). Each has different hopes, and all are to be disappointed. Fred hopes to rebuild his marriage. Colee is lugging a guitar that belonged to her dead boyfriend Randy, convinced it is worth thousands and hoping that it will persuade his parents to take her in. TK has a fiancée whom he worries he will not satisfy sexually. These things only slowly become known to each other, and us, as the film unfolds.

The film opens with TK leading his patrol back in, boasting to loud rock music about how men can arouse their women. Explosion: he realises he is injured in his genitals. On the bus to the airport for recuperation leave, he meets the other two. Arriving at JFK airport they find all planes cancelled. They manage to get the last rental car, and drive at night out of New York. (The rental car man is the first of many who declare 'gratitude' to the soldiers.)

On the road, the talkative Colee draws out Fred's story. Felled by a water-container, he feels lucky/guilty because a week later his platoon got shot up. They all laugh, think themselves 'the lucky ones'. Colee tells them about Randy, how he got into debt in Vegas, stole from a casino and had to enlist to get out of trouble. She is furious when TK tells her the army has standards and does not need that kind of 'trash'. Later, at a bar, Colee gets into a fight with a group of college women watching a new television talent show who mock her limp. This bonds the three of them together. 'Just glad I didn't have my weapon', says Colee. That night in the car: TK has a nightmare, they all wake, battle-ready, are 'back there' for a moment. This is one of the most obvious moments of PTSD-like symptoms.

They reach Fred's house, to a wife who almost immediately announces that she wants a divorce. Fred's son has his own concerns; he needs money to get into Stanford. But the company Fred worked for has gone bankrupt. His life is coming apart; dropping the others off at the airport, he doubles up, crying. Instead, they travel on together. Now it is TK who is full of himself. 'Skills' are his mantra, and his are leadership skills. Colee is worrying about Fred who has passed out in the back. Trying to wake him, they distract themselves and crash – and a pole goes through the car, just missing TK by an inch. Colee's wound is reopened. Finding a clinic, they are met by an uncaring secretary. Once more they talk, this time about lying as TK's sexual dysfunction comes out: how can he hope for true love if he cannot tell the truth, Colee says?

Now Colee's story begins to unravel. She has not told her Randy's parents that she is coming, yet she is expecting them to welcome her. TK: 'That girl's living in a dream. Plus she's got no skills'. Colee, meanwhile, has gone to church. Following her, they find an evangelical preacher who talks of being 'in the love business. And the Lord himself is chairman of the board'. They are embarrassed when Colee asks the preacher to speak to the Lord for them, but it does get them invited home to an evening meal by one of the congregation. The house is egregiously huge and luxurious, full of wealthy people discussing their investments, taking 'positions' on the war, and expecting them to do so. Fred's 'Honestly we were just trying to stay alive' kills the conversation. A young woman comes on to him. Later, when the others try to find him, they hear Fred having sex with the woman. But when her husband comes in – and wants to join in – Fred beats a retreat, and they all leave.

Colee gets a valuation of the guitar, and it is indeed valuable. Fred gets a call from his son, who has decided to join up to get the money for Stanford. Fred says no way: 'They'll send him right over there, I'm not going to let that happen'. TK presses Colee to give Fred the guitar. She cries because her 'dream' is dissolving. To calm her, they promise a picnic. The world is peaceful as they watch the sky darken over a beautiful land. Morning, and Colee has met three sex workers willing to help TK with his 'problem', for free. But TK cannot perform. Colee follows him. They get caught in a storm and have to hide from a twister. Hugging each other, TK gets an erection, to Colee's nervous delight.

But TK stays depressed about his 'luck running out'. At Vegas, they split up, and the film intercuts their three stories. We follow TK to a bar, where he drinks tequilas and watches the war on television. Will he flee to Canada? He stands, undecided, as two police stand by the check-in. When Colee meets Randy's family, her picture of Randy fall to pieces when another former girlfriend enters, with his child. Colee quickly invents another story, how Randy always wanted to make it up to them all, and leaves – but asks if she can keep the guitar. Fred wanders through glitzy downtown Vegas, but spots TK in a police car, and follows him to the precinct. Colee arrives, and they learn that TK has confessed to Randy's casino robbery to get out of the army – except that it turns out that the robbery was another of Randy's stories ... Kicked out, they sit together on the steps of the precinct. TK: 'I'm fucked up. It's official, I'm fucked up'. When Colee tries to give Fred the guitar, for his son's fees, he tells them that he has re-enlisted, for the money ... and more.

Twenty-six days later: at the embarkation airport, men in uniform are milling. The three of them meet. TK is no longer engaged. Colee has kept the guitar, and is learning how to play. We watch them board, back to Iraq. The plane leaves, and diminishes in the sky.

This is a film of incidents and gradual revelations of stored-up damage from the war. The journey across America is one of those symbolic road-trips, creating serial encounters with people who gesture, pretend, and live shallow lives. The three realise as the film proceeds that they are out of sorts, and out of place, and the military has become their only 'friend'. In one DVD Extra, producer Rich Schwartz claims that this film is 'not like the others, don't assume it's an Iraq war movie. It's not really about Iraq, or about the soldiers. [...] It's really about America.' Being damaged soldiers from Iraq gives them a special 'innocent eye' on what America is now. So while the Iraq war experience is there, it is more present as a conditioning factor – in how they are, and are treated: lots of 'thanks' but no real caring or understanding. They have wounds and dreams, in equal measure. Whilst not overtly about PTSD, the idea of concealed wounds and carried damage makes them metaphors for heroism to judge the state of America.

Positive user comments pick on this, seeing this as an unusually optimistic film that made them smile and laugh with the three characters. They expected heavy-handed commentary, and got 'real people handling real problems'; they feared stereotypes, and got complex characters who make for themselves a kind of military family. That sense of nervousness is well-captured here: 'The Lucky Ones is something that could have been obvious and clichéd, but ended up being just the opposite'. Or again: 'What could have been a downer filled with cheap shots and cheap tactics is instead smart and even handed, and above all respectful.' It is as if those who found some kind of hope in the film – even if that hope was to run back into the arms of the military – found this sufficient offset for the implied criticisms of an uncaring, disturbed and fake America.

GRACE IS GONE

Starring John Cusack (whose production company New Crime Productions was involved), *Grace* was a first outing for its director, James C. Strouse, who says that he found a story he wanted to tell, of a man losing his wife and being unable to admit it – and found in Iraq a setting for the story. The film also bears the imprimatur of the Weinstein Brothers, long-time independent producers with a fearsome reputation – although not primarily for the strength of their politics.[9] *Grace* was produced through Plum Pictures, a small independent production house founded in 2003 with the aim of producing two to three 'intelligent and heartfelt' films a year. Cusack's involvement was partly driven by his ambition to have his first hit since *Identity* (dir. James Mangold, 2003). Premiered at the Sundance Festival, *Grace* was snapped up by the Weinsteins, now operating independently of Miramax. *Grace* unfolds the plainly told story of Stanley, a store manager, unable for health reasons to join the military, whose wife has gone to Iraq. Near the beginning of the film, he is visited by two soldiers who have come to tell him that his wife has died – and he shuts down inside, and cannot bring himself to tell their two daughters, Dawn and Heidi. Instead, he takes them on a mad road-trip to 'Disneyland', wanting to give them something to make up for what they can never now have. En route, he encounters his brother, a drunken swearing bum who is opposed to the war. It emerges that Stanley is a Republican ('you voted for this monkey president, I didn't'), but the moral superiority remains with Stanley. As the three travel on, the girls become more tense and disturbed by Stanley's behaviour. The sheer time elapse of him not telling them provokes a sense of impending doom. In the car, with Dawn asleep with exhaustion, Heidi asks him about the war, and her mother. She asks why he thinks the war is worth it. The exchange is significant:

S: Sometimes you've just got to believe.
H: What if you can't?
S: Then we're all lost.

At the next fuel stop, he 'phones home', and leaves a tearful message to his dead wife apologising for last time they went to Florida when he got angry because he was ashamed that it was not him going to Iraq, and now asking her help, because he cannot talk to the girls. At the end of the film, he finally tells them, as they sit beside the sea. They hug and comfort each other, and the film ends on an older Heidi remembering her mother, in a funeral oration.

Two Extras to the DVD demonstrate the tensions within which the film works. On the main 'Making Of' Extra, John Cusack relates the attitudes that drew him to the film:

> The power of this film is, paradoxically, it is an anti-war film, and also I think the politics of it are brilliant. The people who are making the arguments are the people who really have the right to make them.

Note that last sentence. Soldiers and their families are here seen as the only ones with the right to speak on the war. There is an Extra associating the film with TAPS (Tragedy Assistance Program for Survivors), a Pentagon-supported support programme for families of war victims. There is talk of 'victims', and 'people who make the ultimate sacrifice'. Being anti-war is made effectively synonymous with taking the right kind of attitude to those who deserve our sympathy: the American soldiers and their families. And it is striking that the predominant theme of those who respond positively to the film is to describe it as being 'neither pro- nor anti-war'. Suffering somehow becomes apolitical, whatever its makers intend.

BADLAND

Badland is almost the exact opposite of these films, in that by its end there is a world of complete bleakness and despair with no hope or road back. A very personal project, it was written, directed, produced, edited and part-funded by Francesco Lucente. Its teaser opens with a Kennedy quotation: 'Mankind must put an end to war or war will put an end to mankind', and insists that the film is 'inspired by actual events'. The film opens with stills of the Iraq war: tanks, an explosion, a grieving man holding a photograph of his son, weary soldiers, a burial marker. Then a voice declares that a soldier is being discharged dishonourably (we have no idea why). The voice fades as we see a photo of our central character, Jerry. Cut to a bleak landscape, and Jerry about to leave his gas station job. Called in to the boss, he is accused of cheating him on the night shift, and his pay is docked. He leaves, angry but defeated. As he drives home through a wastelandscape of dead fields and abandoned cars, weirdly sublime music soars over his anger. At home, amid dereliction, he greets his two sons, plays for a moment with his young daughter Celina, then goes into the trailer to his wife Nora. She accuses him of having stolen the money, and he is furious at her not believing him. He is blowing apart, and the music quietens to sympathise with him. His rage makes his nose bleed, and his wife demands he clean up.

Evening: we watch Nora concealing a large roll of dollar bills. Jerry, awakened, staggers wearily out to find that his daughter has put her rag doll into his car for company. He returns to gently place it in her pram. Arriving at work early, he discovers his co-worker Louie siphoning off the propane that he had been accused of stealing. Outraged at the betrayal at (as he learns) the boss's behest, he beats up Louie, then drives off, leaving the gas station to its fate. Heading home, he finds his wife asleep. Moved to tenderness, he strokes her breast gently. But this discloses the bill-fold inside her nightdress. Bewildered, he retreats and sits – a man gone dead inside. When Nora is woken by the phone, she tries to brazen it out: 'You should have died over there. We'd have been a lot better off'. Looking up through dead eyes, he pulls out his gun and shoots her, then walks outside and kills the two boys. But he cannot bring himself to shoot Celina and almost shoots himself instead. She begs him not to. The frenetic pace slows, he puts the gun away, places her in the truck, and they drive off.

Beside a river, Jerry lays a false trail. When the police arrive, Celina is convinced that they miss her because she prayed. This conviction will return to haunt Jerry. On the radio as they drive on, a ballad talks of the struggles of life and 'man's inhumanity to man', turning non-diegetic as they pull off with a puncture. The local repairman says they will have to stay over. Thus begins their life in a small, seemingly empty town.

In their room, Celina turns on the television to a news programme about the hunt for them. The back-story now begins to be filled in. Military police are reporting that his unit were accused of a 'My Lai-style massacre' just outside of Fallujah. Upset, she asks about it, and in fragments he tells her. Did he kill a lot of people in Iraq? No. Why did he kill mummy and her brothers? 'They hurt me, and the pain wouldn't go away'. She is fearful, wondering if her love is enough for him now. He tries to assure her. When she asks if he would be happy if they came back, he has of course to say yes – and Celina says she will ask God to bring them back, and her prayers are always answered.

The middle part of the film shows us Jerry's encounter with lonely café owner Oli, who offers him a job and a room (which he accepts), and herself (which he cannot, because of Celina's conviction that her mother will return). Through Oli, Jerry meets Max, local sheriff and stressed-out ex-Iraq soldier. Celina starts wandering because she is lonely and scared. The rising tensions among the four of them culminate in Max discovering who Jerry is, after picking up the wandering Celina. But a dead-drunk Max reveals his complicity in killing people in Iraq: 'We did what we were told. But I don't know why we were there. If I knew, then maybe I could live with it.' Jerry drags him out of town, at gun-point. Jerry's story, now we finally hear it, is different. He had gone to the first Gulf War, then home to marry, but it all went sour. Going back with the invasion, his unit was posted to Fallujah and was ordered to take out a house presumed to be full of insurgents, but actually contained only old men, women and children. Ordered to kill them and clean up the evidence, they refused. So another, more willing unit was sent in and an air strike ordered to destroy the evidence. But their unit was then made to take the blame. Max starts crying, pleading for his life. This enrages Jerry who hits him repeatedly. Jerry begins to rant that he has been betrayed by everyone, even Celina. Jerry rages against the notion that there is a God, because the world makes no sense at all. He yells his defiance at the universe, while Max dies in front of him.

Jerry returns smeared with blood to a terrified Celina, and they leave. Eventually he stops the car and orders her out – she is to go to her Aunt's who will look after her. Celina cries and will not go. Jerry marches her out and drives off – watching her in his rear mirror as she stands there distraught. Distracted, he runs into the back of a car in front of him. As he staggers out, she runs towards him – and is hit out of the blue by a car coming out of a side turn. Jerry gathers her body in his arms and howls.

And now we are back to the 'beginning'. A song bridges us back to Jerry sitting in his trailer, just after finding the money on his wife. She is talking to boss Alex on the phone. The camera stares at Jerry as he listens to her. The song talks of 'fear' destroying the things we love. The final shots are of Jerry looking through the window of the trailer at Celina, who looks back at him/us with almost a smile on her face. Dissolve out to the title in negative, the letters formed of waving American flags.

This is in many ways a minimalist film. A tiny cast and a narrow diegetic space make Jerry's world so circumscribed and empty, it is as if America has been hollowed out. An almost post-apocalyptic setting of rusting cars and barely-populated streets magnifies his sense of hopelessness. He was desperate at the beginning of the film; by the end not an iota of hope remains to him. The denouement of Celina's death by freak car accident shockingly deploys a trope found in a series of recent independent films. The motif of the unmarked, unmotivated crash which turns a narrative is to be found in at least the following independent films: *Pulp Fiction* (1994), *Southland Tales* (dir. Richard Kelly, 2006), *No Country for Old Men* (dir. Ethan Cohen & Joel Cohen, 2007) and *Broken Embraces* (dir. Pedro Almódovar, 2009).[10] But this time, the unmotivated crash goes way beyond being a clever motif. It is as if the car is the ultimate proof of the cruel meaninglessness of life and the universe that he raged against. Jerry has something worse than PTSD. He has a crisis of being, and it puts him in confrontation with everything that America is and stands for. This overwrites the sheer fact that he was a victim of military politicking. His mental crisis expands to a moral and ontological one, from which it is impossible to conceive a return.

CONCLUSION

It is not as simple as that the films just dramatise PTSD, show us characters suffering from it. *Home of the Brave* aside, they do more than this, in their different ways. In *Elah*, the sickness is a shocking discovery which, coming late in the film and after a sharp turn in generic expectations, becomes an acceptable excuse for soldiers' brutality. In *The Lucky Ones*, while there are elements of stress, the sickness resides more in the relations between soldiers and civilians, and only return to their comrades relieves the situation. In smaller ways, the same could be said about aspects of another film, *Stop-Loss*, although the core of that is the simple injustice that traps soldiers into being returned to Iraq even after completion of their official time. In *Grace Is Gone*, PTSD is a virtual infection transferable from soldier wife to guilt-ridden husband, who is saved in the end by his family. In *Badland*, things are far worse; injustice revealed comes too late to redeem terminal suffering, and everything combines to make memories turn into nightmares. Here, we might say that the whole of America is sick with on-going PTSD.

And that says much about PTSD's status as convenient metaphor. With the smell of science and promise of remedies, PTSD has come to function as a key metaphor for America inspecting itself within safe margins. What does it achieve? It offers soldiers a self-justifying account of their situation. It 'explains' abuses as unintentional outbursts. It generates positive-smelling narratives. It helps make suffering 'American'. It provides a bridge across conservatives and liberals in America. And it buffers an entire Foucauldian industry (pharmaceutical industries, hospitals, Veterans Associations, government lobbyists, therapeutic organisations and programmes, research institutes and programmes, and medical epistemologies). What it does not do is actually heal the psychic harm done to individuals and groups by their participation in the conflict.

7
Explaining the Iraq War

Five films generally accounting for part of the Iraq war genre do not deal so directly with the conflict. Instead, they build stories about the politics of the region, and the role of the US, its military and its corporations. Soldiers here play a subordinate role, as we will see. And in another important respect these films differ. Where films centring on the 'experience' of US soldiers tend to be set in a rather timeless present, these five depict the continuing forces in play, and sometimes offer timelines of conflicts. Because of this, they raise rather different questions, and connect with a long set of debates on the boundary between film studies, history and politics, about the role of films in understanding American history.

The debates over this have been widely reviewed. As McCrisken and Pepper (2005) recently explained, they have tended to polarise between two camps: those (often professional historians) who suspect the impact of film on historical understanding, and who assess them in terms of their accuracy, bias, or distortion; and those (often influenced by the 'new historicism' of writers such as Hayden White) who argue that history is always made up of narrative reconstructions, all told from points of view – for whom, therefore, films are to be examined differently. What perspectives do they offer? From what stances do they derive? How are images of the past made use of in the present? McCrisken and Pepper themselves take something like a middle position, seeing the necessity to discuss the accuracy or bias of films such as *U-571* (dir. Jonathan Mostow, 2000), *Pearl Harbor* (dir. Michael Bay, 2001) and *Mississippi Burning* (dir. Alan Parker, 1988), but arguing for also considering films' ideological perspectives. Their accounts of films ranging from *Amistad* (dir. Steven Spielberg, 1997), to *Saving Private Ryan* (dir. Steven Spielberg, 1998), *Malcolm X* (dir. Spike Lee, 1992) and *Black Hawk Down* are valuably nuanced, but there are elements in their approach that are worrying. These emerge at the outset, as they lay out their questions:

When we assess Hollywood's recent portrayals of American history, we shall not simply be looking at the 'authenticity' of what is presented on the screen. We shall consider what kinds of questions, if any, the films raise about the meaning and significance of the events and characters they portray. How much historical contextualisation do these films provide? What historical questions do they engage with? How do they interpret the past? What messages and conclusions are they sending to the audience? Do they provoke the viewer to think about the many ways in which the events being portrayed can be understood or do they simply assert a closed viewpoint? Is there an argument being made about the past in the film? How well does it make that argument and does it indicate that it is important? Do any distortions or uses of fiction in the films undermine our ability to interpret history or can they, perhaps paradoxically, actually strengthen the argument being made and add to the viewer's ability to learn something about the historical period in question? (McCrisken & Pepper 2005:6)

This is an ambitious canvas, with much of value in it. But my concerns about it are these. First, there is that slippage common to this kind of work, to imputing responses to 'the viewer' who remains generic and undefined. Yet we have already seen that all the films not only attract hugely diverse responses, but also come out via distribution routes which steer them to particular audiences and uses. Without investigating those, the claims remain empty deductions from purely textual investigations. This is something I have sought to challenge in previous work (Barker with Austin 2000).

Second, there is a half-hidden 'ideal' in here, in which the best that a film can do is to encourage you not to be 'closed'. That, puzzlingly, sees films as almost operating outside any real settings. But what if they are conscious responses to contexts of likely reception? When considering a film like *World Trade Center*, for instance, my argument was that it came out into an over-determined debate, and its refusal to engage in that debate was itself a political act. Or, as we will see, a film like *GI Jesús* may speak specifically to a Latino population, offering them a committed perspective. 'Openness', while sounding a good liberal ideal, can clash with ideas of *committed* film-making. Third, there is a curious, half-argued claim that well-made films will better embody arguments than poorly-made ones. I want most definitely to challenge that linkage. The very *struggles* for clarity and coherence in a film can point to the stressful and limiting conditions under which it was made; while in the other direction (and I will argue this in the final chapter in looking at *The Hurt Locker*) 'effectiveness' in a film may be an indicator that it has smoothed out conflicts, leaving an unchallenging hollow.

But there is a larger issue dogging this debate: the issue of 'taking sides'. I pointed up some of the problems in Kellner's account. Now, I want to go wider. My argument is that, in terms of understanding Hollywood's films about American history and politics, the issue is not whether they *ought* to be evaluated for their accuracy, bias, and taking of sides, but to consider the fact that they *are* so evaluated. Hollywood, because of its status, is dogged by criticism. This means that when producers are developing a film, they will be extremely aware of potential complaints. They cover their backs as best they can, in advance. Script-development must take such risks into account. Marketing, trailers, interviews, websites will evidence the decisions on how to position a film in relation to such points of challenge.

Sometimes this can be worked to ensure safety and guarantee praise. *Sergeant York* was a classic case of this, with Warner Bros. paying good money to ensure that York, his family, neighbours and comrades would have nothing to complain about. Sometimes it can be in expectation of head-on clashes. *Missing* (dir. Costa-Gavras, 1982) is a good example of this. This film told the story of Ed Horman, whose son Charles was murdered in Chile, possibly with the American connivance, at the time of the CIA-backed overthrow of Salvador Allende.[1] Robert Toplin (1994, Chapter 4), among others, reviews in great detail the case for and against the film's accuracy, against available public records. There is nothing wrong with this, in principle, but Toplin's conclusion reveals the approach's limitations. He writes that,

> [B]ecause important documentation about the US role in the Chilean coup and in the murder of Charles Horman was lacking, Ambassador Davies appears to be correct in his claims that the movie represented 'an assault on the integrity of the US government, the Foreign Service and the military without sufficient justification' (Toplin 1994:24).

This limitation, to whatever has leaked out, forbids a role to a film of challenging secrecy and suppression of evidence (as, for instance, Oliver Stone did with his *JFK*). However, it also limits the debate to the truth or otherwise of this particular story. New historicist critics would point to the larger issue – that it takes one American's death against the hundreds of thousands of Chileans' to provide a motive for a Hollywood film. I now want to add this: that it is the very terms of the debate around a film like this that need examination. What they can reveal, as perhaps nothing else can, is what *count* as the available 'sides'. What interpretive and critical forces are active around a film? This is, in effect, the purpose of the reception studies approach introduced by Janet Staiger (1992, 2000), and developed and elaborated by a number of other film scholars. Staiger argues that the meaning of a film is not given by its textual characteristics alone, but by the cumulative discursive frames of interpretation brought to bear on it, and circulated among viewers.[2] This will prove particularly important in thinking about the judgements passed on two films, *Rendition* and *The Kingdom*.

WAR, INC.

How, then, do my five contextualising films go about their argumentative work? One of them – in some ways a pair to the deadly serious *Grace Is Gone*, in starring John Cusack and coming out via his production company – tackles the war via the notion that it is so crazy that all we can do is howl with desperate, cynical laughter. *War, Inc.* casts a sardonic eye on the whole of America's Middle East involvements by casting Cusack in a wacky reprise of his unhappy assassin role in *Grosse Point Blank* (dir. George Armitage, 1997). The film's humour is so broad it trumps every attempt at accounting. Calling itself an 'absurdist comedy, but with a serious point', it celebrates its cynicism ('Thanks to the 3rd Bomber Squadron for those humane precision strikes that have created this wonderful opportunity to restore clean water supplies'). All mannerisms are exaggerated, all stereotypes play themselves as stereotypes. Villains are Bond-like, but with corporate politics – grotesques.

Cusack plays hired assassin-cum-wedding organiser Brand Hauser – cool and ultra-competent at killing, but with a conscience and bad taste. By the end, we realise he is this way because his wife was killed and his daughter stolen as punishment for trying to get out. Hauser works as cynical fixer for a multinational corporation Tamerlane in fictional Turakistan. No-one is heroic. Even Natalie, the left wing journalist who is exposing Tamerlane's corruption, has a recorded phone message which diminishes her: 'This is Natalie. I'm either unmasking corporate greed or I'm washing my hair'. But when Hauser has to rescue Natalie from a bunch of incompetent kidnappers and finds himself in the war zone, the film turns nasty, offering a vision of a ruined country reminiscent of Hieronymus Bosch, and all jokes vanish. Bleak desperate figures move across an apocalyptic landscape. But the film returns at the end to its unconstrained cynicism. As our 'heroes' fly out celebrating their escape, we see a missile approaching their plane from behind. The final shot is a television image of the former Vice-President of Tamerlane (looking uncannily like Colin Powell) announcing a new war, now that they have identified the source of the recent attacks: 'America will not allow outside forces to interfere in the internal affairs of Turakistan'.

War, Inc. straddles the gulf between the slick rhetorics of American political, military and corporate leaders, and the realities of their actions. There, it bares its buttocks and invites us to think how far we dare go in thinking about the lies we are told. But – as enthusiastic responses on IMDb make very evident – you have in many ways already to be inside this cynicism and to have become good at reference-spotting to get the most out of the film. If you are not so adept, *War, Inc.* is likely to confuse and frustrate. This is a film for cynical cognoscenti.

BODY OF LIES

This film opens on a quote from W. H. Auden: 'those to whom evil is done do evil in return'. Manchester, UK: a radical preacher is under surveillance, but a police raid leads to the triggering of a huge explosion. Cut to Samarra, and a prisoner being beaten to death, leading to the voice of CIA boss Ed Hoffman (Russell Crowe) pronouncing, Bush-like, a war between creeds, future against past. During all this we get glimpses of CIA operative Roger Ferris (Leonardo Di Caprio) watching and blending in, in Iraq. He is in an operation to pick up a man who is terrified of being made to martyr himself and who knows the plans for another UK attack. After getting the information, Hoffman cynically orders the man's release so they can track who kills him.

This cynicism sets the pattern for the rest of the film, in Iraq and Jordan. Hoffman keeps interfering with his crude ideology, while Ferris beds in (eventually literally) with a young Arab doctor, Aiesha. Ferris comes to value the lives and culture of ordinary Arabs, but he is captured, and would be executed except for the intervention of the local Jordanian Chief of Police, whom Hoffman still despises.

The film ends with him walking out on the CIA, watching Aiesha from across the street, summoning up the courage to speak to her. The CIA cut him loose to take his chances, following this exchange – Hoffman: 'Ain't nobody likes the Middle East, there's nothing here to like'; Ferris: 'Just be careful calling yourself "America", Ed'. This simple morality tale depends heavily on the contrasting star-images of the bullying macho Crowe and the softer, engaging DiCaprio. However, the striking thing about the most positive reviews is that, unanimously, they praise *Body of Lies* as a 'Ridley Scott film' (and the film bears the safety-guarantee of association with both Warner Bros. and Scott's own production company). This then is trademark Action stuff. One IMDb reviewer asks, rhetorically: 'is this anti-war?' The answer is almost certainly no – it is just anti-Bush strategies and rhetorics for the war. That is safe ground for a studio (Warner Bros.) project.

THE SITUATION

This film opens at a checkpoint in Samarra. Iraqi soldiers observe US soldiers throwing two teenagers off the bridge, one of whom drowns. Everything thereafter is an aftermath/extension of this. At the centre of the story is American journalist Anna (Connie Nielsen), who tries to explore what happened and finds herself inside the corrupt world of Iraqi politics. Connie's boyfriend is a weak American political officer who is trying to arrange the refitting of a hospital, hoping thereby to win over halfway friendly Iraqis. Much turns on a contact, Rafeeq, who has insurgent sympathies because he feels let down by the Americans. Rafeeq is eventually killed and dumped outside his house – but by whom?

The tone is set from the outset as an Iraqi photojournalist speaks to Anna: 'I used to dream of a life after Saddam, and a McDonalds in Baghdad'. They are going to visit Rafeeq. They talk about 'the situation' (corruption, bombs, mujahideen and criminals now back in power, because of the Americans). In Baghdad, politicos and military take opposite views on handling the situation, the latter favouring direct action to clear out the insurgents. The arguments are stalling rebuilding efforts. A new enthusiastic recruit argues the need to bring 'democracy by force'. We learn through conversations about the many splits, Sunni/Shia, regional, Muslim/Christian and so on. They watch a US raid on a house opposite – 'it happens all the time', the photographer says as he documents the soldiers' brutality. We see the mayor paying off associates, then bringing in prostitutes for his men. A 'retired diplomat' (an old Ba'athist officer) offers the Americans information on condition of being relocated, to Australia. Their conversation touches on Saddam: 'He understood the need for discipline'.

After Rafeeq is killed, Anna pledges to find out what happened to him and insists on going to Samarra. But she cannot get the story – the police will not talk. Finally kidnapped after getting caught up in a seizure of guns by the local insurgents, she and her photographer/ translator are bundled into a basement when two Saudi/Al Qaeda operatives suddenly arrive. Eventually freeing her, their local leader tells her he wants her to know the true story – of the corrupt lines between the ex-criminal chief of police, who shot Rafeeq so he could marry his daughter, through the sheikh who put him there, back to the Americans who have supported the sheikh. She promises to bring the story out. Meanwhile, her politico boyfriend has called on the military to rescue her. In the ensuing firefight, many on both sides die; the photographer is shot and dies, with a parting kiss from Anna. We see the local insurgent leader emerging from the river, having just escaped. Anna's now ex-boyfriend finds his hospital equipment dumped in a field by the outside toilets. The film ends on Anna preparing to leave looking at the last photos (including of her) taken by her Iraqi friend.

The themes are hardly hidden in this: Anna's disaffection leading to her increasing detachment from the American side; the corruption linking American occupiers to those they installed after defeating Saddam; and the impossibility of differentiating insurgents from ordinary disaffected Iraqis. Nothing is resolved at the end, and Anna's departure with her token photographs promises little.

RENDITION

Rendition is a considerably more complicated film. Merging two accounts of real renditions (Maher Arar and Khalid El-Masri), the film was released by New Line Cinema in its final year before it was reabsorbed by Warner Bros. after over-reaching itself. New Line had begun in the independent film sector but, with *Lord of the Rings* in particular, had moved into blockbuster cinema – then crashed badly with *The Golden Compass* (dir. Chris Weitz, 2007). This wobbly balance was reinforced by choice of director, South African Gavin Hood, himself in transition from independent international film-making to Hollywood mainstream (in 2009 he directed *Wolverine*). With star input from Reece Witherspoon[3] as an expectant wife, Isabella, whose husband, Anwar El-Ibrahimi, vanishes from a flight into the US, the film interweaves her attempts to uncover what has happened to him, in the face of denials and hints of his terrorist involvement, with two other narrative lines: the story of Douglas Freeman (rising star Jake Gyllenhaal), a fresh CIA analyst who becomes disillusioned as he is forced to watch Anwar's rendition to torture by a dubious US ally Abasi Fawal; and the story of two young Arab lovers, Fatima and Khalid, caught up within a repressive regime, one of whom we learn (very late) to be Fawal's daughter. That late revelation comes as part of a major narrative twist in which we have suddenly to understand that events which we saw near the beginning of the film are in fact out of temporal order. Time gets shuffled. At the film's climax, when Fawal's men are chasing up the stairs to find his daughter, she is rushing down the stairs to follow her boyfriend. Yet they do not meet, because the events are actually a week apart. The boy was heading for the town square to try to blow up her father in a suicide bombing. This twist is critical, because it suggests that events are caught in an almost unstoppable loop, sustained from afar by the cynical interventions of America's spymasters.

The film ends with Fawal encountering the grieving grandmother of Khalid, realising his daughter has been dead for a week. Freeman cuts himself off from his boss from Washington and puts Anwar on a boat. The closing shot of the film is an exhausted Anwar reuniting with his wife and son. A DVD Extra counterposes long interviews with two rendered men about their torture, commentary from a judge on its illegality and from a former CIA chief on its uselessness, against 'statements' from George W. Bush and Condoleeza Rice insisting that the US never tortures anyone. For the film's enthusiasts, as one IMDb review nicely captures it, the film is happily non-preachy: 'The movie's message seems to be (as stated by Jake Gyllenhaal's character in the film) that by abducting and torturing suspects you create many more terrorists'. What the makers have done is to absorb the argument of the film into its structure. Borrowing from the inventions of recent puzzle films (see Buckland 2009), it embeds the politics in the 'time-loop' structure. But for many (including those who appreciated its politics), there was a generic conflict in the film. Its linear, mainstream narrative and star-led performances set up expectations which sat awkwardly with its sudden use of an indie, puzzle-film-based time-loop motif. Then, reverting to a 'happy ending' for which Gyllenhaal's character Freeman has to become a barely believable good guy standing up to his CIA bosses, did not just strain credibility – it left you unsure of the very grounds on which this might be secured. This unease is present in bits and pieces in many of the IMDb comments, but was crisply summarised in one television review of the film:

> The [torture] scenes are effective, and upsetting, and Hood slams his point home. The sight of that Abu Ghraib hood still makes the stomach twist. Valiantly, if not successfully, the script circles the question of whether or not torture breeds more violence. In a head-scratching, disjointed back story, the police chief has a daughter who becomes unwittingly involved with a group of budding terrorists. The film hints that the machine-gun-wielding boys are machines manufactured by violence for violence. I wanted to know more about these boys, as I did almost everyone in *Rendition*. Hood needed to spotlight the real, live people at the centre of this political debate, but who are they? Witherspoon isn't terrible, but she's only stoic; her blankness doesn't really look like fortitude. Meanwhile, jockish Freeman is suddenly quoting Shakespeare. Worse, El-Ibrahimi himself is given no complexity or ambiguity, and thus, no humanity. And without humanity, as this period of history surely shows, there's nothing. (Onstad 2007)

New Line's positioning of *Rendition* as a mainstream, star-studded film, coupled with its play with indie techniques, thus set up frustrations within its reception frame.

THE KINGDOM

Perhaps the most interesting of this group of films is *The Kingdom* – not so much for what it is, but for debates it inspired. A studio output (Universal), this movie is universally called things like a 'high intensity action thriller'. It made almost as much from rentals ($77 million) as it did at the box office ($86 million), confirming its place in the 'action DVD' market. Starring popular action players Jamie Foxx (as Team Leader Ronald Fleury), Chris Cooper (Grant Sykes) and Jennifer Garner (Janet Mayes), it begins with a fast-cut timeline of the complex political tendencies inside Saudi Arabia since the 1940s, leading through the rise of Wahabi Islam and the growth of militant tendencies (including Bin Laden). This timeline displays America's oil dependency on Saudi Arabia and the long, dubious political links this has fostered, and ends with Saddam's invasion of Kuwait and the outline of a plane about to crash into the Twin Towers. Thereafter, while the narrative maps onto the real attack on oil workers in Riyadh, it is thoroughly fictionalised, setting up a crack FBI team who effectively blackmail their way into the country (threatening to expose dubious financial deals if not allowed in), crafty politicians on both sides trying to cut deals (because of oil, it is made clear), and establish a growing liaison with a genuinely patriotic Saudi police officer, Colonel Faris Ghazi. It results in a huge shoot-out, the deaths of dozens of militants and of the Saudi officer. The most striking thing, apart from its battle scenes, is the ending. After the fighting, there are emotional scenes when Fleury visits the dead Ghazi's children, and assures them that Ghazi was his good friend, then at the airport affectionate farewells and thanks from grateful Saudi officers. Back home, they are briefed about how they should respond to the inevitable inquiry – and told to lie if asked whether they were briefed – and praised for an 'outstandingly good job'. The film closes with a precise doubling of closely intercut scenes, in which the Americans recall a moment when Fleury whispered to his wounded compatriot Mayes: 'Don't worry, we are going to kill them all', while in Riyadh the grandson of the militants' leader Abu Hamza recalls his grandfather's dying words: 'Fear not, in the end we will kill them all'.

Fascinatingly, the film was read almost universally as pro-US. One IMDb critic of the film put it very strongly: 'it's a simplistic, gung ho, neocon piece of wish fulfilment. It appears to open with a criticism of USA military interference and lust for oil, but by the end shows that overt, Rambo-style military action will solve all problems. Yeah, right.' Another angrily reported the responses of audiences he had observed:

I don't know if Peter Berg has had a chance to sit in an advanced screening in the South, but he would be appalled. The audience clapped and cheered with every Saudi killed. It was truly more grotesque than any of the unnecessary images being shown on screen. As a filmmaker, he had the opportunity to redeem this message in some way, but he took the low road and fueled hatred. The movie ends with this nugget of advice being passed down from both the Americans and Saudis: 'Kill all of them.' Nice message.

This misses the equivalent Arab comment, which at least ambiguates Fleury's. A third, also strikingly, refused to watch the whole film after even the opening led him to conclude that it was entirely set up to be pro-Bush:

The lead-in history of the world in 2 minutes (from an edited western perspective) irritated me somewhat, but I persevered. But when I saw Fleury in a classroom/grade school setting, calmly 'taking it easy' as the director displayed in juxtaposition, scenes of Americans dying and all hell breaking loose at the Saudi/American compound, when I watched Fleury calmly conduct a cell phone conversation with a [G]round [Z]ero victim, showing little or no emotion, and then casually continue a conversation with his student/son, all my suspicions were confirmed. I flipped it off. It appeared to me that someone was subtly (or maybe not so subtly) trying to justify or lend plausibility to President Moron's incredibly stupid conduct while being informed about the 9/11 crisis during his photo-op classroom visit.

Press reviews reveal another striking connection. In all the discourse around the Iraq war movie cycle, this is the only case I have found where 'John Wayne' is used as a measure. Several reviews compared it with Wayne's *The Green Berets*, arguing that the film might count as a lone pro-Bush case. One instance: the *Deseret Morning News* admonished the film, finding it weak and unconvincing:

> At first it appears that director Peter Berg's thriller is going to depict a few of the Saudis – in particular, Ashraf Barhom's sympathetic colonel character – as being at least as heroic as the Americans. But then Matthew Carnahan's script quickly changes and turns Foxx and the others into modern-day John Waynes. (The similarities between this movie and the even more heavy-handed 1968 Wayne vehicle 'The Green Berets' are many.) (Vice 2007)

The description is odd in that a key premise is that the corruption of Saudi Arabia has been sustained by America's thirst for oil deals.

Some of its IMDb defenders respond by deleting the film's politics from attention altogether, as here:

> It seems most of the negative comments are from people who think this should be an historically accurate picture of culture and politics in the middle East. That's the wrong approach to take from the start! I know a little more than the average American, being Jewish and having an aunt who taught this subject at the college level, but I didn't sit there taking notes about what

was unrealistic like some folks did. And I enjoyed it! Isn't that the point of a movie like this? The story was good, the dialog interesting, the action top-notch, and as an Alias fan, I even get a thrill seeing Jen Garner doing makeup commercials. Hang loose, fellas – this is an action-adventure, not a PBS news documentary.

How do we make sense of this? The criterion best able to make sense of this determined disambiguation of the film is quite simply this: if American soldiers win, little else matters.[4] Politicians can lie and deceive (and by the time this film emerged, the tale of the links between the Bush family and the Saudi royals had been widely discussed)[5], but if US forces do their 'action thing' and win, nothing else matters. Even knowing that you have made yet more enemies doesn't matter. 'We' won.

CONCLUSION

How, then, do these films 'tell' American history, politics and Middle Eastern policy? With the exception of the ill-balanced *Rendition*, both narratives and cinematic strategies are simpler, because (I would argue) of the distance from the figure of the 'American soldier'. But these films do create a virtual equivalent: a non-heroic, ill-prepared 'innocent' who has his or her eyes opened to something they simply had not understood. One is relatively neutral, a journalist, three are FBI or CIA operatives, one a political fixer-assassin. These figures operate as stand-ins for us, and we see their perceptions of the world of politics undone by the brutalities, frauds, and lies that they encounter. By keeping the working soldiers at a safe distance, these exposures can almost be seen to be on their behalf. The films effectively expose deceit, but all the time it feels like we are a step ahead of the central characters – to appreciate their learning, we have to begin and remain more cynical than them.

8
Producing a 'Toxic Genre'

The title of this book is taken from a report in *Variety* in which Anne Thompson (2008) reported Kathryn Bigelow's plans for *The Hurt Locker*, but wondered if she knew what she was letting herself in for. The epithet 'toxic genre' is a passing reference among notes of other new developments. The implications are left implicit, but assumed to make sense to readers. So, what exactly does it imply?

Certainly there is plenty of evidence to show that other commentators thought Iraq movies constituted a *type*. Here is part of one promotional account of *The Lucky Ones*, evidently trying to fend off a risk: 'People will be surprised by what they see. It's not really about the war, or about the soldiers, it's about the country now. The word "Iraq" is not mentioned in the movie'.[1] This collation of phrases from news items, reviews, alerts and commentaries from this period was found by searching the US press under the phrase 'Iraq war movies':

> Don't let any bias against Iraq war movies stop you from seeing … the late, unlamented anti-Iraq war movies. … Iraq war movies have been box office poison … There seems to be a jinx on Iraq war movies – even when there's a good one, audiences are reluctant to see it … Iraq war movies have typically fizzled at the box office … Thankfully not just another one of those antiwar Iraq war movies … the somber moralizing that has afflicted the recent crop of Iraq war movies … Just when I thought I'd seen enough of Iraq war movies along comes … The great Iraq war movies will come in time … Iraq war movies don't sell … whether marketing the film more as a thriller will be enough to overcome auds' resistance to Iraq war movies …

All these comments evidence an awareness of a troubling category: anti-war, disliked, audience rejection and probably just not very good. Sometimes the advice is to see past it – but that just re-emphasises its potential power. This category emerged early, perhaps even before the first of the films, as evidenced by this remark on *Home of the Brave*: 'more interested in being among the first Iraq war movies than being a well thought-out one'. This was a signally effective challenge.

In this chapter, I explore the significance of this category in two ways. First, how should we understand the very appearance of these films, given that it was clear they would meet with such scepticism or hostility? Through what production structures, histories and practices did they come to be, and how did these shape the kinds of films they became? Second, how should we understand this very process of labelling and what might be added to our understanding of the films to see them labelled a 'genre'? Tackling each of these questions requires an excursion into a much wider body of theory and research.

THE POLITICAL ECONOMY OF FILM

In the broadest sense, political-economy approaches to film, and to Hollywood specifically, turn on asking: in what ways do the economic and industrial processes involved in the making of films impact on their cinematic shape? Answers to this question range from macro-accounts of the general tendencies inherent in capitalist production or the market system, to more localised histories of the Hollywood studio system.

Because of its financial scale and its self-importance, Hollywood has long fascinated critical thinkers who have wanted to understand the drivers that might explain the kinds of films made by the studios, and what thereby is marginalised or left out. One starting point is the widely acknowledged fact that nine out of ten Hollywood releases make no money, while the successful tenth is capable of spawning vast (if often well-concealed) income. Another is the much-quoted remark by screenwriter William Goldman (1983:39) that in Hollywood, 'Nobody knows anything'. How do the studios guess winners from losers, and how do they seek to manage the losses on the latter? There have been several competing approaches to this. There is, on the one hand, a broadly monetarist approach, often produced by people advising the studios themselves, which looks for a 'rationality' in the overall structure of their decision-making. A significant figure in this is Arthur De Vany:

> 78 per cent of movies lose money and only 22 per cent are profitable. Profit is unevenly distributed among those movies that are profitable: just 35 per cent of *profitable* movies earn

80 per cent of total profit. Losses are more evenly distributed. Among *unprofitable* movies, 56 per cent accounted for 80 per cent of total losses. The most dramatic statistic is this: just 6.3 per cent of movies earned 80 per cent of Hollywood's total profits over the last decade. [italics in original] (De Vany 2003:214)

De Vany sees the process as one of managed chaos, with the producers second-guessing the decisions of unpredictable individual consumers. His account in the end confirms to the studios that it is worth surrounding films with marketing 'noise', because this can produce 'statistical herding', with people following each other to the cinema on the basis of the perceived popularity of films. Thus does an initially individualistic account (everyone makes his/her own choice to see a movie) turn into an econometric proposal (you can get them to respond in a mass, like this).

Exact opposites of De Vany's account are proposed by two sometimes interlocking approaches, which see Hollywood as a cynical money-making machine, willing to sacrifice art to money at the least, but possibly going further by producing the kinds of art designed to persuade people to accept the US model of money-making. Croteau and Hoynes (2005) well exemplify the first of these. Their study of contemporary US media emphasises the rise of multi-media corporations, their search for economies of scale, and for the mass market multiple-release cultural objects which can be merchandised through multiple routes – all multiplying the return to the corporation. This leads them to focus on a series of tendencies within corporate America: conglomeratisation, horizontal integration, vertical re-integration, government de-regulation, the centrality of market/political relations, and near-monopolisation. The related approach emphasises the role that the films themselves can play as carriers of an appropriately persuasive ideology. Perhaps the most outspoken representatives of this approach are Michael Ryan and Douglas Kellner (1988). They largely take as given the arguments of people such as Croteau and Hoynes, and turn their attention to the films themselves, analysing them for overt political messages and sub-texts. They certainly score some hits, in relation to films such as *Top Gun* (dir. Tony Scott, 1986), which was produced in close cooperation with the military in order to glamourise the fleet air force and its hardware, and indeed succeeding in raising recruitment among young men who wanted to be like Tom Cruise. Whether they work as well on most others is arguable.

There is another, less well-known approach, best illustrated in the work of Nicholas Garnham (1990). Garnham begins with three factors that are special to cultural production. First, unlike cars, clothes, foods and so on, for which long production lines can be planned, every cultural release has to be prototypical, that is, sold on the basis of its difference from previous releases. Second, the very factor that drives the newness of these endlessly changing prototypes – its makers' creativity – is the hardest to predict and control. Third, creative goods are not burnt up by being enjoyed; their value as intellectual property potentially goes on. For these reasons, the economics of cultural production – and Hollywood film-making is just a special case of this – is necessarily different from other industries. The fundamental imperative behind Hollywood therefore takes a peculiar form: 'It is cultural distribution, not cultural production, that is the key locus of power and profit' (Garnham 1990:161–2). This leads Garnham to emphasise the many ways in which producers try to manage risk through, for instance: control of distribution channels; intellectual property control; creating dependency relations between hardware and software; selling its audiences as commodities to advertisers; in-built obsolescence and need for repeat purchases; creating franchises, genres, sequels; and generating cultural obligations to participate.

These varying approaches have different implications for understanding Hollywood. But each, of course, is primarily focused on the Big Players, who make most and the largest products, and largely control distribution systems. Here, the work of Bordwell et al. (1985) on the Hollywood studio system becomes important. Bordwell and his colleagues explored the ways in which the studio system regularised all processes of film-making, from script production to star contracts and release patterns, producing also a set of predictable narrative forms. Their 'classical Hollywood formula' typically includes: a single narrative thread, set around a dilemma requiring solution within a constrained time; a central hero, who has to discover something about him/herself in order to meet the challenge; relatively clear moral lines; a 'reward' for the hero, often in the form of romantic coupling; and so on. This overall pattern then found regional variants in a series of on-going generic formulae. Both Thompson (1999) and Bordwell (2006) have gone on to explore the changes in the studio system, post-1949, arguing that there are strong continuities to the present day.

Whatever the strengths of these varied accounts, each faces problems when applied to the Iraq war cycle. De Vany's account will struggle to cope with films which appear to have been produced without any especial concern with making money – they are what I will call Statement Films; that is, films primarily produced to make a point. Croteau and Hoynes will have trouble addressing films that are not marketed in the synergetic fashion that the studios mainly employ; Ryan and Kellner (as we indeed saw in Chapter 1) also simply carve films into pro- and anti-positions. The difficulty with Garnham is that he treats Hollywood as essentially an economic entity, yet here production motives are complicated by political intentions. Bordwell and Thompson's powerful account, too, primarily relates to *internal* systems, and how these shape cinematic and narrative strategies, rather than Hollywood's external relations with politics.

One author seems to me to have opened promising new lines of enquiry, particularly relating to the sector of 'independent' film-making. Across three books, Geoff King has explored the ways in which the contemporary structures of US film production have shaped the genres, narratives, and formal strategies of the films produced. Following his (2002) general study of contemporary Hollywood film-making, King (2005) explored the tradition of US independent cinema, tracing its inception alongside the origins of Hollywood itself, but focusing in particular on the period from the mid-1980s. King's argument is, contra several purist authors, that there cannot be a normative definition of 'independent'. Systems of production, distribution, and validation have altered over time, and very much by relation to the moves of the Big Brother studios. These have proven well capable of acquiring styles, narratives, and successful names from the independent sector, or even (as in the early 1990s) directly buying into the sector, either through the creation of specialist subsidiaries (King particularly considers Sony Picture Classics, Fox Searchlight, and Paramount Classics) or through the acquisition of formerly independent companies (most notably, Miramax, and New Line Cinema).

If in his second book King stressed that, 'During the 1990s, independent production became concentrated in the arms of fewer and larger companies' (King 2005:26), his third (2009) book studies the formation which emerged from this, widely known as 'Indiewood'. King's powerful study of this phenomenon is based on some dense industrial research. In case studies of films ranging from Charlie Kaufman's and Steven Soderbergh's output, to *Shakespeare in Love* (dir. John Madden, 1998) and *American Beauty* (dir. Sam Mendes, 1999), he explores the ways in which compromise narrative and formal strategies emerge from the kinds of requirements and pressures these films come under. His study of *Three Kings* (1999), one of the key critical films about the first Gulf War, is exemplary in this respect. King argues that the film cut a path that avoided too much controversy whilst gaining the cachet of critical independence, by combining 'controversial politics, stylised textures and shifts of modality, but underpinned by conventional group-quest structure coupled with doses of melodrama' (King 2009:236). He evidences moments of controversy in the writing of the script, as these compromises were struck. The inclusion of George Clooney, for instance, came largely at Warner Bros' insistence (against the wishes of scriptwriter David O. Russell) – although that rebounded when Clooney was one of those to complain at the watering down of the script.

King's conclusions are worth noting. He argues that while Indiewood is a distinctive phenomenon arising out of specific conditions, its various players carve up this specialist territory. It is hard therefore to find many distinctive norms. There is a tendency to what he nicely terms the 'mixed resonance ending' (King 2009:271), and to play with artistic/cultural resonances. But their central feature is the films' balancing acts.

The most important lesson from King's studies for mine is his insistent attention to the institutional and decision-making frameworks within which the films are made. The completed films are to be seen as the outcome of negotiations and struggles between various parties involved in their production. The complications in the case of the 'Iraq war genre' seem to be these. Many of the films, as we will see, are driven by highly individual intentions and funding regimes, and by a will to make Statements about the conflict. In this sense they are the precise opposite of what Mike Hammond (2002) discusses in his study of recent studio-derived combat films. Hammond focuses his discussion around William Friedkin's *Rules of Engagement* (1999), a film geographically relevant since its main events are set in Yemen. The narrative begins from a siege of the US embassy, in the course of which the Marines commander Colonel Childers (Samuel L. Jackson) orders his troops to fire into the crowd, killing many, and is put on trial for murder. There is a back-story to Vietnam, where Childers (serving alongside the man now asked to defend him) was involved in the brutal execution of a prisoner. Hammond is particularly interested in the fact that on the DVD Friedkin reveals that the ending was altered, after test screenings, so that Childers is unambiguously seen as innocent (contrary to the trend for leaving such things ambiguous, for fear of alienating

sections of viewers). Hammond argues that these films set out to
involve audiences in terrible events immersively, following the model
of *Saving Private Ryan*, and then through investigative narratives
to get them to consider the events' significance. Memories thus
become key to finding answers. All of these can then bring 'closure'
to psychic wounds such as Vietnam.

This very will to closure, and the use of test screenings to find
out 'what audiences want', are the precise opposite of what I
am identifying in many of my films. There is a will to challenge
viewers and to provoke rethinkings about the war and the US's
involvement in it. To achieve this, they provide 'reality guarantees'
that I discuss later in this Chapter. At the same time, many of
them deploy cinematic devices that are common currency in recent
independent cinema. But while these devices have there been used
as demonstrations of artistry, in the Iraq war films they function to
provoke challenges to audience assumptions. They *aim to undermine
presumed ways of understanding the war*, and to *provoke disquiet*.

I want to make a point that should be so obvious as to seem
almost trite, but which is often forgotten, its implications set aside.
Films are made for many very different purposes, and in many cases
are mixed together. These different purposes shape, for those who
engage with them, their ways of participating in them, the criteria by
which they assess them, and the ways that canons of best and worst
examples are generated. Without any wish to make a finished list,
consider the following. Educational film-making: seeking to embody
complex ideas in accessible forms. Propaganda film-making: aiming
to win and hold recruits. Worshipful film-making: offering emotional
participation in valued, religious experiences. Art film-making:
generating complex experiences to be valued for themselves.
Experimental film-making: trying out new formal devices within
the medium. To these broad categories could be added many more
specialist kinds of film-making. Visceral films (aiming to arouse,
amuse, scare and so on).[2] Trade films (advertising your wares, as
a company, specialist, or other).[3] Brand-recognition films (keeping
your image in the public eye). Apprentice pieces (putting out a
film that will prove your worth to potential employers). Putting
it very baldly, it is daft to think that there can be one measure of
'success' or 'failure' across all these. But, just as importantly, the
sheer variety of kinds of films and film-making means that there are
likely to be specialist audiences, places for sharing, discussing and
evaluating, as well as distinct production and distribution regimes
and routes. Religious films are a very good example of all this.

Largely hidden from general view, there is in the US in particular a large corpus of films which are promoted by and circulate through churches. Used often as part of services, they are measured for their appropriateness to achieving a sense of spiritual uplift and enhanced belief. Occasionally these may spill into the domain of general circulation, as with Mel Gibson's *Passion of the Christ* (2004). But the imprimatur of those closed circuits carried over, as when, for instance, some preachers block-booked cinemas and insisted their congregations attend.

These are by no means the same as film genres, even if some of these do map quite well onto one of these kinds ('horror' as a type-case of visceral film-making, for instance). Of course only some very specialist films fall tidily under just one rubric. Audiences encountering most films, which mix kinds, have, as David Bordwell (1979) has argued, to learn (be trained in) the appropriate ways of making sense of them. And it is via this that I am making my claim about positive responses: that the responses of those who engage most positively can allow us to see the kinds of 'training' that particular films demand of their audiences. Positive responses become a special kind of mirror, allowing us to examine the operations of a film for those most receptive to its impact.

Among all the kinds hinted at above, one film-making purpose has particular importance to my Iraq war films: the will to make a Statement. By this I mean that these films, of course among other things, frequently intend to mount an argument and propose a position on the conflict. The striking thing is that they have chosen to do this through the medium of fiction, albeit fiction which constantly emphasises its reality-links. To the extent that they are, and are judged as, Statement films, 'success' and 'failure' become inherently more complicated. While we can be sure that film-makers want financial success, this will be only one of their measures. Like a political speech, adherents may hear a different 'message' than opponents. But also like political speeches, films partly take on their meaning from the ways in which dominating voices name, judge, and categorise them.[4] The struggle to shape debates over the purposes and achievements of films is crucial. Producers, directors, actors make statements, give interviews, and add Extras to DVDs in which they make their pitches. But these are not transparent access to a film's purposes, as experienced by those who engage with it.[5] They are positions in the terrain of debate.

Nonetheless, one important feature of Statement Films is the way their makers and promoters emphasise their relevance to contemporary events and thinking. And it is here that we can further answer the question I posed at the outset: why use fiction, instead of documentary? Linking the benefits of using character types and typified events with careful grounding of these in relation to real events might maximise the emotional possibilities of fiction, with the applications of those emotions to the lived world. In light of this, consider Table 3, which shows how often within my 23 films three forms of what I would call 'reality guarantees' are presented. (1) Films can be overtly rooted in something real beyond Hollywood (real individuals, events, an organisation, or a named problem). (2) Symbolising quotations can be used, to lock the film onto some over-arching moral point, thus turning Iraq into something of wider pertinence. Or, (3) films can diegetically introduce moments of captured politics (clips from speeches, television coverage or the like) which remind us of the rootedness of the fictional events in the real world. (Ticks, dashes, and crosses mean the same here as in Chapter 3.)

Table 3 'Reality guarantees' within the films

Title	Beyond Hollywood	Symbolising quotations	Captured politics
American Soldiers	✓	✓	–
The Jacket	–	–	–
Home of the Brave	✓	✓	✓
The Situation	–	–	✓
GI Jesús	–	✓	✓
The Marine	✗	✗	✗
Badland	–	–	–
Battle for Haditha	✓	–	✓
Grace Is Gone	✓	–	✓
In the Valley of Elah	✓	–	✓
The Kingdom	✓	–	✓
Lions for Lambs	–	–	✓
The Mark of Cain	–	✓	✓
Redacted	✓	–	✓
Rendition	✓	–	–
Day Zero	✓	–	✓
Conspiracy	–	–	–
The Lucky Ones	✗	✓	–
Stop-Loss	✓	–	✓
War, Inc.	–	✓	–
Body of Lies	–	✓	–
The Objective	–	–	–
The Hurt Locker	–	✓	–

Nine of the films make explicit reference to some real event or organisation as the ground of their narrative. These include: *Grace Is Gone*'s association with the 'Tragedy Assistance Program for Survivors', a Pentagon-backed support programme for families of war victims; *Stop-Loss*' dedication to a named dead soldier, contextualised by figures for the number of soldiers forced to return to Iraq up to 2007; and *In the Valley of Elah*'s association with the Richard T. Davis Memorial Fund. *Redacted* manages to combine these provocatively, with its opening declaration that the entire film is a re-imagining of the real rape and murder in Samarra, its construction as if it were entirely made up of other people's bits of filmed evidence, closing with a long series of photographs of dead Iraqi civilians. Seven of them deploy a summary quotation which proposes some kind of wider meaning or significance to the film's narrative. These include: *Home of the Brave*'s 'Wars begin where you will but they do not end where you please' (Machiavelli); *Body of Lies*' 'those to whom evil is done, do evil in return' (W. H. Auden); and *American Soldiers*' quote from General Zimmi (2000) that 'its serving soldiers are America's greatest treasure, not to be used lightly and without good cause'. Thirteen of the films at some point allow moments of actual news or politics to penetrate the fictional diegesis, as reminders of actual events and debates. They include: *Rendition*'s quotations from speeches about the 'War on Terror' (along with which should be mentioned the DVD Extras in which, among other things, a US judge presents a long argument on the uselessness and illegality of torture); *Day Zero*'s direct recollection of the Vietnam draft, using news clips; and *The Lucky Ones*' insertion of real news clips as TK Poole sits in a bar, pondering whether to desert to Canada or return to Iraq. And nine of the films use two or more of these devices.

Table 3 raises the difficult question: what counts as delivering a 'message'? In some of the above cases, it seems that the extra-diegetic reference points operate as a safety device, to try to defray possible complaints. The most obvious case of this is *Redacted*, where funding was made conditional on De Palma fictionalising his characters, even while he reminded us that everything was based on real events. In other cases, they function as optical glass for an emergent idea, but in the case of *Elah* this is paradoxical because (as we saw in Chapter 7) the real case of Richard Davis had complexities that the film denied. Only two of the films use none of these devices. Yet I do not believe this entails a lesser 'message' element in them. The two films are *Conspiracy*, and *Badland*. *Badland*, as we saw in

Chapter 6) is an interesting example in that its narrative intensity runs so far that the DVD Extras try to shuffle off some of the emergent threats this could pose, over the issue of its implications for god and religion.

CONSPIRACY AS A TEST-CASE

Conspiracy is a good test-case of these complications. The film tracks a naïve US soldier (played by a rather plump Val Kilmer) from his return at the end of a tour of duty in Iraq, damaged physically and mentally, to America. His platoon buddy Miguel Silver encourages him to join him in building a new life in New Mexico. Eventually, almost against his will, he goes – to find his friend vanished, and a town taken over by a development company, Halicorps, whose billboard proclaims it to be 'Keeping America safe at home and abroad'.

Costing $18 million to make, the film was destined not for cinemas but for the 'direct-to-DVD' market, a system that has grown and sedimented in the last decade. Its main distributor was Sony, via their recently created subdivision 'Fight Factory', which specialises in 'high concept, star-led direct-to-DVD action movies'. But funding came through a variety of routes, including through Kilmer's own production company. Trying to understand the ways in which the production circumstances might shape a film of this kind, we need to attend to at least four distinct forces. First is the Iraq war aesthetic, that showing of bewildering battle situations, and the associated focus on the costs to US soldiers, most typically in the form of PTSD. To these, the film pays its homage.

Alongside these influences comes Kilmer himself, a left-leaning maverick (he endorsed Ralph Nader's bid for the Presidency in 2008) who has been living in New Mexico since the 1980s, where he likes to make his films, and is involved in some local environmental campaigns. In 2010, it was rumoured that Kilmer was considering running for the State Governorship (see Adams 2008). One of the hottest political topics along all the border states is immigration, as is the status of Mexican–Americans. It is hardly surprising that this becomes a further theme in the film. Then there is the film's director, Adam Marcus. Marcus comes from a 1980s New York film-school background, but came into prominence with his 1999 film *Let It Snow*. The film was the Official Selection at the 2000 Sundance Festival. But this film did not follow that route. Written, directed and acted in by Marcus, with his partner producing, it was

Figure 8.1 'Fight Factory' (Sony) logo. Dismissed as 'failures' (whether with pleasure or concern) by most American commentators on the evidence of their weak box office, what was missed was the often unusual routes to release these films took. *Conspiracy*, for instance, never sought cinema release, instead entering the curious world of the Sony subsidiary *Fight Factory*'s 'Direct to DVD' system, finding itself thereby alongside films combining macho display with cynical politics.

clearly a very personal project. But it depended on a distribution deal, which he got with Sony's Fight Factory label – a deal that made it essential for the film to play up not only its 'action' qualifications but also its star-lead (leading to snarky reviewer-comments about Kilmer's weight).

Being sent straight to DVD does not necessarily connote death as it once did. The distribution of action films is now heavily played through this route, and increasingly known to aficionados. But equally it does not entail a catalogue of scenes of conflict. Rather, these films typically contain strong strands of cynical politics. Take as a clear illustration *Zombie Strippers!* (dir. Jay Lee, 2008), also distributed by Fight Factory. A 'zombie comedy', the film claims a serious heritage, being loosely based on Eugene Ionesco's classic play *Rhinoceros*. The movie's official website describes the film thus:

This movie opens with a news montage explaining that it is set in a dystopic near-future in which George W. Bush has been elected to a fourth term. The United States Congress has been disbanded; public nudity is banned; the United States is embroiled in wars with France, Iraq, Afghanistan, Iran, Pakistan, Syria, Venezuela,

Canada, and Alaska. With more wars than there are soldiers to fight them, a secret laboratory run by Dr. Chushfeld (Brad Milne) in Sartre, Nebraska, has developed a virus to re-animate dead Marines and send them back into battle. However, this virus has broken containment and infected test subjects and scientists, and they are at risk of escaping the lab. A team of Marines codenamed the 'Z' Squad is sent in to destroy the zombies.

As the virus takes hold, a series of conflicts-to-the-death erupts among the strippers and their clients, with appropriate levels of nudity and mayhem:

The remaining humans in the club struggle to survive until the 'Z' Squad burst in to destroy the zombies. But they discover that the zombies were allowed to escape by the Bush Administration, in the hopes that the ensuing zombie plague would distract Americans from their gross mishandling of the war effort and the economy.

Joyously pitching itself as a ludicrous B-movie, the film nonetheless takes as given a deep distrust of the motives and actions of the Bush regime. And this surely is quite typical of this tradition of films. But *Conspiracy* – with its more evident element of Statement film-making – has somewhat more politics than this background cynicism.

How do these influences mesh to shape the resultant movie? The film opens directly to 2005 Iraq, and we are straight into a piece of 'Iraq war experience'. A deliberately unclear cinematic presentation half-conceals what is going on, so we cannot be sure of sides, or experience, until its outcome: a smiling little girl with a teddy and a rucksack on her back – with wires protruding. There is an explosion. Our central character, McPherson, is injured. Thereafter, the film keeps flashing back to Iraq to remind us of the clobber McPherson is carrying within himself. We learn in fact that he has almost lost the ability to fight at all, so that when the local thugs beat him up he can hardly defend himself.

On his journey to find Silver, we are shown bits of 'America' in a state of moral collapse, and without respect for a veteran. In one scene, he outfaces trouble-seeking teenagers by catching their firecracker in his bare hand and throwing it back at them. McPherson heads off on a bus to the lonely outpost of New Lago. This looks like a frontier town in a Western – but with that giant Halicorps billboard. A general opposition emerges:

ex-military men are respectful but reserved, while the locals are crude, dismissive, cynical and provocative. No-one in New Lago will speak to him about his friend, until a Mexican worker agrees to take him out to his land ('New Hope'). The sheriff watches them go, suspiciously. At the address, McPherson just finds marks for a planned building. Back in town, the son of his driver has meanwhile been 'accidentally' run over. McPherson tries to get information from the local store-cum-library, but its girl owner, though she wants to help, is scared. McPherson, recognising his friend's name in a book, *The Red Badge of Courage* (an 1895 war novel by Stephen Crane), makes off with it (we have kept seeing clips of Silver as an obsessive reader). Checking into the hotel, he finds that his ID has been run and a local deputy is able to tell his history: half-Cherokee, ex-Marines, no social security. The local law decide to run him out of town, leading to a brawl, in the course of which they discover that he has an artificial leg. They take his leg away, and humiliate him by hosing him down. The local Halicorps boss, Rhodes, pontificates to him about 'trying to protect God's country' from illegals, immigrants and non-whites – although we by now know that he is using them as virtual slave labour. Rhodes offers McPherson a job putting his military talents to use for the company. When MacPherson refuses, the boss accuses him: 'A working man held out his hand in friendship and you turned him down', to which McPherson replies: 'The only work your hands ever did is counting money'. This is one of several markers of a class discourse running through the film.

The rest of the film is the build-up towards the Western-style showdown. McPherson, chased out of town, is shot on the edge of the ravine leading over into Mexico, waking to find himself in the girl's care. They learn about each other, and about the depth of the corruption Halicorps has brought in. When her house is shot up, they have to fight back. McPherson heads on in to the final shootout and, of course, wins against incredible odds. The sheriff turns out to be another comrade from Iraq, and the shooting a fix because he was wearing a bullet-proof vest. At the end McPherson decides to stay, at the place that his friend had started to build – and the beautiful Hispanic girl might just be by his side.

There are some distinctive politics in here attending to class, immigration, exploitation, border patrols and vigilantes – all viewed through the lens of the Iraq experience. These wider politics use the frontier town to stand for 'America', and political corruption, to play out what cannot be said directly. The shift to a Western-style ending is presaged by McPherson's accusation that the local boss has a 'John Ford obsession'. Here, in other words, is a film trying to manage the tensions between the making of a political Statement, Marcus' independent credentials, Kilmer's career, and the need for the film to fit within a high-concept/conspiracy/action tradition now finding a main outlet through DVD. The reception of the film, assessed through IMDb, shows all the signs of these strains. Enthusiasts treat the film *only* as an actioner:

> *Conspiracy* is a great film, with good actors. Val Kilmer plays William McPherson an ex-veteran of war and his acting is fantastic. Jennifer Esposito is good in her role, and the supporting cast is excellent. Also the direction is good and the director, Adam Marcus is a great director. The film is an action explosive film, and the story is location in New Mexico (Arizona in the film plot). For me this film is a great film, and the action scenes are very, very good. ... The return of Val Kilmer!

The focus is on the 'explosive' action scenes; that is enough. Others praised with more qualifications. They were aware how widely the film had been dismissed. One writer tried to meet those criticisms head-on:

> I think a lot of us are being too harsh! I thought Val Kilmer did a great job. He came off depressed because his character WAS depressed: trying to integrate back into society after going through what he did would be unimaginable, and even worse when suffering from PTSD. He seems distracted because he is constantly fighting old battles in his head. I thought when he was being intimidated by the evil Rhodes in the diner his attitude was perfect: This is NOTHING compared to situations he's been through and Rhodes does not even matter to him. Yes, the plot was a bit predictable but wasn't it just oh so satisfying when he cuts off the disgusting E.B.'s fingers and shoots out his knee? And I think this story does have political significance. I'm Canadian but it still deeply disturbs me to ponder how companies like Halliburton make their billions. I agree with others who say that this movie most likely lost some of its lustre in the editing room. Another element I didn't care for was the undercover deputy. It just didn't quite come off quite right and I would have preferred MacPherson to kick ass by himself.

Another defender relishes the very simplisms that others dismissed:

> The good guys are good and the bad guys are real bad. Val Kilmer plays a one-legged Billy Jack in a nice twist on a story that will continue forever. Former special forces bad-ass who doesn't want to fight no-more gets roped into an evil environment (with a Dick Cheney clone as Darth Vader) and he finally gets pushed a little too far. He moves fast invisibly 'Like a ghost' – with one leg. Works as well here as in old-fashioned radio theater. Low-budget and thus sparse but well done with myriad close-ups and all characters as caricatures. There is no pretense of realism and thus it works as a comic book on screen.

The pleasure in being a critic who can see all the flaws and simply not care is characteristic of this kind of knowing action-audience. And its reduction to a deliberately low-budget, non-realistic comic book populated with caricatures allows *Conspiracy* to take its place alongside other pop-melodramatic movies.

The film succeeds well enough for this kind of audience, but at the price that its Statement-strand becomes game-like. Cartoonish villains get their asses kicked and their knees smashed. The film is rescued from its toxic genre associations by being received within another tradition of responses. In this case, then, the attempt to create a Statement by looping into fiction did not by and large succeed; its cynical reality 'hints' (the name 'Halicorps', the pointers to race and immigration debates and so on) could too easily be treated as genre-hints: this is 'just a dumb actioner'.

THE 'TOXIC GENRE'

In light of all these complexities, what should we say about *Variety*'s expression 'a toxic genre'? Should it perhaps simply be regarded as a careless attribution? To see why this is not right, we need to ask: what is added to our understanding of a group of films by labelling them a 'genre'? Debates about genre have a long history within film studies. At their best, it seems to me, genre-investigations have achieved three things. They have allowed scholars to take what might appear to be ordinary items or moments within a film, and see within them a wider significance. So, a horse is not just an animal, it is a symbol of power and grace if it appears within a Western. A car crash is not merely a hurtful collision, it can be a motif that evokes wider currencies about civilisation, technology and progress, especially if it occurs at a key moment within a Road Movie. Genre-analysis, in other words, is part of the wider will to locate elements and conventions whose meaning is an outcome of how they are portrayed and constructed across an array of films.

The second big gain has been the light it has thrown on studio practices (and while not limited to Hollywood, it is these films which have most submitted to genre-analysis), in particular, the tendency to repetition, to playing to audience expectations which depend on knowing in advance the *kind* of film a studio is publicising. So, to think what is promised when a studio announces a 'thriller', or a 'melodrama', is to unlock a shared set of recognitions. Of course, as a number of researchers have shown, the studios in fact spend as much time trying to avoid generic placement – wanting instead to stress the distinctiveness of their films (and especially any expensive, prestige ones) – as they do playing any genre-games.

The third gain is the emphasis it potentially places on audiences' recognition of conventions and thence the role of expectations when they go to watch a genre film – although this is a deeply paradoxical point, since so much of film studies has shied away from any direct exploration of audiences. Instead, as Barry Langford (2005:11) notes:

> [I]n most genre theory and criticism the audience has remained a somewhat elusive presence, notionally an indispensable interlocutor in the generic process but in practice, the general absence of clear evidence about its historical composition, remaining largely a project and undifferentiated function of the text (or rather, of the meanings ascribed to the text) its response 'read' at best largely in terms of the spectator 'implied' by the genre text.

But beyond these, genre-theory can too readily become a kind of labelling game, part of a hermetic world of film studies. In his 2000 overview, Steve Neale provides an exceptionally clear summary of the history of debates about film genre. He traces their early manifestations in the *Cahier du Cinema*'s dismissive comparison of genre film-making to the transcendent work of Hollywood's 'auteurs' – a view that, as Gledhill (1985) showed, was challenged as early as 1963 by art critic Lawrence Alloway who, among things, was a champion of Pop Art. Alloway celebrated the transient cycles of popular films precisely on grounds of their popularity. By the 1970s, as film studies emerged as a substantial academic domain, scholars began to study in depth the major Hollywood genres (the Western, the Gangster, the Musical and so on), identifying distinctive iconographies in each, their narrative formulae, and locating the industrial imperatives driving their evolution. Individual genre studies (the Road Movie, the Slasher Movie and so on) abounded. Interest in genre declined across the 1980s. Sometimes debates would erupt over the inclusion or exclusion of particular films from a genre – this happened, for instance, following the publication of Jeanine Basinger's (1986) study of the World War II Combat Film. Basinger proposed a very tight and restrictive definition of the Combat Film. Others challenged her, Neale (2000:130), for instance, worrying that she ends up having fewer films within her definition, a greater number counting as marginal. Barry Langford makes what seems to me a more valuable argument, arguing that the war film can *never* be read in this kind of enclosed way because 'the evolution of the war (or combat) film is marked perhaps more directly than any other by developments in the world beyond the frame' (Langford 2005:107).

But what is at stake in these debates? Why does it matter whether films like *Wake Island* (dir. John Farrow, 1942) or *Destination, Tokyo* (dir. Mervyn LeRoy, 1944) are to count as combat films? What is at issue if a film like *Chinatown* (dir. Roman Polanski, 1974) is named as a detective thriller, a neo-noir, a pastiche, as part of its own Chinatown cycle, or simply as a 'Roman Polanski film'? Sometimes claims about genre do come laden with implications. The work of literary-inspired analysts like John Cawelti claims that genres constitute the expression of a quite fundamental 'national imaginary'. So, Cawelti (1970, 1976) roots the Western in the distinctive American frontier experience. In direct opposition, Will Wright (1975) turns the Western into a distinctive ideological phenomenon, tied to shifting mythologies of American business. In these cases, we can see clearly what difference genre-labelling makes. That is not always the case. Often it seems that this is a game for academics, a kind of induction ritual for our students.[6] We can see this also in the recurrent interest in the internal evolution of genres, with suggestions that there is a kind of 'natural cycle' to genres as audiences become used to their formula. This leads to increasing intertextual referencing and, ultimately, to parodic plays with formulae, marking the close (for a time) of the genre cycle. This sees genre films as essentially closed exercises, with little purpose beyond continuing the game – whereas, as Neale notes, the War

Film genre appears to have a series of rather exceptional features, including allowing its male heroes to show deep emotions:

> This is not the only conventional but otherwise unusual feature of the Hollywood war film. Its close relationship to US foreign policy, its regular stress on cooperative goals, its frequent critiques of extreme individualism and its routine emphasis on the extent to which its characters lack knowledge and control of their environment, their activities, their enemies and their fates all tend to make it the exception rather than the rule among Hollywood's genres. (Neale 2000:133)

The War Film genre is also an odd one out in having much less intertextual referencing between films, and less sense of knowing evolution.

But in the reawakening of genre studies that has come in the last decade, an approach has emerged which asks a different set of questions. Associated in particular with the recent work of Rick Altman and Steve Neale, this strand asks: to whom do genre names belong? Who does the naming, and for what purpose? This strand of work recognised that genres emerge, they rise and fall, and the significance of their names can change. So, Altman (1999) shows how in early Hollywood a number of genre names emerged by a process of adjectives turning into nouns. So, 'the musical' emerged at the point when critics decided musical romances, comedies, thrillers and so on were becoming predictable. The adjective became separated, and turned into a (dismissive) label. Neale (1993), meanwhile, demonstrated how the term 'melodrama' – by the 1980s strongly associated with what were argued to be women's sensibilities – had in the 1940s and 1950s been strongly associated with appeals to male viewers.

An important contribution was made by Barbara Klinger, in a 1994b essay on what she terms 'local genres'. Klinger is critical of the ambition within film studies to 'devise "master" definitions of genres' that will cover big ranges, when – as scholars often acknowledge – their sources are often reviewers, and lay commentators. Klinger argues for historicising our approaches, addressing 'how films were labelled in the past and, in the process, to grant that generic definition is a potentially volatile or at least contingent phenomenon, conditioned by social, institutional and historical circumstances (p. 135)

Klinger's own study is of a group of films labelled 'adult' in the 1950s, sold on a promise of emotional and sexual 'frankness'. What Klinger does with these has been done in other cases. My own and Julian Petley's (both 1984) work on the creation of the category 'video nasties' has been taken on by Kate Egan (2007), who shows that what began as a censorious label was taken up by fans as a basis for collecting, list-making, and distinguishing between originals and copies. The genre-label in important senses *changed hands*, and new layers of signification were added in the process.

It is this coupled emphasis on historical placement, and the purposes shaping the naming of genres, on which I am building. In particular, I take from Altman's work the notion that there are distinctive 'Games' associated with different players in the film business: producers, publicists, distributors, exhibitors and (professional, citizen and academic) critics. Let me illustrate the difference this approach makes. In 2010 Robert Eberwein published a survey of the Hollywood war film, covering a century of films including a brief mention of a few of the films I study in this book. Useful in many ways as an overview, it nonetheless presents problems. Eberwein adopts a version of the 'myth' theory of genre – that genre films do more than entertain and, in the case of the war genre, they 'assuage fears' by showing events 'realistically'. This allows him to make easy references to the audience, and coat-tail in what watching a film must mean. So, of *Hearts of the World* (dir. D. W. Griffith, 1918) he tells us that it was 'popular' – but presumes that that means it did a job selling the war; of *The Best Years of our Lives* (1946) he says that 'its themes and concerns hit a collective nerve' (Eberwein 2010:22), but is thus presumed to have calmed them. These chickens come home to roost when he says (Eberwein 2010:55), 'War films seem real, in part because they actually use material taken from the battlefield, but also because the reality of the actualities bleeds into the reenactments. The authenticity of the one guarantees an ontological authority for the other.' This notion is then applied to, among others, *Redacted*'s use of mobile phone-style filming. While Eberwein is right to take note of this feature, I query his assumption that 'realism' is the mythic heart of the genre. De Palma's borrowing of multiple modes of filming becomes, I have argued, one of the *filters* through which his Statement about the war is announced. It offered a *way of looking back* at the war, effective to the extent that it persuaded some people that the army's and the soldiers' self-accounts *should not be taken on trust*. The extent to which it was reviled hardly attests to any authority, ontological or otherwise, managing to attach to it. *Redacted* ran up against the buffers of what was culturally allowable; and that, not a 'mythic realism', was the force constituting the Iraq war genre.

Genre-theories matter. They tell us what we are supposed to attend to in the films, and then slide in claims about how this matters. My argument is that the labelling of the Iraq war cycle as a 'toxic genre' constituted a prime case of Altman's 'Critics' Game'. Almost always reviewing the films in groups, comparisons very frequently begin by considering likely criticisms, and the failures of previous examples. To be named an 'Iraq war movie' was to have to struggle against the threat of controversy, and of being judged bad.

This was not, as far as it is possible to judge, a *viewers'* genre. I am not referring here to the low audience figures, but to how ordinary viewers grouped the films. A useful pointer can be gleaned from the 'Others who bought this also bought ...' facility on online stores. Reviewing purchasing evidence at Amazon.com, it emerges that 17 of the 23 films show no cross-connection at all.[7] Aside from a few apparently random, one-way associations, the only clear evidence of cross-purchases is between *Haditha*, *Cain* and *Redacted*. This is interesting inasmuch as these three are arguably the most overtly critical films, in particular challenging the core image of the 'American soldier'. But that is the extent of purchaser groupings.

If the 'toxic genre' is a critics' label, then, the production and reception environment already guarantees a struggle for any film. To pitch such a film in this period would be an uphill battle to persuade anyone that it was worth trying. To seek cinema release for it would be a struggle against expected apathy/hostility. Most importantly, to write and direct such a film would always be against a backdrop of fears of criticism, therefore creating a difficult balancing act between the wish to make a Statement, and careful drafting and presentation.

9
Free-riders and outliers

It would be wrong to ignore exceptions, occasional films which do not fit at all the general pattern I am outlining. Actually, I want further to argue that their very exceptional status can throw a reverse light on that central formula. Three films stand out as having many crosses and few ticks in Table 2. But I also briefly consider one other – *Day Zero* – which on inspection is further outside the formula than at first appears. Among the key features which separates them from the main cycle is their adherence to older versions of 'the American soldier' – with curiously incoherent results.

THE OBJECTIVE

Directed by Daniel Myrick, one of the two student film-makers made famous by *The Blair Witch Project* (1999), *The Objective* was put out by a small start-up company JAZ Films, whose owners had both previously worked within Studio subsidiaries. *The Objective* inevitably owes much to *Blair Witch*. The film opens with a voice-over (which overlays the film all through, not unlike someone speaking into a diary), matched by sombre music over a map-shot of Afghanistan, recalling how the events began three days after 9/11 when evidence suggested that Al-Qaeda might have got hold of a nuclear weapon – or was it, as a trusted local source suggested, something even worse? Agent Ben Keynes enters a hut in Afghanistan filled with Afghan and US soldiers. Voice-over: 'I feel like every time I come to this country it tries to spit us back out'. The local commander, Hamer, insists he is in charge of their mission, which is to seek out a local anti-Taliban leader Mohammed Aban. What he only gradually learns, is that Keynes has other orders.

They move out across an arid landscape, cautiously approaching a small run-down village. At the chief's house, they learn that Aban left for the mountains because the Taliban will not go there – the mountains are sacred. Keynes asks if he can film his home for people to see back in America. We see that he uses a heat-registering camera, and that he pockets a model of a plane: a toy, or evidence, he wonders? Next morning, they set out aboard an old truck guided by the chief's grandson Abdul. The ever-returning voice-over provides commentary on the kind of place this is: 'There are few places on earth that are as unforgiving as this desert. Whole armies from Alexander to the Soviets have paid the price for wanting to make it their own. I can only hope we aren't as foolish'.

They enter a canyon, cautiously. It's blocked ahead, by an overturned cart. Suddenly, men appear on the skyline with guns, and there's a fire-fight. One of the soldiers is shot, as are several attackers. But they can find no bodies: 'The only body from that fight was one of our men. That doesn't make sense. Ghosts don't fire real rounds'. With a dead comrade on their hands, they try for an extraction chopper, but the radio has stopped working. Night, and strange noises are heard. A pair of headlights is seen approaching, which split and shoot over their heads. That night, they hear a chopper, but can't see it even through night vision glasses – and the sound just stops dead overhead. The next morning they scout and find their dead comrade's body reduced to his viscera, and then, in the distance, a strange triangular construction of wood. Following Abdul to a watering-hole, they spot a cave opening, and the soldiers insist on checking it. Inside, they discover candles, a small altar, and an old man who offers them food and water. As they sit with him, Hamer spots that he is wearing bits of a very old uniform. Keynes recalls an impossibly old legend, of an 1844 British expedition: '60,000 went into the pass, only one came out'. That night, one of the soldiers, casually using his night vision glasses, watches the old man chanting in front of the cave. Adjusting his glasses, he sees five other men, armed with swords, blurred with blowing sand. Seizing his gun, he fires wildly, and the others wake – to find nothing but the old man, dead.

The next day, all the water the old man had given them has turned to sand. At Keynes' insistence they carry on. But Abdul, believing them cursed, refuses to go any further and, when Hamer tries to force him, steps off the cliff to his death. Keynes now sees something ahead: a triangular shape that glows in his heat-camera view, then lifts and vanishes. Now he tells them his CIA mission, to find out about a perhaps legendary 'force' concealed in this dead area – dead, in that no radios or other equipment seem to work there. They are in effect a suicide mission, whose only purpose is to send out the images he has been recording. Hamer is desperate: 'I'm willing to die for my country, but this? I don't know if this is life or death. Maybe it's something in between'. By the next day, they are down to just two fit men, and one sick one. As they enter a canyon, suddenly ahead of them appears the 'shield'. One trooper shoots wildly at it, but vanishes when touched by its light. Keynes now leaves the sick man beside the road, to go on to his doom and death. 'You're a good soldier. Your country would be proud of you', he says to him. 'My country will never know who I am', the man replies. Keynes drags himself towards the mountain. Suddenly, there ahead of him is an oasis – with trees, and flowers, and a pool. He drinks desperately from it, and passes out. Awakening, the camera shows first the little toy plane, then we hear a plane. Desperate to attract attention he fires his last flare. But in response a firework display of flares go off all round him. Keynes screams, and looks up to see a silhouetted figure coming towards him. Duty-bound to the end, he points his special camera at it. A finger extends, arrows light into his head – and we see a stream of images (memories, symbols and a picture of the plane in his hand). They resolve into a shadow of the 'plane' flying over the empty desert, to a high chanting soundtrack. And this resolves into Keynes' head, eyes fixed wide, electrodes clamped to him: he is in a hospital, still clutching the plane. His final gnomic words are 'He'll save us all'. As the captions roll, an inset image shows Keynes' wife being interviewed about the whereabouts of her husband and his special mission. She doesn't know, doesn't understand: 'I just want to know if he's still alive'.

Several themes run with and against each other in this odd film. First, is a theme of Afghanistan as so utterly foreign and unconquerable that 'we' perhaps shouldn't be there. Second, is a conflict between soldiering and staying alive: can soldiers simply be sacrifices to secret plans and a supposed 'greater good'? The problem is that the soldiers never become distinguishable characters with lives or stories, they are simply duty-machines unto death. The result is that the film effectively depends on its third theme, which is simply a post-*Blair Witch* 'let's spook people out' tale of the inexplicable, redolent with an image of Afghanistan as completely alien and 'Other'. At this level its dull repeating even of images from the earlier film irritated many viewers. If this film belongs in any broader sensibility, it is the vague and generalised fear of government conspiracy that found expression in for instance *The X-Files* (1993–2002).

In fact *The Objective* gained more attention *before* it emerged, than after. This is partly because a new film from Myrick, ten years after *Blair Witch*, was newsworthy in itself. But just as important was horror publications' and websites' interest in proving their currency by being the ones to carry stories, rumours and interviews – more, in fact, than ultimately reviewing the film. So, a series of interviews with Myrick appeared, in all of which the central question is: what kind of horror film will this be? Iraq/ Afghanistan hardly get a mention.[1] Mainstream commentary, meanwhile, while interested in the horror dimension, often still grouped the forthcoming with others in the Iraq cycle. So, the *Los Angeles Times*, after discussing the post-*Blair Witch* aspect, could not forebear adding: 'Still, given the way the subject matter dovetails with the recent disappointing box-office performance of films either literally or tangentially related to the wars in Iraq and Afghanistan, "The Objective" will be a tougher festival sell than "Blair Witch".' (Brownfield 2008) This kind of comment aside, *The Objective* vanished into its own black hole.

THE MARINE

The Objective's free-riding oddity aside, the connecting thread of the other outliers is, in a strange way, Vietnam. Most films in my cycle hardly touch Vietnam except perhaps in the figure of a wise veteran. In fact, it is generally as if there is a careful avoidance of the topic and comparison, as too risky. But in the other fringe films, Vietnam does play some role. And this very feature may be a substantial factor in disrupting their capacity for coherence.

With its world premiere held at Marine Corps Base Camp Pendleton to a cheering audience of soldiers and their families, *The Marine* unapologetically presents itself as an homage to the military. Created as a spin-off to World Wrestling Entertainment (WWE), which likes to show its stars 'in the kinds of activities our fans would like to see them in', the film was joint-funded by the WWE and Twentieth Century Fox. The WWE even arranges annual tours to Iraq and Afghanistan to entertain the troops, where the stars do demonstrations of their ultra-masculinity.[2]

The film opens outside Tikrit, Iraq. Marine John Triton, played by wrestling champion John Cena, is trying to rescue comrades facing execution by Al-Qaeda forces. Triton has to disobey orders to delay the rescue until other troops arrive. Discharged even though the Marines know he is a hero, he is shattered: 'It's not about work, it's not about a job, being a Marine means everything to me'. He goes home to his pretty wife Kate and takes a job as a hotel security guard. There, he encounters a very arrogant and aggressive local rich man, but loses his job because of his physical handling of the situation. The news coverage pointedly makes him out the villain: 'They're hired to protect us, who will protect us from them?' Meanwhile, a diamond heist is carried out nearby by some evidently Very Bad Men led by psychotic Rome (Robert Patrick) who casually shoots his own inside man, then blows up the police when they arrive.

Triton and his wife go travelling, and cross the path of the jewel thieves who take Kate hostage and drive off. Triton chases them in an abandoned police car. The local police chief lets him go. The rest of the film is the hunt through the swamps, as Triton uses his military skills to track, find, fight and kill them. Rome even comes back zombie-like for one last attempt to kill Triton, to be duly disposed of. The film ends with Triton tenderly holding Kate, against a backdrop of fire and destruction.

The film is awash with chase sequences, proofs of bodily strength, giant explosions and impossible escapes from injury. Fights are extravagant fist-fests, yet Triton comes through them all with but a few scratches. The Bad Guys fight dirtier, but inevitably lose. Triton is an über-masculine man, with a rugged face and chin that would scare Desperate Dan, rarely showing emotion. This of course makes him a true American, while all around is corruption. Kate, meanwhile, is as tough as a woman can be, and cat-fights the bad girl. Even the local police prove corrupt – later on we learn that the police chief was in on the diamond robbery, and only let Triton go after the thieves because he was being double-crossed.

The film does not even return at the end to the question of his Marine position. Iraq merely provided a general premise and a 'personality' for him. This is fairytale stuff, revelling in its simple oppositions of villainy versus virtue. The film is replete with movie in-references. Triton, proving unstoppable, is discussed by Rome: 'This guy is like the Terminator' – a comment which took on extra meaning because Rome's actor, Robert Patrick, had famously played the second Terminator. Later, there are knowing references to bayou horror films, to *Scarface* (dir. Brian De Palma, 1983) and to *Deliverance* (dir. John Boorman, 1972). But the most significant intertextual reference is less overt. Pitched as being 'like an 80s action-flick', 'with a hero we know you want to see', the film uses Iraq as a setting for a bloodless re-emergence of John Rambo. Its opening makes this clear: to martial music, and from a posed shot of Triton in full dress uniform saluting, it goes straight to the rescue mission at an Al-Qaeda training camp. Inside, hooded men are readying three American captives for filmed execution. We see a camouflaged Triton watching, yet getting orders over his earpiece to delay action. 'No time', he whispers, and charges in. A brutal fight leads to all the terrorists being killed by fist, knife, gun and immolation. As the compound quietens, he asks the Marines: 'You guys ready to go home?' This is pure *Rambo II*, and these are virtual Vietnam MIAs. Triton, like Rambo, is made a disillusioned political victim – but the rest of the film quietly sheds all the politics of that, to make him just a saintly fighting machine. This is all that Iraq contributes to the film. In a direct echo of Rambo, Triton does what is necessary, whatever the politicians and lawyers say. Like Rambo, he is simply an ultra-male body obedient to the idea of 'America'. But in becoming a ghostly version of Rambo, Triton loses the resentment and danger that Stallone's character portrayed.

Responses to the film turned on two things. To the dislikers of the film, it was not simply that they found the plot desperately weak and the action sequences absurd; it was that (as one put it directly), 'Neither Cena nor Cena's character in this movie deserve to be called The Marine'. To love the film, you needed to be willing to forego all such requirements and take this as little more than a WWE event itself:

> But what I liked about this movie is that it is NOT an action movie, it is a comic action movie. Just sit back and enjoy some great explosions, fighting scenes and snappy comic remarks. I couldn't stop laughing through the whole movie.

A whole different style of enjoyment is required – your mates round, a few beers, and the brain switched off:

> Why are you guys hating on this film. It had action galore, comedy, hot girls fighting, a fast camera, explosions and a freakin terminator. As for the comments on the fight scenes not being true to real life. Well I don't know about you but I go to the movies to watch films for their realism ... NOT! I wanna see an indestructible bad-ass rippin through the bad guys.

Or, as one female enthusiast summarised it: 'It's a funflick. No questions asked'. 'Funflick': now there is an interesting vernacular category!

The only question worth asking about it, in fact, is about the provenance and significance of that incorporated Rambo, and the interesting small light it throws back onto the Iraq war cycle. Here is a film without any of the signature elements or motifs. There is no split between camp and street experience. The officer who discharges Triton apologises, knowing he is a good Marine. But Triton bears no resentment, and is dangerous to no-one, except Very Obviously Bad Guys. This film is not about Iraq, it is about World Wrestling star John Cena playing at the idea of being a Marine – after a short course from Sylvester Stallone on how to appear on screen without needing to act.

DAY ZERO

This slightly oddball film (another very low budget Independent production) imagines Iraq as an exact re-run of Vietnam, with civilians facing the Draft, opening with a sequence of documentary clips of how this operated. It returns to the Vietnam frame in another way, in putting class at the core of its narrative, with three friends in New York receiving their call-up papers: Feller (Elijah Wood), an aspiring but unhappy writer; Dixon (Jon Bernthal), a New York cabbie; and Rifkin (Chris Klein), a successful lawyer. The film tracks their uneasy relationships and very different responses to call-up, with Dixon welcoming a chance to fight for his country, Dixon trying to buy his way out (as of course so many wealthy men did during Vietnam), while Feller is tipped over the edge and ultimately commits suicide – leaving a note summing up a ten-point wish-list for his life, number nine reading 'Get head shaved' (this he has done) and number ten reading: 'Serve with honor'. The film is interesting for the arguments it stages between the characters over whether and why they should fight. This is the story of three ordinary but differently-classed men, and works as a contrast between the ludicrous political rhetorics they encounter (their call-up papers say: 'Our nation has embarked upon a great quest. It's up to us to light the path ahead and make the world a fairer and safer place for all'), and hard decisions about patriotism versus resistance.

It is interesting to compare *Day Zero* with Kimberley Pierce's *Stop-Loss*. That film (which opens with cycle-standard bewildered filming on patrol in Iraq) then suddenly returns to America. It tracks the responses of Corporal Brandon King to his discovery that although he has served his full time in the military, he can be forced to continue and return to Iraq. The film follows his inner turmoil, his attempt to flee to Canada and his conflicts with friends who feel he is deserting them (one commits suicide when he is on the run). Ultimately, King returns, defeated, and the closing shot is of him, his surviving mates and a new young generation of soldiers, loading to go. *Stop-Loss* is the Iraq conflict's version of the Draft, a very visible unfairness, so that King's return to the army takes on tragic moral meanings (as we will further see in Chapter 10). But it is hard to see the closing sequence of *Day Zero*, as the two remaining friends go to sign up, in the same way. This is just a tough decision they make, almost out of respect to their failed friend.

THE JACKET

The Jacket tells the story of Jack Starks, a soldier returning from the first Gulf War (opening with fragments of participatory war footage – this time, though, as night-vision of supposed 'clean strikes'). Starks is falsely accused of the murder of a policeman after getting caught up with an escaping prisoner. His problems are compounded by memory loss, from a combination of a blow to the head and a suggested 'Gulf War syndrome', leading to him being found insane and incarcerated in an asylum specialising in such disorders. Here, Starks finds himself subjected to treatments which take him to the edge of insanity: enforced drug therapies coupled with periods of enclosure in a coffin-like drawer. In these, and in scenes which flash-mix moments of recall of battle with almost psychedelic experiences, he starts having visions of encounters with a young woman, Kathy, who turns out to be a grown-up version of the child he helped shortly before being caught up in the policeman's shooting. Starks gradually realises that this is an impossible future, attainable only through these barbaric treatments, since in her world he is already dead. Thereafter the film riffs on the meanings of disturbance, and the maltreatment of patients, very reminiscent of another Vietnam-influenced film, *One Flew Over The Cuckoo's Nest* (dir. Milos Forman, 1975) – using treatments the film describes as having been 'banned in the 1970s'. And it is revealing to learn from the DVD Extras that the original script was indeed conceived to involve a Vietnam veteran. Updated at Maybury's insistence to the Gulf War, it nonetheless retains a 'Vietnam feel'. Here, veterans are feared as dangerous, explosive, even if their diagnosis is now Gulf War syndrome. But these themes are contained within a moralistic science-fiction format. The film closes enigmatically with Jack and Kathy impossibly meeting for one last time to a lingering voice-over near-metaphysical question: 'How much time do we have?'

The film fits snugly into Geoff King's 'Indiewood' category.[3] The main DVD Extra describes the film as an exercise in introducing 'influences from avant-garde cinema' to the Studios. Made on a $29 million budget and released by Warner Independent, the film stars Adrien Brophy, Kris Kristofferson and Daniel Craig, whose involvement was made possible by George Clooney's interest in the project. Maybury was brought on board by the much-feted Steven Soderbergh precisely because of his experience alongside another hero of the independent sector Stan Brakhage (in preparing the film, Maybury made his crew watch some Brakhage films) – but at the price of accepting the studio's casting of star Keira Knightley as Kathy. The film then strikes a precarious balance between the political and the fantastical, in both themes and cinematic methods. *The Jacket* works like a puzzle film, in using a time-loop narrative, and also in not disclosing motives of key characters, in particular the controlling Dr Becker. It makes heavy use of extreme close-up, aiding these with digital effects which, Maybury insisted, had to be made not to look like special effects. Not in any significant sense a Statement about Iraq, rather, it is a riff on fate, time, and how to stay human in an insane world.

CONCLUSION

So what light do these outlier films throw on the core genre of Iraq war films? Each is in its different way an opportunistic film. *The Objective* tried to re-run the impact of *Blair Witch*, with an add-on layer of a conspiracy sensibility and its soldiers as bit-part sacrificial victims. The film sank without trace, in the teeth of Myrick's assertions that he expected it to be a box office hit. The others take fragments of a 'Vietnam' comparison, and try to structure this into their narratives. *The Marine* is hardly more than a sham exercise in self-promotion, for Cena and the World Wrestling Federation (and a year later, *The Marine II* (dir. Roel Reiné, 2009) was rushed out, fronted by a different WWF star). *Day Zero* ends by stripping out the initial class resonances of Vietnam, and replacing it just with loyalty to personal friends. *The Jacket* engulfs what politics it has in a flurry of indie motifs and mannerisms. The most striking absence is any hint of the shifting representation of the suffering 'American soldier' that I identified in Chapter 4, and to which I now want to return.

10
Latino Grunts: the new victim-heroes

In a 2002 essay carried on the militant Latino website 'La Voz de Aztlan', Ernesto Cienfuegos denounced the Bush administration's preparations for war, not simply in the name of Iraqis, but in the name of the soldiers repeatedly thrust into the front line of fire. They were 'La Raza', the 'Grunts of the US army'.

The presence of large numbers of Latino soldiers among US forces in Iraq and Afghanistan has for some time been the topic of considerable controversy. Among the very first US troops to die in Iraq were two Latino recruits: Lance Corporal Jose Gutierrez, a 28-year-old Guatemalan orphan who moved to America in the mid 1990s, and Corporal Jose Garibay who emigrated from Mexico as a 2-month-old (see Filner 2008). The recruitment process itself has been fiercely debated. With high unemployment, high incarceration rates and low life prospects, military policy-makers have targeted a proportional rise from 10 to 22 per cent Hispanics. This, in a context of falling recruitment among African–Americans.

One commentator, Richard Hil for *New Internationalist* (2005), summed it up thus:

> They have been variously described as 'working class mercenaries', 'green card troops', 'non-citizen' armies, or desperate recruits of the US Government's 'poverty draft'. They are the huge contingent of Hispanic personnel who – for personal and economic reasons – have been recruited into the ranks of the US military. According to US journalist Jim Ross, by February 2005 there were 110,000 of them. The biggest single contingent of such troops is made up of Mexicans and Mexican descendants. Many were in the marine units from Camp Pendleton in San Diego that participated in the initial stages of the invasion of Iraq in March 2003 and later fought 'insurgents' in Falluja. Puerto Ricans, Dominicans, Central Americans and Ecuadorians are also well represented. Since the start of the war about a third of the US forces stationed in Iraq – between 31,000 and 37,000 troops out of a total of about 130,000 – were non-US citizens serving in the navy, Marine Corps, army and air force.

Recruitment has been accompanied by 'promises of green cards, scholarships, post-service employment, and various medical and pension benefits'.

> [T]he number of non-citizens in the military has risen — there are now about 35,000 'green card' service members, an increase from the 23,000 who were serving in 2000. And more than 32,000 have become US citizens since the Bush administration announced expedited citizenship for members of the armed services in 2002 (Spicuzza 2007)

As the death toll rose, anti-war movements grew within Latino communities, as did the number of cases of refusals to serve in Iraq. A generalised distrust of the Bush administration's policies led commentators to link liberalisation of migrant laws with a convenient deepening of the military recruitment pool.[1] In fact the precise proportion of Hispanic recruits within the army is a subject of debate, because global figures are not far out of line with overall population statistics (Somosierra 2007). But as one report (Berkowitz 2003) argued, it was not simply a matter of numbers:

> Referring to a March 2003 Pew Hispanic Center Fact Sheet titled 'Hispanics in the Military,' Prof. Mariscal said that Latinos made up some 13.5% of the civilian labor force 18–44 years old – the age range for military service – and as of September 2001, they made up nearly 10% of the military. 'These numbers are deceiving,' said Prof. Mariscal. 'In reality, nearly 25% of Latinos in the military are involved in combat or hazardous duty occupations. They are basically the grunts'.

And as a result, Latino troops 'died at a rate disproportionately high for their representation in the active forces and among the deployed troops' (Davey 2004). These statistics provide a raw context for the role that Latinos came to play in the Iraq war film genre.

HISPANICS ON SCREEN

The previous history of representing Hispanic characters on screen does not bode well. This history has been usefully summarised by Allen Woll (1993). Woll recounts the early emergence of 'the greaser', a sneaky, rapacious stereotype who provided easy enemies for white heroes to confront in the Silent era. Films such as *Tony, the Greaser* (dir. Rollin S. Sturgeon, 1911) and the short *The Greaser's*

Revenge (Frontier Motion Picture Company, 1914) laid down a pattern which did not change greatly until the 1920s, when – partly under pressure from the Mexican government – the emergent studios began to avoid such ethnic indicators. By the 1930s, Woll shows a few films were developing a new representation: of a stylish, dangerously romantic figure (of which Rudolf Valentino was of course the early exemplar) – or, if female, a hot-blooded temptress. Washington's Good Neighbours policy before and after World War II was taken up by Hollywood, who retold aspects of Mexico's history, and even (as in *A Medal for Benny* [dir. Irving Pichel, 1945]) to confront white prejudices against Mexicanos. But the new-wave Westerns of the late 1960s–1970s reverted to type, with films such as *The Wild Bunch* and *Bring Me the Head of Alfredo Garcia* (both dir. Sam Peckinpah, 1969 and 1974, respectively) creating a new version of the slick but deceitful 'greaser' who speaks distorted English. Of course there is a small separate tradition of films made by and for Hispanics, but these have influenced Hollywood's practices far less than, say, 1970s independent Black cinema did.

An illustration of the dominant mode is well captured in a story David Robb (2004:287–96) uncovered: the case of the 1955 Warner Bros.' *Battle Cry* (dir. Raoul Walsh), which recounted the experience of Marines fighting in the Pacific in World War II. The film was important to the Marines, in their struggle for recognition, who therefore could do without revelations of anti-Hispanic racism within their ranks. Written by the liberal Leon Uris, the screenplay for *Battle Cry* did just that, including a closing scene where Private Pedro Rojas, having won a Silver Star for bravery, is abused by a white soldier as a 'Spic'. The scene was shot, and was so powerfully performed by actor Victor Millan that there was spontaneous applause from cast and crew. But the scene vanished from the released film, and Millan never knew how or why. Robb uncovered memoranda from the Marine Corps and the Pentagon film office to Warners, urging its deletion on the grounds that it might be used as 'anti-US communist propaganda'. Warners complied, silently. 'Heroes' are best when no structural issues accompany them.

By 2005, and this cycle of films, circumstances had changed. I have already noted the presence of such characters in significant roles in several of the films: Sergeant TK Poole in *The Lucky Ones* and Private Salazar in *Redacted*. Private Rodriquez and his family in *Stop-Loss* act as figures revealing white political deceit, while staying narratively off-centre. *In the Valley of Elah* offers a complicated case. Although the central family is white, the unnamed flag-raiser is

Latino, as is the soldier blamed for but innocent of the son's death. There are of course other 'minorities': black soldiers and female soldiers. But the role played by a Latino character is marked and charged in special ways, as is particularly revealed by three films.

Examples of Latino soldiers within the cycle

Figure 10.1   Hank Deerhurst (*In the Valley of Elah*) meets Private Ortiez, whom he earlier assaulted (convinced he was involved in his son's death) and insulted as a 'wetback prick'. Now knowing the truth of his son's death, he has to listen to a Latino soldier's experiences.

Figure 10.2   Home of the Brave: Two soldier buddies – one Latino, one black – are preparing to make the ultimate sacrifice, as they try to prove to 'America' that they are valuable citizens.

Figure 10.3   From *Battle for Haditha*, we see media coverage of Corporal Ramirez before he is blamed and sacrificed by the military authorities for his part in the murder of an Iraqi family.

Figure 10.4   *Redacted*: Corporal Salazar films himself on an Iraqi street. Moments later, his camera will record his being snatched by insurgents. All through the film all he has wanted is only to make a movie to get into film school back home. Salazar will be shown being beheaded in a webcast.

BATTLE FOR HADITHA

This film was controversial for its open critique of American soldiers' involvement in rape and murder – but ends with a hint of redemption for its main Latino character, Corporal Ramirez. It opens with components of an 'Iraq war experience': four US soldiers being 'interviewed' on their views of Iraq. 'The only thing I'm fighting is to get home each day without being killed. Because I don't know why we're here.' To these soldiers, Iraq is the 'asshole of the world'. *Haditha* declares its grounding in real events there in November 2005. Loud rock music cuts in as three US patrol vehicles bucket over the desert sand. The soldiers go on patrol, through a city filled with people going about their lives: women with children buying chickens; soldiers buying DVDs from a man, who leaves suddenly – and we see that he's off to plant a roadside bomb.

The film sets up a contrast between the motives for becoming a US soldier ('to get out of Philadelphia'), and a bomber ('they disbanded our army after Saddam, gave us nothing'). Haditha, once a place for honeymoons, is now the 'City of Death'. At the barracks amid hyper-masculine jostling, Ramirez tells a new recruit: 'Nobody gives a fucking shit about you, except you. The Marine Corps don't, this country don't.' The story then tracks the planting of the bomb, its explosion killing an American, and their officer-licensed revenge mission into a house where they suspect bombers might be holed up. Their Rules of Engagement are, basically, if anyone in the house moves, they are enemy. We are shown the soldiers' attitudes and their wild killing spree. We see the Iraqi fury in its aftermath. Back at the barracks afterwards, Ramirez is sick physically and psychologically: 'I fucking hate the officers that sent us to do that', he says, thinking of the women and children they killed. But when the story leaks months later, George Bush (shown in the film) blames 'rogue soldiers'.

Ramirez is hung out to dry by the very officers who had sanctioned and encouraged his actions. The ending is critical. It jumps forward to March 2006: across the desert again come Humvees, rock music blaring. Ramirez and his colleagues are being court-martialled. Their captain lines them up and denounces them : 'It is my job and your job as Marines to protect the reputation, the honour and the future of this Corps, and I will not let a band of reckless Marines ruin that future and that reputation.' And now, as Ramirez prepares for his inevitable sentence, we see inside his head his recall of the assault. The officer's voice fades out over a close-up of Ramirez's face, and the vision cuts to him remembering (truthfully? or wishfulfilment? we are in no position to know) going through one of the houses, seeing a dead child in a bed, then finding a small girl hiding in the bath. He takes the girl's hand and begins to lead her out, while another soldier shouts to him, checking that all is OK. With bell-like music tolling over, his echoey voice recalls how young he was, yet this was already his third tour: 'We've all seen things that will haunt us in the rest of our lives. And I guess after a while you just get hardened. And become numb'. The final shot is of him leading the girl out of the house into a light that strengthens and finally burns to white. Ramirez was, and was not, guilty. He was villain, victim and hero all in one: the perfect Latino grunt.

It is interesting to note that in IMDb's user comments, while there is considerable praise for the film – and in particular for 'giving all sides', for not 'demonising' US soldiers (despite what they did), and for using non-professional actors ('using real Iraqis and a lead Marine who's an Iraq war vet were master strokes') – I could not find one response directly noting the significance of Ramirez's ethnicity. It is as if this is contained within and covered by his 'ordinariness'. To the (many) haters of the film, no matter that the events behind the film were real, it was simply an exercise in America-hating: 'Insurgents are less than human. They are barbarians while American Soldiers are some of the most honorable people in the world'. There is truth, and there is 'truth'.

LIONS FOR LAMBS

If ever there was an example which had to be described as a 'statement film', this surely is it. A joint enterprise between United Artists, Robert Redford's production company Wildwood Enterprises and a small recent independent production outfit Andell Entertainment, the film gradually interweaves three stories. It opens with a news report on continuing casualties in Iraq and Afghanistan. Story 1 involves a journalist (played by Meryl Streep) invited to the office of a bright young senator (Tom Cruise at his smiley, shining best) who is trying to sell a new initiative on Afghanistan. She is an old hand at uncovering the rhetorics and flaws in such initiatives. The film unfolds his persuasive speech, interspersed with segments of the other two stories, as he meets her challenges, and challenges her back – not least on the promotional role her own previous reporting has played. Redford leads Story 2, as politics professor Stephen Valley challenging a clever but disaffected student Todd, who is disillusioned about the point of political study when he feels powerless in the face of injustice and corruption. Valley urges the necessity of making choices and commitments. Story 3 follows the launch of the new Afghanistan initiative, to land US soldiers on mountaintops just as spring is due, so that they hold the commanding heights and can drive Al-Qaeda out. Two soldiers are singled out for attention – who we eventually learn are ones who *did* take the professor seriously, but not as he had intended. They volunteered to serve, so that they could return as 'Black and Mexican combat vets with an education – they gotta listen to us then, doc'. But failed by bad intelligence and weak officers, the two ultimately die pointless deaths. The issues all through are about choices, in the face of the senator asserting that 'we have everything we need except the public will'. To the professor addressing his student, it is being able to say 'At least you did something' even if unsuccessful. To the soldiers it is winning the *right to be heard* by going into combat for 'their country'. To the journalist it is telling the truth, rather than being a mouthpiece for the administration. Each has to make a choice, a commitment. The film ends on the journalist facing her choice to tell or not to tell.

The striking thing here is the choice of the buddy partners: one African–American and one Latino, joining up to become living proof of their peoples' commitment to 'America'.[2] In the face of the rhetorics and duplicities of politicians and military leaders, 'ordinary folks' – black and Hispanic – still go and make their sacrifice. But again, this dimension does not become directly visible in IMDb User comments. Receiving the usual mixture of praise and dismissal, even its most enthusiastic reviewers never say the obvious – even, as here, a reviewer from Mexico:

> *Lions for Lambs* is a movie about conscience and the effects of politics and the government in society, it also touches several aspects of the American society, such as student issues, the manipulation of media for political propaganda ends. It also invites the viewer to reflect on very important ethical and moral issues of modern society[.]

Important, indeed – but perhaps the most important has not here become visible.

GI JESÚS

The third film is the most unusual for its contribution to the Latino victim-hero, both in its themes and the cinematic devices it uses. *GI Jesús* tells the story of Jesús Feliciano (Joe Arquette) returning home after a tour in Iraq. The film opens in Iraq with soft 'Arab' sounds. Stock shots show us trucks moving, a shepherd beside the road, then night-time. An officer instructing his men to be careful of IEDs. Then, a cut-in of television 'Breaking News', and they are on the plane home, being adulated as heroes. Arriving at Los Angeles, Jesús is greeted by his ecstatic family: his ten-year-old daughter Marina and Claudia, his sexy 'Dominican Princess'. At their home, a trailer park, Claudia shows off the 'new goods' she has acquired for them through the generosity of his Colonel. But as they start to make love that night, Jesús gets flashbacks to Iraq. The next day, he also 'hears' some family life in distorted fashion, as when his daughter asks him, 'Did you kill people?' At a petrol station, he has an odd encounter with a man who appears to know him, whom he does not remember.

Driving Claudia to work, the radio talks about the CIA's role in overthrowing Allende in Chile. Jesús connects this with his daughter buying Pepsi, who were among the companies 'funding' the overthrow. When he begins to question why he went to Iraq, his wife says: 'Baby, you went to Iraq just to get us legal'. Discomfited, he asks: 'You mean I killed a lot of people just to get us legal?' Back home, as he tries to repair his old car, the odd man appears again, and finally says his name: Mohammed. But to an old friend, Fred, visiting him, it appears Jesús is talking into thin air. Taking Marina for an ice cream, he again flips back to the war, holding conversation with his former officers (filmed in sepia) while she watches, worried. He begins to speak, it goes wrong – and he wakes up suddenly and with a jerk.

Jesús and platoon-mate Jorge visit a hospital where their colonel's son is recovering from injuries. He's angry at being dragged by his father into the military. It was assumed he would join, but 'What the fuck has the military ever done for me?' The doctor takes Jesús aside, telling him that the boy has classic PTSD symptoms: seeing people, having conversations with them ... He offers Jesús some pills as well – why not? He has a quota to use, provided (he explains) by the pharmaceutical industry who see the military as the ideal test-bed for new products. As they exit the hospital, the colour again flips to green as Jesús hears a helicopter go over. That night, he tells Claudia the Colonel wants him to become a recruiter, which would mean they could stay in America. When that is settled, he wants them to have a boy. She makes him promise he will not leave her again. Again as they begin to make love, again he 'sees' a figure watching them from the other car.

The next day at the Colonel's house turns surreal. Jesús is offered $10,000 as a down-payment for a house. The Colonel then delightedly shows them a film of high-precision killing taken from the helicopter gunship, which suddenly intercuts with images of a topless woman in fatigues and smeared in mud. He tells him the real mission: a black ops brigade, raising money so the military can fight in Latin and South America without political interference. Now a bizarre game of musical chairs begins – which cuts without warning to a screen in Marina's school. Her class are watching their game, their teacher saying this is evidence of animal primitiveness, that the war in Iraq has no point, the soldiers murderers. Next day Jesús goes to the school, seeking an apology from the teacher. The Head promises to 'look into it'. Mohammed now reappears to him, and his story emerges. He was there in Fallujah, where he, his wife and daughter were all killed. From a reverse angle we see again that there is no-one there. Cut back to Iraq, and we see US soldiers at night bursting into a house and shooting people. Jesús awakes in a panic. Going out into his garden he again meets Mohammed. Mohammed accuses him of the killing and dismisses Jesús' apology. This time, Claudia too sees him talking 'to himself'.

Jesús hears that he is being recalled to Iraq. When he suggests going to Mexico to escape this, she rebels. Everything she wants is in America. In despair, he goes to his recruitment fair, and we see him give a DVD to two small boys – and its blatant promotionalism. Horrified at what he is becoming, Jesús heads to Mexico alone, only turning back at the last minute. Returning, he finds Claudia with Fred, and he is touching her up. There is a fight. Claudia blames him, saying, 'I do what I have to do', so he drives off and leaves her. Everything is coming apart. Claudia goes out for dinner with Fred, who declares his love for her. Jesús returns, to find them almost naked in Fred's jacuzzi. In green film we see Claudia teasingly feeding grapes to Fred. Jesús seizes a high-powered sniper rifle, and (in distorted sepia filming) takes aim. Suddenly the filming goes chaotic, fast-intercutting scenes from Iraq, night-vision filming, and a maelstrom of fractured bits of film.

Out of the confusion we cut straight to Jesús opening his eyes, on a plane. Only gradually does it become clear that it is a re-run of the opening sequence of their arrival back from Iraq – but with differences. Now it is Jorge who is injured, not the Colonel's son. They are no longer adulated: the air stewardess even insists that Jesús use the economy washroom. At home, his wife has no new goods to show off – indeed, not even lights, as power has been cut off by the electricity company. Jesús tells them that he is due to go back in a month, and suggests Mexico. After a long pause, Claudia agrees. They make love, tenderly, that night. Then, as Claudia packs their few goods, he says goodbye to his friends, including Fred who is now just another trailer resident. They cross the border, and arrive at a beach cantina – poor, but rich with family and friends. Jesús walks onto the littered beach, and once more meets Mohammed, who welcomes him to 'paradise', and asks: have you made the right decision? Yes, says Jesús. The film ends on his return to the cantina.

Jesús' Latino status is crucial to the film. It informs his motives for being in the army. It shows in their life-chances in the trailer-park, and shapes what they aspire to. It motivates his unease at being asked to join the black ops squad. But the twists and repetitions in the film are also essential to its nature. GI Jesús is no simple morality tale. The central characters, Jesús and Claudia, are interesting in and of themselves. Both very attractive, they maintain all appearances – sharp clothes and looks, good car and so on – against the odds of their trailer-park life. Their lives are orderly, despite being caught in the trap of an American poverty life. They keep their pride, in other words. The film then fashions around them a layered narrative, with abrupt shifts and surprise elements.

There are moments which swing very close to docufiction: for instance, Jesús' induction into the politics of the war, when he hears the radio debate, and links this to their buying of junk food; and at the hospital, where the doctor instructs him on the official symptoms of PTSD, and on the pharmaceuticals' cynical use of military personnel – after all, the military have all kinds, all races, 'except the rich, of course'. This encounter with white official cynicism counterpoints Jesús' determination to live a good life. Camerawork shifts without warning between various modes, signalling stress and distress in Jesús. It switches repeatedly from standard to hand-held, half-bleached or sepia 'amateur' filming in Iraq (but also sometimes in an apparent present-day), to green night-vision filming (sometimes back to Iraq, on occasion showing the ongoing narrative). At the crisis point at the jacuzzi, these jumble together into a fast-cut chaos of images. Two linked sequences veer to absurdism. When Claudia and Jesús visit the Colonel's home, there is the switch, without reaction from the characters, to the soft porn performance, followed by the game of musical chairs, which shifts without warning to Marina's schoolroom, the game becoming a strange teaching aid.

Figure 10.5 Closing sequence in *GI Jesús*. In the closing scene of *GI Jesús*, even after an apparent 'real' restart of the narrative, Jesús once more encounters the 'ghost' of Mohammed, whose family he killed while in Iraq. Mohammed now approves his decision to leave America for Mexico. Is Mohammed 'there'? His daughter Marina's friend appears to talk with him. Yet Marina challenges Jesús for talking to no one. His wife sees him talking to empty air. But his importance supersedes his 'reality' as Jesús turns to look to 'us' in the final shot.

His nemesis Mohammed first appears as an apparently diegetic character, introducing himself then wandering off. It is only on his third appearance that we are given a direct indication that he may be unreal. Then there is the narrative twist near the film's close, where Jesús suddenly awakens on the plane – but to a different scenario. So what status did the first have? If this is Jesús' dream sequence, how can it be that we see him from others' perspective, and see Mohammed's unreality? Then there is Mohammad's final appearance. On the beach in Mexico they talk one last time, and Mohammed apparently forgives Jesús for his family's deaths. Marina apparently cannot see him ('Who are you talking to?', she asks challengingly), yet for a long moment her new Mexican friend looks at the camera as though she can. In all these ways the film refuses to provide us with a stable, comfortable 'reality' logic and position. It deploys a range of cinematic devices borrowed from independent cinema to destabilise our viewing. But these are not distancing devices. They are trying to take us inside Jesús' dilemma in a quite startling new way.

To the enthusiasts on IMDb, it was clear what made this a fine film, as in this example:

> This deeply touching film explores the effects of what soldier Jesús Feliciano saw and did in Iraq. A Mexican national, Jesús joined the army to get his United States citizenship. He felt becoming an American would better himself and his family. This was his chance. The U.S. military told him this was the right thing, so he went and he fought. Jesús is now returning to his home in California. He is a wounded man. He isn't physically hurt, but he is mentally and emotionally. He is confused, depressed and fearful. He feels guilt and is plagued with anxiety. He has to work through his emotions and finds himself wondering if taking the lives of others is worth becoming a legal American. Shot on HD with actual war footage cut into the movie, 'GI Jesús' offers a surreal look at the psyche of soldiers caught in the system trying to better themselves and their families, but shameful of what they've seen, done and have become in the process.

Here, to a small degree, we see recognition of the relevance of his marginal Latino status. The film appears to have been released primarily in areas with high Latino populations. Its one Award was at the CineVegas Festival, one of whose judges subsequently wrote of it: 'As a Mexican who enlisted to secure US citizenship, Jesús suffers further when he's ordered back to Iraq. He will absolutely lose his family if he leaves them for another year. As these pressures become murderous, writer-director Carl Colpaert never loses his balance, despite the David Lynchian leap of faith he asks us to make midway, in a twist so bold as to be a backflip. If anything, this extra layer in the story effectively illuminates the moral choices Jesús must navigate' (Feeney 2007). Jesús becomes a hero *by virtue of* being torn apart with guilt, and the film's indie techniques help to accentuate this. He comes to embody the dilemma of an outsider wanting the American Dream, being bribed to fight and kill 'people like himself', and discovering that the Dream means betraying what he is. His sickness is most definitely not reducible to PTSD. It is a moral and political crisis of the soul.

CONCLUSION

The Latino as victim-hero is a new development, I believe. And that is surely the reason why it has hardly yet become visible. While the role of black troops was the softly-spoken truth about Vietnam, here, it is at least making the margins of cultural image-making. How long this theme will last, and how far it will lead to a new core image of the 'American soldier' it is impossible to say. But even if very short-lived, it is surely a highly significant development.

These films allow us to see further what is gained by tackling Iraq via fiction, as against documentary. Fiction can give us heroes. It can find among the mass of characters one or more who embody the best that can be imagined. Where documentary would struggle to find such idealised people, and would risk much if it claimed to find them, fiction typically focuses, cleans up and simplifies motivations. Removing characters from the possibility of a real checkable history, fiction films, even where they give us a back-story, can suggest and build clean lines from past to future, uncomplicated motives, and attractive hopes.

11
The Hurt Locker and beyond

In several senses, Kathryn Bigelow's *The Hurt Locker* closes my cycle of films. I believed this before the film won its six Oscars at the 2010 Academy Awards. That merely became another dimension to the closure, which is mainly the result of how it differs from the others. Bigelow collaborated with Mark Boal, whose earlier film *In the Valley of Elah* was, as we saw, based on a tidied-up version of real events. Boal spent time as an embedded journalist with American forces. *The Hurt Locker* is based on research among the technical specialists who defuse planted explosive devices. The film is constructed as a series of semi-connected episodes, following the arrival of new Specialist Sergeant William James to replace one killed at the film's outset. He gradually transforms the other members of his unit, Sergeants JT Sanborn and Owen Eldridge, by his apparently uncaring attitude to risks. But James has thereby lost his ability to live a 'normal life'. The film closes on his returning for yet another tour of duty in Iraq, after finding that he cannot live a civilian life with his wife and child.

Bigelow's film was being made as the 2009 presidential election was taking place, which marked the defeat of the Republicans. Released after Barack Obama's victory, its reception context was therefore markedly different. Even this did not make it a financial success. Until its Oscars success, *The Hurt Locker* was well short of the required box office take to cover its costs. Since then, it has achieved a substantial 'bounce' in pay-per-view, DVD rentals and sales. But the film anyway did two things very differently than the others. It does present bits of an 'Iraq war experience' (soldiers' respectful public appearances coupled with wild barracks behaviour – in this case most apparently in a drunk fighting session). But the bewilderment at Iraqi hostility that usually accompanies these is altogether absent from James – and in that, he becomes something of a role model to his platoon mates. Along with this, the film stripped out almost every single moment that might be judged political. I cannot recall seeing one US flag in the entire film – usually the first marker of such politics. There are no moments of inserted speech, or television coverage, or soldiers' debate about why they are there.

Just two components of the political gestures of the other films make it into this one. First, officers are presented as somewhere between stupid and brutal. One stupid colonel relishes the risks that James takes, exclaiming 'Hot shit!' over them. The same man executes a wounded insurgent, coldly telling one of his men 'He's dead anyway'. The other, a well-intentioned 'Doc' who wants to help the soldiers deal with the stress, proves foolish when he ventures outside, and gets himself blown up.

The second element comes right at the end of the film, after a scene in which James cannot save an Iraqi man padlocked to explosives. Sanborn, in shock, wants to get out. 'I'm not ready to die', he declares, close to tears. Earlier he could not bear the idea of having a son, now this becomes his dearest wish – so that someone will care if he dies. As it is, 'Nobody will give a shit'. It is not particular groups, or politicians, or attitudes that are against him. A generalised sense of being deserted by everyone pervades the scene, which closes with shots of laughing small boys pelting their vehicle with stones. So, why are the soldiers doing this? James' role-model response is a shrug of the shoulders. He is untouched by it.

It is here that the real politics of the film lie. Soldiers like James do it because that is what they do: *finis*. What this film celebrates, is a character who is the *living embodiment of post-traumatic stress disorder*, but who is treated by the film as not disordered at all. James is an 'adrenalin junkie', who lives off the risks he takes. James displays the full canon of symptoms by which PTSD is defined. He has just forgotten how to be its victim, and thus becomes a poster-boy of the Iraq war generation. Seen in this light, he can be an attractive and fascinating character. But the film goes even beyond that.

Consider the 15-minute scene, at the heart of the film, where their patrol encounters a stranded British contract team, with prisoners. It opens with a series of long tracking shots, as their armoured vehicle tracks towards and across our vision. Its antennae rise up above a rocky crest like some giant insect. A pulsating rock track, heightened with a slight wailing noise, rises, then dies out as an SUV and moving figures are spotted. Camerawork shifts to a series of longish medium or close-up shots, some of them whipping into focus (like someone adjusting binoculars too fast) as we experience the nervous encounter, then recognition of the figures as British. Now camerawork becomes more generically hand-held, long unsteady shots. The prisoners are given water, a damaged wheel is repaired, conversations go on. The camera swivels from speaker to speaker like a listening participant.

Suddenly, one such shot showing a British soldier is punctuated by a thud, and he falls dead. After a one-second pause, editing speed doubles as they take cover, marshal themselves, locate the source of the threat, and begin to fire back. The camera shoots from beside, above and below in smash zooms, crazy tracking actions, cutting between fragments of faces, guns being fired, random small ins-and-outs on bullet cases falling, an upwards shot of the machine gunner firing from his turret, who then drops, himself shot. A calm falls as two of the British officers identify and line up shots on a small house, seen only through heat haze. This is more than a point-of-view shot. Sounds become accentuated and distorted. There is a vague registration of wind noise: deep, slowed breathing. A shot fired at the building produces a long-delayed, silent spurt of dust from its wall. Now we cut to inside the building and two Iraqis silhouetted against its window, performing the same routine as the British soldiers. Switch back to the Allied side, and a heard popping sound produces the death, a pause later, of the British team leader. Fragmented camerawork returns, as the remaining British try unsuccessfully to call in support. James and Sanborn take over, and the same slow, almost contemplative camerawork and sound resume. Over six minutes, James instructs Sanborn in how to take out the insurgents. A panicky Eldridge is instructed on how to spit and clean blood off sticky ammunition; again, the more frenetic filming is calmed as James tells him, 'You're doing good, man, you're doing good'. They resume their targeting, James unhurriedly guiding Sanborn's shots. The only overt sound is their calming breathing, punctuated by the rifle shots. As the penultimate man is taken out, his head exploding silently from afar, James quietly comments: 'Good night, and thank you for playing'. The chess game is almost over. One final shot of this sequence becomes aestheticised as a spent cartridge cartwheels in the dirt, overlaid with sounds like wind chimes.

Cinematography, sound and editing here play crucial roles. They never just observe the action. Nor do they simply participate in it. They build its meaning in three ways. They enact the chaos, putting a rhythm to the challenges the soldiers face. They detail it as a kind of deadly game, in which James' skills, both military and emotional, steady its presentation. And that attaches a fascination to its manoeuvres and tactics, and to the fine use of deadly weaponry. In all this, James becomes the one lead character in these Iraq war movies who is never once bewildered. He is a calming epicentre for characters and cameras alike.

Figure 11.1   Still from *The Hurt Locker*. A symbolic moment in *The Hurt Locker*: Sergeant William James stands amid wreckage and flames. A 'still centre' to the film, he has, but is untouched by, post-traumatic stress disorder. He alone cannot be 'burned'.

THE OSCAR WAR

Hollywood, and the media that feed its needs for publicity, love a personalised conflict – especially with a ring of sexual history to it. So the fact that the 2010 Oscars pitched divorced couple James Cameron and Kathryn Bigelow against each other for the Best Film award was perfect copy. But while the films could have been thematically counterposed as well – two films addressing military action 'abroad' – that was not initially done. Rather, the early tone of coverage was of a woman, Bigelow, making serious and committed independent films, versus Cameron making financially-indulgent 3D entertainment. This was serious apolitical film-making versus bloated blockbuster, plain-speaking versus special effects, film versus movie. A Google search for references linking *Avatar* with 'Iraq' produced a third as many hits as with 'Blockbuster', a sixth as many as with 'Special Effects', and one ninth as many as with entertainment.

But gradually people began to ask, is *Avatar* not every bit as much about Iraq as *The Hurt Locker*? Even if the setting was fantastical, it showed US Marines being sent in to steal another world's resources, it adopted wholesale the Marine's mannerisms and modes of talking. The native peoples have to resist at cost of their lives. These reports were often aware of going against the grain of coverage.[1] One

London-based Iraqi journalist Mamoon Alabassi (2009) presented the strongest account, in a much-cited article:

> Ironically, and contrary to official film labelling, for many Iraqis 'Avatar' is seen as the most accurate Iraq war movie so far, while 'The Hurt Locker' might appear as more alien to them. The link to Iraq in 'Avatar' is apparent to many from the outset of the film, but it is further entrenched with the use of terms like 'shock and awe' and 'fighting terror'. However, the plot thickens. The blue humanoids in 'Avatar' appear more humane than their human invaders, who came from earth to steal the resources of their planet. In 'The Hurt Locker', where we follow an adventurous US bomb squad in Iraq, the Iraqis in the movie appear to serve just as a background that shows how heroic the film's stars are. Almost faceless and voiceless, they are – as in the world of politics – robbed of their humanity. It would be more accurate to say that 'The Hurt Locker' is an action movie that uses Iraq as a background than to brand it as an 'Iraq war movie', and less so as the 'Iraq war drama'. The film does not really address the Iraq war, the reasons for the presence of the US squad or even the bombs they are supposed to defuse, and most importantly it ignores the views and feelings of Iraqis.

Cameron himself was more guarded. He acknowledged in interviews that there were important parallels with Iraq, as indeed with Vietnam, and all the way back to America's colonial wars. But the key to *Avatar*, he insisted, was the environment:

> Referring to the 'shock and awe' sequence, he said: 'We know what it feels like to launch the missiles. We don't know what it feels like for them to land on our home soil, not in America. I think there's a moral responsibility to understand that. 'That's not what the movie's about – that's only a minor part of it. For me it feels consistent only in a very generalised theme of us looking at ourselves as human beings in a technical society with all its skills, part of which is the ability to do mechanised warfare, part of which is the ability to do warfare at a distance, at a remove, which seems to make it morally easier to deal with, but it's not'. (Hoyle 2009)

But this was not something just for journalists and publicists. In the West Bank, Palestinian activists saw something of their own situation in the film, and staged a demonstration in which they painted themselves blue to resemble Cameron's Na'vi. The same happened subsequently with a tribe of Amazonian Indians resisting the building of a dam on their ancestral lands.

One general press website reviewed the debate – and its tone revealed that the American Right was worried by the film's success. Up until now opposition had been known lefties like Susan Sarandon and Tim Robbins holding up placards, while the films they produced about Iraq died. Now, with *Avatar*, it seemed that a successful anti-military formula had been found:

> As for the anti-military message, many military members and their families see this movie as a metaphor for the Iraq war. Defenders are quick to point out that Cameron wrote *Avatar* in the mid 1990s so its reference to the current Iraq situation is unfounded. Although since the first Iraq war began in 1991, Cameron did have a war time reference then as well. However, Cameron himself seeks an interpretative stance for his movie. If this is his intent, then the seemingly marauding Marines, ordered to secretly invade under false identity and therefore infiltrate a peaceful realm all the while carrying the evil intent to pillage its natural resources can only be interpreted as it is represented. (Aikens 2009)

With its overt references to 'shock and awe' and 'using terror to meet terror', and with its presentation of the Marines helping the strip-mining of other lands/worlds by US corporations, *Avatar* paints a merciless anti-portrait of the American military.

But while mainstream commentators were debating whether the film was entertainment (look at the special effects!) or anti-military propaganda (listen to the messages ...), an oddly opposite but parallel phenomenon was emerging on the American left. The prompt was a pair of polemical commentaries by Slavoj Žižek. Žižek is a kind of rock-star theoretician whose writings (rooted in a combination of philosophy and Lacanian psychoanalysis) are taken terribly seriously by many on the intellectual left. Žižek published two commentaries. In the first, a comparison of *Avatar* with *The Hurt Locker*, he appears to come down strongly on the side of the former: 'For all its mystifications, *Avatar* clearly sides with those who oppose the global Military-Industrial Complex, portraying the superpower army as a force of brutal destruction serving big corporate interests' (Žižek 2010a). Bigelow's film, by contrast, mystifies the war by excluding all its politics. We are only asked to care about the soldiers (although Žižek is careless in claiming that *The Hurt Locker* never shows American soldiers killing people). In this review, theory is lightly applied, smuggled in via notions of audiences 'identifying' with American soldiers, with a resultant 'obfuscation' of the war's politics. But these are in passing.

But even as he was writing this, Žižek (2010b) was also arguing a near-opposite position, damning *Avatar* for helping to maintain a 'reactionary myth', a white man's fantasy that natives need help to survive from a noble outsider – who will then marry the local princess and rule. Here, the theoretical dosage rises. Žižek argues that the problem is the particular construction and interweaving of reality and fantasy which constitutes the danger. We have to adjust our fantasies to the reality of the situation, he argues, or it becomes a hideaway. Cameron's 'Hollywood Marxism' is so disconnected from the realities of struggles, it cozens its viewers. His article generated a wave of critical debates, the best of which point up his delight in taking contrary positions, his assumptions about audience reception and his empty purism.[2] All these I agree with, but want to add one more. Žižek also continues the long film studies of seeing special effects as *devious additions distracting attention* from a film's message. Calling *Avatar* fundamentally conservative and old-fashioned, he writes that 'its technical brilliance serves to cover up this basic conservatism'. Here, the IMDb responses simply give the lie to his claim. Enthusiastic respondents there make clear that the force of the special effects was to multiply their experience this constructed world. They dissolved the reality/fantasy divide in a way that made them care all the more about the threat to that, and our own, world. To quote just one:

> It was as if the viewer sat down in a chair, put on glasses, and was literally placed on Pandora, spaceships, and floating mountains. The viewer can feel so engulfed by the imagery, you feel like you can smell the leaves from the trees. *Avatar* is utterly hypnotizing. James Horner's score is some of the best work done in his career. It offers a variable of devastation that moves the viewer to near tears.

This is not engulfment *preventing* (mystifying, obfuscating, enclosing, debarring) wider thoughts; it is an *intensification* with which people have a new resource for feeling and thinking. The difficulty here is the operation of that much wider set of claims about 'fantasy'.[3] The fascinating thing is to see how sections of the

Left ended up bemoaning audiences finding resources for thought and anger about America's military, because it was the 'wrong kind of trigger'.

HOLLYWOOD AND THE IRAQ WAR

Hollywood has, of course, not finished with the Iraq war, yet in at least four ways *The Hurt Locker* appears to me to close the cycle. Its timing (running over the 2009 election); its 'overcoming' of PTSD by having James absorb it into his personality; its deletion of all Reality Guarantees; and when the film won the Oscars, in important senses it ceased to be an Iraq war film, being celebrated instead as: the first Oscar-winning Best Film by a woman director; an indie art film; and an anti-special effects accolade. It is interesting to note that the next film to emerge – *The Green Zone* – does things substantially differently. Paul Greengrass's film was released under the 'thriller' tagline 'Bourne goes epic', its DVD proclaiming, 'We wanted to make a popcorn movie' but set in Iraq; and very many reviews and commentaries make that comparison their point of reference for evaluating the film. Drawing on the action figure of Matt Damon as Jason Bourne from the *Bourne* film franchise, the film presents John Miller as a heroic military man who is willing to work entirely outside rules and discipline because of his commitment to truth.[4] He discloses a conspiracy – standard fare, of course, for action movies – to fake the evidence about Weapons of Mass Destruction, which apparently runs right up to the top of American politics. Yet it is left to the audience to make the jump to who, precisely, is leading this conspiracy, and indeed why. We are shown one suggestive television fragment of George Bush but, that aside, no *real* American political figures are even named. Oil, Middle East policy and Israel are never mentioned. Iran slips in once. Miller, meanwhile, relates nobly if uncompromisingly with local Iraqis, as he tries to save a Ba'athist general who is the supposed 'source' of the false intelligence about WMDs, and whom the conspirators now want dead, so he cannot point the finger. If there is any bewilderment in Miller's character, it is with his own side. *The Green Zone* locates itself elsewhere.

A PROPPIAN FORMULA

In Chapter 3, I introduced the notion that this cycle of films might profitably be seen through the lens of Propp's work on Wondertales: that they are constructed, albeit loosely, around a formula. I want now to cash in this claim and delineate a journey which overarches the whole cycle, within which each film selects some parts. The formula is complicated, with many variants, but some real constants.

1. There is an implied story-arc, from over here to over there and back again. There is a real opposition in all the films between 'over there' and 'over here'. 'Over there' is taken to be unknown, unpredictable, governed by rules that 'we' do not understand and inexplicably hostile. 'We' who go there will at some point find that who we are and try to be is thrown into disarray. A running *question*, often articulated openly in the films, is 'why are we there?' The question is not answered. That very failure to answer constitutes the ground for all that follows.

2. 'Over here' comprises three strands. First, is deceitful officialdom. This can be in the personae of officers and military leaders, politicians and other elements of the governance system. They can be incompetent, self-aggrandising, or corrupt, but they all seek to mislead and hide. Second, is a glib uncaring civilian population, who do not understand what is happening 'over there'. The third strand is a more generalised 'America', which appears emptied of opportunities, of relationships, of fields of meaningful action.

3. 'Over there' focuses on several kinds of actor, who will be differently visible. The locals will rarely be visible at all, except as they might threaten 'us'. Soldiers will be very visible. Soldiers take with them weaknesses, prejudices, wild behaviours which constitute them as 'ordinary us' over there, and we accompany them. Other actors (officers, staff, politicians and so on) will be filmed more dis-passionately – our encounter with those over there is not constituted in a cinematically special way.

4. Individual films select a part of this journey from home to away and back again, and choose protagonists who all share one characteristic. They are all, at some point and some narrative juncture, *bewildered*. The responses of local people over there just do not make sense: why do they hate and attack us? how do we tell a bad one from a good one? Soldiers cannot make sense of their presence in this world. They *believed* that things had purpose and point, but become disillusioned. Encounters confuse and mount up to increase bewilderment to the point of damage. They may begin to experience symptoms similar to PTSD: dissociation of emotions and behaviour, fantastical imaginings and violent outbursts, swings between helplessness and hyperactivity.

5. This bewilderment and damage comes home, where it will run back up against those three strands of 'over here': deceitful officialdom, glib and uncaring civilians, and an American 'desert'. This intensifies the bewilderment.

6. The films face a choice. Either they follow a protagonist's journey into and through bewilderment, and offer that in itself as evidence to viewers. Or they use some of the repertoire of cinematic devices developed by the tradition of independent cinema, to step back from the character and bewilder *us*. As Statement Films, these techniques are always in the service of unsettling our existing assumptions and understandings. They try to provoke us into rethinking, and making a positional decision.

The decisions on which parts and how much of the arc, and how many of the resultant tensions to display, how if at all to resolve them, and where (if at all) to find heroism, constitute the key political decisions by the film-makers.

RAYMOND WILLIAMS: DOMINANT, RESIDUAL AND EMERGENT THEMES

What does this Proppian formula amount to? I want to make a link, finally, to three ideas from the work of Raymond Williams. It is not common to use Williams' ideas in film studies – indeed, they have become somewhat unfashionable in the broader cultural-studies domain. Yet I believe they have real potential. Williams, surely the most important twentieth-century British cultural critic, wrote widely on everything from drama, the novel, the rise of mass communications and working class life in Wales, to the struggle for democracy. Williams insisted in all his work on exploring cultural forms for the ways they related to on-going struggles for life, community, and justice.[5] Within the political-theoretical frame which he developed, Williams put forward three concepts which I want to use here: 'structures of feeling'; 'conventions'; and the distinction between 'dominant', 'residual', and 'emergent' cultural forms. The concept of 'structures of feeling' was used by Williams from his early work on drama. Williams used it to capture the idea of people's everyday experiences: the way the world seems and feels in particular periods, the senses of directions being taken, the expectations, hopes and fears that go with this. A great part of these, he believed, arises from tensions between official, formal ideologies, and the practicalities of life. But they can appear shapeless, like a cloud of steam – except, perhaps, in the imaginative fiction of a period. Art takes on the role of putting form on the otherwise inexpressible. It thus can embody the sense of a whole society: 'It is in art, primarily, that the effect of the totality, the dominant structure of feeling, is expressed and embodied' (Williams & Orrom 1954:21).

As Williams himself acknowledged, this raises many problems. In any period, how many distinguishable structures of feeling can there be – especially when there is rising conflict? Does all art and culture equally embody and express such totalities? If people live most of their lives within national-linguistic boundaries and associated structures of feeling, how do international cultural influences bear on this? In interviews with *New Left Review*, Williams acknowledged the concept's methodological risks. If structures of feeling can effectively only be known through works of art, is there not a circularity, in that 'the concept is only going to be articulated and available in fully expressed work' (Williams 1979:158)? But the concept remained with Williams across his intellectual life because it allowed him to explore the political significance of culture without *either* reducing culture to ideology, *or* relegating it to an autonomous domain. Identifying and studying 'structures of feeling' may be complex and difficult, but that's life.

Cultural forms at their best, then, contain and express the tensions and demands in people's lives, and do so not just through characters, motives and narratives, but also through the distinctive 'conventions' of different genres and periods of an art. Williams addressed two aspects of conventions. They provide the conditions for audience participation (in the theatre, an aside or monologue can be overheard by audiences but not by other characters on stage; in a film, a matching edit between two characters establishes their dialogic relationship). But the *general character* of conventions in a period and art-form establishes the kinds of imaginative universe and the kinds of relation they proffer to audiences' lives. And of course this will be particularly true as and when conventions are challenged and changed. So, the disruption to people's perceptions of cinema induced by the arrival of the French 'New Wave' ('naturalistic' characters and dialogue, unsteady camerawork, jump cuts and so on) would be, for Williams, more than artistic shifts. They registered a new instability, the emergence of new social actors, new significant social settings, and the like.

Williams' third idea was that cultures are always in flux, and because of this must contain within them the marks of change. Thus, we should expect to trace, within any cultural formation, three tensely-related components: the 'dominant' modes of thinking and feeling; 'residual' elements of old movements, formations and classes; and new 'emergent' ones, holding out potential for new and future developments.[6] Culture was for Williams *deeply historical*, caught up in a restless encounter between competing social forces. Because of his own background within English Literature, Williams' primary interest remained literature and drama, although he did write still-valuable works on mass communications, and specifically on television. But I want to propose a link between his ideas and those of Vladimir Propp who, in a very different context, explored what we might call the social construction of narrative formulae. Propp is another who has become unfashionable as an intellectual resource. Partly this is because he has often been understood very mechanically, through the interpretation offered by Claude Levi-Strauss, an interpretation Propp himself repudiated strongly in the last years of his life.[7] Where Levi-Strauss and others sought to co-opt Propp to a structuralist enterprise, seeking in him an early version of attempts to theorise the *general nature of formulaic fiction*, Propp insisted that he was trying to characterise one very specific phenomenon: the imaginative world of Russian peasants. He was not even dealing with all folktales, only Wondertales. He would never, therefore, have suggested that we should seek some formula which could be applied to all narratives.

The great virtue of studying narratives with some generative formula is this: their conventions, in Williams' second, broader sense, become especially accessible and analysable. Long-standing or evanescent, the implications for drawing out their generative structure of feeling should be clear. If we stitch together, then, the ideas of Williams and Propp, we can formulate a distinctive question: at moments when, in response to felt changes, recognisably different forms of cultural expression emerge with new characteristic (uses of) conventions, can we diagnose the shifts in broader sensibilities or 'structures of feeling' which generate them? Putting this into the context of this book, can we see within the linking elements of these 23 films the symptoms of a broader struggle to articulate a way of responding to the 'Iraq crisis' in the US? And can we thus distinguish marks of the old, the current, and the new within them? I believe we can, in at least the following ways:

- The adoption of a 'soldiers' eye-view', through the borrowing of their war video aesthetic: incorporating that as a distinctive formal device turns that eye back onto the soldiers themselves, becoming a basis for examining the authenticity of that way of seeing. In its *dominant* mode, it ramifies into an image of stress, leading on to admiration, concern about stress, and demands that soldiers be seen as victims. 'PTSD' then becomes the 'official' discourse locking down the meanings and implications of it all. In its *residual* mode, it looks back to Vietnam, putting meaning back into that war, but then carrying forward to Iraq the sedimented debates over that war. But in its *emergent* mode, it becomes the beginning of a new critique. Limited by its initial commitment to the soldiers as the arbiters of the situation in Iraq, it cannot travel very far – and the barrier that de Palma's film hit attests to this. The most powerful addition, suggesting new but as yet unfulfilled directions, is the creation of the figure of the Latino soldier.

- A number of the films borrow formal devices and techniques from Indiewood cinema. But in the act of borrowing they often transform them. Whereas in Indiewood films they function primarily as artistic gestures, through which film-makers and their audiences acknowledge each others' cultural knowingness, in *dominant* mode they become formal means to disturb and disrupt otherwise-easy narrative directions (*Rendition* is a clear example of this). *Elah* on the other hand uses its generic instability to warp unease back into the dominant mode of understanding. In *residual* mode, they either just appear clever devices that are irrelevant to the issues of Iraq (*The Jacket* is an instance of this), or they signal simply frustration and helplessness (*American Soldiers* might best be seen in this way). In *emergent* mode, they go in a number of directions: sometimes towards empty despair and the loss of meaning (*Badland*), sometimes towards transformations of fantasy (*GI Jesús*).

My argument is that this formula emerged out of a compromise, a way of speaking when something had become almost unsayable, a way of making Statements in a highly embattled situation.[8] A few films did break away – mostly evidently *Redacted* – and paid the price in furious denunciation. Others found space by never seeking cinema release. Outcomes often prove crucial. It is a special feature of fiction that stories somehow resolve. Films address the uncovering of deceit or treachery, of seeking to answer the narrative question, 'Why are we there?' That gives rise to several possible outcomes, based around choices between *despair* versus *hope*. If there are no solutions, the deceits and concealments will continue, the 'American landscape' will continue as bleak and hopeless as it first appeared. In which case the only hope may be to return 'over there', with your only remaining true and trustworthy friends: other soldiers. The other possibility is the finding of heroes, who might just make and lead to other decisions; and the emergence of the Latino victim-hero is surely critical here.

This cycle of 'toxic' films contains some poor films and some small gems. Weaknesses, I believe, are often a function of films' struggles to be seriously political under very constrained circumstances. The strengths could just be signs of a renewed politicisation of independent cinema in America which may, in future, produce new challenging work.

Notes

1   THE DISAPPEARING IRAQ WAR FILMS

1. One example of this kind of reflective coverage: on 25 March 2008, the *Washington Post* asked: 'A spate of Iraq-themed movies and TV shows haven't just failed at the box office. They've usually failed spectacularly, despite big stars, big budgets and serious intentions. The underwhelming reception from the public raises a question: Are audiences turned off by the war, or are they simply voting against the way filmmakers have depicted it?' (Farhi 2008).

2. All figures in this table are taken from IMDb.com.

3. New Line Cinema played safe with the possible political implications of *Lord of the Rings*, not least because of the wide circulation of images of George Bush wearing 'The One Ring'. National Geographic was licensed to produce a promotional DVD, 'Beyond The Movie', which was also widely shown on TV, before being incorporated as an Extra into the Special Edition of *The Fellowship of the Ring* (2001). It invites us to consider the relevance of Tolkien's story to our world, but in sufficiently abstract terms as to attach to no particular conflict – except, perhaps, the threat to our environment (at that time, the Bush administration's inaction on climate change was not yet so overt).

4. In saying this I am disagreeing with Douglas Kellner's estimation in his *Cinema Wars*. Kellner, using a critical measure I discuss in detail shortly, judges Stone's film in particular to constitute a 'conservative take on 9/11' (2009:104) through not being overtly critical of the Administration's response ('failing to deal with the political context' [Kellner 2009:117]), through sentimentalising, and through the inclusion of the character of the ex-Marine who rejoined for the invasion of Iraq (which, as Kellner rightly insists, had no links with bin Laden or Al-Qaeda). The film would simply have lacked credibility as an account even of the 'local' events if it had not acknowledged that some did respond in this way. Indeed, the importance of these two films seems to me precisely in their *refusal* of any political frame – beginning the process of detaching the events of 9/11 from the Bush narrative of 'terror'. The account that comes closest to seeing this is Jeffrey Klenotic's essay on *United 93*. Klenotic acknowledges that in important ways the film functioned to 'bear solemn witness' to the events by, as it were, living inside them. But Klenotic still finds it necessary to tag on some unconvincing claims about the films 'naturalising the war' (Klenotic 2008:101).

5. Within a few months of its release, two Republican-supported counter-documentaries had appeared: Michael Wilson's *Michael Moore Hates America*, and Alan Peterson's *Fahrenhype 9/11* (both 2004). See also, among many others, Ralph Reiland (2004). For an examination of the controversy over Moore's film, see Robert Brent Toplin (2005).

6. Some of the ambiguities of this raising of hopes and rousing the opposition are captured in this article from one of the very small American socialist organisations:

> Across the country – and, indeed, in much of the world – this film seems to have fallen like rain on a cultural landscape thirsting for the unvarnished

truth. People are clamoring to see it – from Joplin, Mo., to Crawford, Texas, to cities in Australia and US Army bases in South Korea. Go to Google News and type in 'Fahrenheit 9/11' and you will read reviews from hundreds of small-town newspapers across the US. Most report a standing ovation and cheers when the film ends. Audiences laugh and cry, and few are unmoved. In Joplin, Mo., 60 people signed a petition to their local theater demanding it be shown. In Crawford, Texas – where Bush has his "ranch" – nearby movie houses are afraid to offend the don, but local peace activists intend to show it outdoors, on the side of a barn. They don't have a building large enough for the expected crowd. Audiences go far beyond those already opposed to Bush and the war. Dale Earn Hardt Jr., the NASCAR racing-car icon, took his crew to see the movie. It is especially popular in towns near military bases. Republicans are being offered free admission in some areas to test their faith in Bush. (Griswold 2004)

7. That same year, looking immediately back, one critic observed nothing but a wave of anti-intellectual 'affect' dominating American political thinking (Ó Tuathail 2004).
8. For perceptive critical examinations of this documentary tradition, see Carruthers (2006, 2007), Grajeda (2007), Gaines (2007) and McGrath (2009).
9. On the history of this fallacious charge, see in particular McDonald (1985).
10. See Barker (2000).
11. See for instance Barker et al. (2001), Cronin (2009), Hagen (1999), Schoenbach (2001) and Schiappa (2008).
12. For a discussion of the rationale for this, see the report Barker et al. (2007) produced for the British Board of Film Classification, on audience responses to screened sexual violence. In fact, a number of early works in the cultural studies audience-research tradition built on a realisation of the exceptional importance of positive responses. For example, Janice Radway's *Reading The Romance* (1991) uses the tactic of taking readers' favourite stories and extracting a formula of what is required for readers to enjoy them. Ien Ang's *Watching Dallas* (1985) explores the fragmented character of those who most enjoyed the series, arguing that this is because the other main frames of response – a mass culture-rejection and a cynical pleasure at the programme's 'badness' – both bring to bear outside constraining discourses.

2   *NO TRUE GLORY*: THE FILM THAT NEVER WAS

1. Amusingly, one website was in 2009 still giving a release date of December 2008, and managed to give a star-rating to the film (4.5 out of 5). See Anon (2008).
2. As examples, at the same time that the stories about *No True Glory* were circulating, at least two other projects were being discussed – a Disney movie about 'Navy seals', literally about the use of the mammals in military operations; and *The Bomb in my Garden* (ostensibly deploying Johnny Depp to tell the story of an Iraqi nuclear scientist escaping Saddam Hussein). Neither emerged.
3. Contrast this with his reported 'official' advice to his Marines, in a 2003 leaflet: 'For the mission's sake, our country's sake, and the sake of the men who carried the Division's colors in past battles – who fought for life and never lost their nerve – carry out your mission and keep your honor clean. Demonstrate to

the world there is "No Better Friend, No Worse Enemy" than a US Marine' (Mattis 2003).

4. It is interesting that at this point commentators are picturing 'audiences' as keen and eager for these screened stories. Yet within two years many would be expressing no surprise that the films performed very badly at the box office. For a slightly contrary view, but one which arrived at the same conclusions, another academic was quoted in another of these long reflective articles:

> With the war still raging and the country divided over how to end it, Robert Thompson, media professor at Syracuse University, said he was amazed at the speed with which popular culture was tackling the subject. 'The Vietnam War was one that pop culture virtually tried to erase, with the exception of news and a few comedy/variety shows'. ... In contrast, Thompson noted, '*The West Wing* was plowing 9/11 themes into its story line just weeks after the attacks'. McGrail, of Susquehanna University, thinks the public is ready for war as entertainment because it already feels connected to the subject. 'The first Gulf War was a masterpiece of military message control and people didn't know anything about what was going on. Now, we have embedded journalists and a lot of news coming at us all the time, so people feel they are intimately familiar with the topic. (Gillin 2005)

5. In a personal email (18 March 2010), Bing West simply said, 'Beats me', when I asked whether he could throw any light on the film's non-appearance.

6. 'If Matt Damon can't sell an Iraq war film, perhaps this is a lost cause for Hollywood. One week after the tiny war drama *The Hurt Locker* claimed the best-picture Oscar, Damon and Paul Greengrass – who directed the last two Bourne films – were expected to bring the Iraq war feature into the mainstream. Instead, *Green Zone* put up little resistance to the competition this week, mustering just $14.5 million.' (Bowles 2010)

7. 'Producers at Universal Pictures are developing what would be Hollywood's first feature film about the war in Iraq'. (CNN 2004)

8. 'As the wounded warriors of Iraq and Afghanistan arrive in Los Angeles for the Iraq Star Foundation, "A Night of Honour" fundraising gala, they find themselves being treated like the celebrities who are honoring them. The Military Connection and Universal Studios have invited the arriving troops and their caregivers to enjoy the day at Universal Studios Theme Park before their big night of honor.' (Universal Studios 2009)

9. See, for instance, Crawford (2007).

3   CONSTRUCTING AN 'IRAQ WAR EXPERIENCE'

1   A good example of this kind of writing can be found in Burgess and Green (2009). A useful critique of these optimistic accounts is given in Hess (2009).

2. See for instance Poole (2008). Some of the concerns of the military are well-captured in an insider essay by Dauber (2009).

3. The soldiers were not alone in this. According to Astley, the magazine *Vogua Italia* reshot many of the most iconic Abu Ghraib photographs with models.

4. On this, see also Andén-Papadopoulos (2009a).

5. Stewart's essay is peppered with uses of the word 'we', implying that his judgements are obvious and shared. His essay – the only extensive consideration apart from Kellner that I have found (Stewart writes about twelve of the films)

– is its exact opposite. Kellner's considerable virtue is that he makes absolutely explicit what theoretical and political approach underpins his claims, making it much easier to evaluate. Stewart (who belongs to a long line of literary scholars who want to write about film) delivers lordly pronouncements in a fashion that presumes a host of concepts and claims, but in a perversely impenetrable way.

6. This easy dismissal has spilled into academic commentary. Paul Arthur (2007) excoriates *Redacted* for offering blatant 'Hollywood stereotypes' of reactionary soldiers (comparing it with *Battle for Haditha*, which he describes as 'balanced'). It is interesting to see this deploying of 'analytic' language to cover what is essentially political outrage.

4   FROM DOUGHBOYS TO GRUNTS: THE 'AMERICAN SOLDIER'

1. Michael Hanlon (2000) gives three most likely sources: getting covered by white dust during the Mexican–American war of 1846–47; the stodgy diet given to soldiers in the 1850s; or even the distinctive domed shape of soldiers' buttons in this period.

2. This summary of the film is helpful: 'Bosko is a doughboy in the Great War. Bullets and bombs are everywhere. (A bomb even blows up the title card.) Bosko and his fellow infantrymen are hardly safe in their trench. Bosko is happily eating from a pan full of beans when a bomb hits the pan and destroys his meal. Bosko misses Honey; he pulls out her picture and kisses it. A cannonball tears through it, making her head a gaping hole. Now Bosko is angry. He vows revenge but the moment his helmet appears above the trench, it's hit with dozens of bullets, knocking him back down. Another soldier (a horse) briefly cheers him up with harmonica music. Bosko gets his chance to be a hero when his buddy (a hippo) swallows a cannonball.' (Spurlin, n.d.) Little of real soldiering survives this cartoonisation.

3. The title (so similar to *Meet John Doe* [dir. Frank Capra, 1941]), a classic 'plain American confronts the political machine and makes things change' Hollywood story) suggests this is surely in the tradition of the spoof renditions of major films so well crafted in the Dogville Comedies.

4. On *Sergeant York*, see also Chapter 3 of Toplin (1996).

5. Thomas Myers' (1986) review of Lewis rightly argues that it is flawed by its exaggeration of this consistent theme, and its insistence on a 'need for consensus' on the war.

6. Thomas Doherty (1993:274) quotes part of a marketing release for the film:

> Throughout the nation, the United States Marine Corps is on the alert – ready to give you (the exhibitor) every possible cooperation to help put *Sands of Iwo Jima* across! Every Marine Corps Unit in the country is ready to work with you on crowd-building promotion.

7. See for instance Goldberg (1993:142–7), Hartley (1996:216–21), Bertelsen (1989), Edwards and Winkler (1997), and Hariman and Lucaites (2002). More generally, the flag fetishism, which many have argued the photograph helped engender, has been superbly analysed in Dubin (1992; see Chapter 5, 'Rally round the Flag').

8. The full story of the photograph's taking has been told in several places. The key part of it is that there was indeed an earlier (small) flag, but the US Command

wanted a larger and more visible one – hence the 'replanting'. See, for instance, Marling and Wetenhall (1991).

9. Roberts and Olson (1995:318–21).

10. The bulk of the studies were eventually published as the four-volume *The American Soldier* in 1949–50.

11. This story has been well told by a number of historians, most notably by Glander (1999) and Simpson (1996).

12. There is not the space here to deal properly with these films, and moreover others have done so very well (see Koppes & Black 1987, for instance). But it has to be noted in passing that the 'knowledge' they offered was itself of course a very particular ideological distortion. The second in the series, for instance, portrays the problem and purpose of the war to be stopping Germany from enacting its 100-year-long mission of world domination – with seizure of 'freedom-loving America' as its ultimate ambition.

13. See Marken (1995:70–1).

14. The materials and figures for this and the next table were gathered through searching the online press database Nexis, using its 'All US Press' option. I am here drawing on the set of approaches which have become widely known as reception studies: that is, the study of circulating reviews, debates and commentaries for the ways in which they reveal the *discursive frames* through which people are interpreting things such an event, object, or icon. For valuable works in this area but taking rather different orientations, see various publications of Janet Staiger (especially 1992, 2000) and Ernest Mathijs (especially 2003). Staiger builds primarily upon the tradition of reader-reception theory. Mathijs builds more on the work of Karl-Erik Rosengren and his work on 'mentions'.

15. John Fiske, in his widely-known *Television Culture* (1987), devotes a whole chapter to *The A-Team*. Disappointingly, he is so concerned to introduce large transhistorical categories of race, class and gender into his account that he manages not to think about the historically-specific context entailed here. He writes, for instance:

> The voice-over tells us that the A-Team escaped from their army accusers in Vietnam. These images of male power breaking free are metaphors for masculinity's desire to break through the laws and the social constraints with which society tries to contain it' (Fiske 1987:206)

This tendency to lose all sense of history is a weakness of this kind of approach to 'popular culture'.

16. One harsh indicator of this fear of vets was their appearance as psychopathic rapists in a number of the sexploitation movies of the early 1970s. See for instance *Forced Entry* (dir. Shaun Costello, 1973; remade by Jim Sotos, 1975), in which a returned Vietnam vet, seemingly an innocent petrol pump attendant, rapes and murders women, each time seen against a backdrop of Vietnam carnage images.

17. This short overview has the added benefit of also covering a number of lesser known films. His comments on a later cycle show this: 'The warrior/hero also appeared in combat films like *Hamburger Hill* (dir. John Irvin, 1987), *Platoon Leader* (dir. Aaron Norris, 1988), *Siege of Firebase Gloria* (dir. Brian Trenchard-Smith, 1989), *Casualties of War* (dir. Brian De Palma, 1989) and *The Iron Triangle* (dir. Eric Weston, 1989). All of these films rationalise the violence that

occurred in Vietnam. *Siege of Firebase Gloria* and *Platoon Leader,* for instance, condemn the violence of the Communists as aggressive while justifying equally outrageous American violence as defensive, while the more egalitarian *The Iron Triangle* assumes that both Communist and American soldiers are just trying to survive in a violent world' (Muse 1993:91).

18. See also John Pilger's 1970 BBC documentary *The Quiet Mutiny* in the course of which Pilger said: 'The war isn't over, but it is ending. It is ending not because of the Paris talks or the demonstrations at home. It is ending because the largest and wealthiest and most powerful organization on earth – the American Army – is being challenged from within. From the very cellars of its pyramid – from the most forgotten, the most brutalized and certainly the bravest of its members. The war is ending because the grunts are taking no more bullshit.'

19. It is worth noting that the title of the leading alternative newspaper circulating among American soldiers in Vietnam was the *Grunt Free Press*, a monthly paper which debated the war, and became an organising point for a number of the soldiers' mutinies.

20. 'A US sniper uses the Qur'an as target practice in Baghdad. A US Marine hands out coins to residents in Fallujah that ask in Arabic on one side: "Where will you spend eternity?" The other side is inscribed with a Biblical verse: "For God so loved the world, that He gave His only begotten Son, that whoever believes in Him shall not perish, but have eternal life. John 3:16." An American soldier who performed two tours in Iraq is denied promotion when his superiors learn he is an atheist, after he refuses to pray during Thanksgiving dinner. An anti-Islamic poster adorns the door of the Military Police office at Fort Riley, Kansas, featuring a quote from conservative pundit Ann Coulter: "We should invade their countries, kill their leaders and convert them to Christianity." And as the *New York Times* reported this week, some cadets at West Point and the Naval Academy feel pressured by their schools to adopt a Judeo-Christian worldview.' (Harwood 2008)

21. See Alan Moore's *Ballad of Halo Jones* (1991) comicbook series for a stunning example of this.

22. See, for instance, the *Space Grunts* series (Ward 2008, 2009; Hightshoe 2009).

23. See, for instance, Mary Gentle's *Grunt* (1995).

5   UNDERSTANDING FILM 'FAILURES'

1. In an earlier book, Carruthers (2000) has written interestingly about the ways in which war films are insistently – but inconsistently – measured for their 'pro-' or 'anti-war' stances, only rarely with open debate about the nature of the criteria being used.

2. An interesting example of this tactic is found in a review of *Redacted* in the left-leaning *American Prospect*:

> The interplay between the naked emotions at the heart of *Redacted* and the stylized method in which the story is told does make the film interesting to watch, or at least difficult to dismiss. Early reports suggest that *Redacted* is failing at the box office like its predecessors in the Iraq War film genre, but for a film that offers little nuance and does everything in its power to provoke and appal, it does a much better job of engendering internal debate

about one's political positions than its more high-minded counterparts. (Muralidhar 2007)

3. The point should be noted, mind, that film studies has not had a great deal to say about the reasons for success. We have tended to treat success as virtually self-explanatory rather than either as a warrant for aesthetic unpacking, or for investigations into ideological dangers.
4. My thanks to Peter Krämer for drawing Anderson's book to my attention.

6   BRINGING THE WAR HOME

1. See on this Kirk and Kutchins (1992).
2. Christopher Frueh, quoted in Dobbs (2009:68), from which much of this section is drawn.
3. The longer history of the relations between military and psychiatry in different countries has been brilliantly recovered in Shephard (2002). Shephard well demonstrates the shifting struggles over models for understanding the mental injuries of war, and the manoeuvres between military leaders and doctors over appropriate treatments.
4. I am very grateful to Allan Horwitz who pointed me to this resource, and for allowing me to read his own latest work in draft.
5. 'The film concludes by cross-cutting between the two men in Fonda's life' (Devine 1995:157): as Bob Hyde (played by Bruce Dern) admits defeat and prepares to walk into the sea to drown himself, Luke Martin (Jon Voight) is making a speech to high school students about the prevalence of death in Vietnam and the need for them to make a choice.
6. See Trudeau's (2005) *The Long Road Home: One Step at a Time* (Foreword by Senator John McCain). The next book of Trudeau (2006) has a Foreword by retired General Richard B. Myers (*The War Within: One More Step at a Time*).
7. It is worth noting here the challenge within the PTSD community to the reliability of 'flashbacks' as indications of trauma. Researchers have reported cases where people realise that they are getting flashbacks of things that they know have not happened. This has led, curiously, to the suggestion that the very idea of 'flashbacks' may derive its force from their use in films, which, if correct, completes a very curious circle. On this, see Frankel (1994).
8. Susan Carruthers throws a passing blast at the film in an otherwise careful essay on the documentaries. (Too) quickly summarising the film, she latches onto Tommy's decision to return to Iraq at the end of the film, judging it to be 'the only argument [Winkler] cares to muster in the war's defense. It must continue so that it can end – like Vietnam, except this time no one even tries to append "with honor"' (Carruthers 2006:36). This rushed judgement badly misses the point. He has gone back because he has nowhere else to go. The war is without point or motive. Only being in the military has.
9. On the Weinsteins generally, see Biskind (2004).
10. The motifs of cars, travel and crashes have long fascinated film scholars. For two recent valuable discussions of the meanings of crashes in other contexts, see Paul Newland's (2009) discussion of their role in mainstream Hollywood and Catherine Simpson's (2006) study of their very different role in Australian mythology.

7   EXPLAINING THE IRAQ WAR

1. There are some striking similarities between *Missing* and *In the Valley of Elah*. Both films present central protagonists who begin as strong supporters of the military, but become disillusioned as they encounter concealment and deceit.
2. See also, among others, Klinger (1994a) and Erb (1998).
3. *American Prospect* dubbed the film a 'Reece Witherspoon vehicle' (Muralidhar 2007).
4. While no doubt this tendency has deep roots, Young and Jesser (1997) suggest a recent source for revival. They point out the media's essential unpreparedness for the 1991–92 attack on Iraq. As a result, they participated almost uncritically in the demonisation of Saddam Hussein and the celebration of America's role. Micro-managed by the military, and fighting each other for journalistic access, they allowed the war to become stage-managed – with motives unquestioned, lacking casualties, a 'painless, bloodless, sanitised success' (Young & Jesser 1997:188). As long as America *won*, its motives must be fine.
5. See for instance Ungar (2004).

8   PRODUCING A 'TOXIC GENRE'

1. These sentences come from Bonus Materials on the DVD for *The Lucky Ones*.
2. Linda Williams' (1991) investigation of body genres broke important ground in thinking about these.
3. John Caldwell's (2008) study of industry films is particularly valuable here.
4. I believe we showed these processes at work in our study of the UK controversy over David Cronenberg's *Crash* (1996) – see Barker et al. (2001).
5. One very concrete example of this: the DVD of *Badland* (discussed in Chapter 6) offers an Extra in which members of the production crew discuss the film's attitude to religion, in face of its central character's anguished rejection of the whole idea of meaning in the world. There is a real sense of nervous backing off, an insistence that this is just a character's anguish, no-one is being anti-religious. Every viewer must 'make up his own mind' about this.
6. A book of which this seems to me particularly true is Grant's (2007) *Film Genre*, which it is possible to read in its entirety and come away unclear *why* genre matters.
7. All evidence gathered from Amazon.com, accessed 4 April 2010.

9   FREE-RIDERS AND OUTLIERS

1. See for instance Mr Disgusting (2007), Rotten (2007) and Brew (2008).
2. Information gleaned from Extras to the DVD.
3. The importance of considering this cycle of films as a whole shows clearly here. In an essay in *Jump Cut*, Justin Vicari (2009) mentions many of these films but, for reasons he never explains, then chooses to analyse only two: *The Jacket*, and *Harsh Times* (dir. David Ayer, 2005) – the latter being so far outside the themes of the cycle, I took the decision not to include it at all. Yet Vicari offers general judgements on American films' relations with Iraq on the basis of these two.

10   LATINO GRUNTS: THE NEW VICTIM-HEROES

1. Craig Hulet (2010) spelt out the link quite precisely:

    > Every alien, illegal or not, denoted immediately above, that registers for the
    > new three year immigration status will be simultaneously (though likely
    > without knowledge of it) be registering to be selected for service in the United
    > States Army or Marines. They will, along with other Americans chosen, be
    > selected by a lottery system most are familiar with.

2. Jeanine Basinger (1986) gives extensive consideration to the way World War II
    movies frequently assemble a culturally mixed and multi-ethnic group of soldiers.
    But in this case the principle is always the *overcoming* and *subordination* of
    their ethnicity as they become a fighting unit. This difference highlights the
    specificity of these films.

11   *THE HURT LOCKER* AND BEYOND

1. See for instance Gardiner (2009), Chapman (2009) and Hoyle (2009).
2. See the extensive debate at the Kasama Project website (2010), but also in
    particular Max Ajl's (2010) trenchant critique.
3. On this broader set of issues, see Barker (2009).
4. Chris Hewitt captured the intended mix perfectly in his *Empire* subtitle:
    'Bourne's dream partnership, Director Paul Greengrass and star Matt Damon,
    take their gripping action aesthetic to the streets of Baghdad to prove that Iraq
    thrillers and popcorn can mix' (Hewitt 2010:71).
5. For a clear and thoughtful account of Williams' life and work, see Higgins
    (1999).
6. It was striking to me to re-read the main source for this idea, Williams' essay
    'Base and superstructure in Marxist cultural theory', which was republished in
    his *Problems of Materialism and Culture* (1980). There, Williams (1980:11–30)
    also pays respect to the work of Lucien Goldmann, another thinker who has
    fallen out of fashion, and in particular acknowledges Goldmann's related ideas
    on literature and social totality, his emphasis on cultural *form* as the link
    between these, and his distinction between actual (how far an idea is developed
    and used in cultural expressions) and possible (how far it is capable of taking
    people) consciousness. It's clear that Williams feels a real connection between
    his own account of structures of feeling, and Goldmann's. From much further
    off, I want to join that comparison.
7. See Propp (1984) for both Levi-Strauss' review and Propp's response, and see
    Barker (1989, Chapter 10) for a discussion of some of the issues involved.
8. One superb essay coming from an entirely different angle effectively arrives
    at the same conclusion. Three American academics have argued that the main
    anti-war movements in the US have become trapped by their felt need to appear
    to be 'on the side of the soldiers'. See Coy et al. (2008).

References

Adams, Guy, 2008. Val Kilmer, aka Batman, the next Governor of New Mexico? *The Independent,* 17 September.

Aikens, Margaret, 2009. Is *Avatar* anti-military? *Examiner,* 30 December. Found at: http://tinyurl.com/ylgwbpy (accessed 5 April 2010).

Ajl, Max, 2010. Žižek on *Avatar.* 19 March. Found at: http://tinyurl.com/2uhtvnu (accessed 24 June 2010).

Alabassi, Mamoon, 2009.'*Avatar*' & '*The Hurt Locker*': Two 'Iraq War' Movies Compete For Awards. Found at: http://tinyurl.com/6z9ehtr (accessed 15 February 2011).

Altman, Rick, 1999. *Film/Genre.* London: British Film Institute.

Andén-Papadopoulos, Kari, 2009a. Body horror on the internet: U.S. soldiers recording the war in Iraq and Afghanistan. *Media, Culture & Society,* Vol. 31, No. 6, 1, pp. 925–6.

——, 2009b. US soldiers imaging the Iraq War on YouTube. *Popular Communication,* Vol. 7, Issue 1, pp. 17–27.

Anderson, Chris, 2006. *The Long Tail: Why the Future of Business is Selling Less of More.* London: Hyperion.

Ang, Ien, 1985. *Watching* Dallas*: Soap Opera and the Melodramatic Imagination.* London: Methuen.

Anon, 2003. Exposing the Lynch mob for what it is. *Monterey County Herald,* 16 November.

——, 2004. Letter to the Editor: Michael Moore film is treason. *The Advocate* (Baton Rouge, Louisiana), 4 August.

——, 2005a. Distributors' description of *A Message from Fallujah.* Found at: http://tinyurl.com/3yg3ep4 (accessed 12 May 2010).

——, 2005b. Propaganda movie to be released in 2006. 20 February. Found at: http://tinyurl.com/38tvh73 (accessed 12 May 2010).

——, 2007. *Six Days in Fallujah* cancelled. Right decision? Found at: http://tinyurl.com/36tcyb4 (accessed 11 December 2009).

——, 2008. *No True Glory: Battle for Fallujah* movie. Found at: http://tinyurl.com/38dakyb (accessed 7 December 2009).

——, 2009. Top 10 Iraq war-inspired horror movies. Found at: http://tinyurl.com/3374egj (accessed 9 December 2009).

Arkansas Democrat-Gazette, 2004. Death of a hero [Pat Tillman]: above and beyond duty's call. [Editorial] *Arkansas Democrat-Gazette* (Little Rock), 28 April.

Arthur, Paul, 2007. Atrocity exhibitions. *Film Comment,* November/December, pp. 52–5.

Associated Press, 2005. General rebuked for saying it's 'fun to shoot' enemies. [*Online*] World News on msnbc.com, 4 February. Found at: http://tinyurl.com/33qm345 (accessed 14 May 2010).

Astley, Mark, 2010. *Meatspace: the body as spectacle and cultural artefact in contemporary actuality body horror and death media.* Ph.D. University of Manchester.

Aufderheide, Pat, 2007. Your country, my country: how films about the Iraq War construct publics. *Framework*, Vol. 48, No. 2, pp. 56–65.

Auster, Albert & Leonard Quart, 1981. Man and Superman: Vietnam and the New American Hero. *Social Policy*, Vol. 11, Jan/Feb, pp. 60–4.

Barker, Martin (ed.), 1984. *The Video Nasties: Freedom and Censorship in the Arts*. London: Pluto Press.

——, 1989. *Comics: Ideology, Power and the Critics*. Manchester: Manchester University Press.

—— (with Thomas Austin), 2000. *From* Antz *to* Titanic: *Reinventing Film Analysis*. London: Pluto Press.

——, 2009. Fantasy audiences versus fantasy audiences. In Warren Buckland (ed.), *Film Theory and Contemporary Hollywood Movies*. London: Routledge, pp. 286–309.

Barker, Martin, Jane Arthurs & Ramaswami Harindranath, 2001. *The* Crash Controversy: *Censorship Campaigns and Film Reception*. London: Wallflower Press.

Barker, Martin, Kate Egan, Russ Hunter, et al., 2007. *Audiences and Receptions of Sexual Violence in Contemporary Cinema*. Report to the British Board of Film Classification, June. Found at: www.bbfc.co.uk/downloads/index.php (accessed 6 February 2011).

Basinger, Jeanine, 1986. *The World War II Combat Film: Anatomy of a Genre*. New York: Columbia University Press.

BBC1, 1997. *Reputations: John Wayne – The Unquiet American*. (dir. James Kent), 25 May.

Belson, Ken, 2006. As DVD sales slow, Hollywood hunts for a new cash cow. *New York Times*, 13 June.

Berkowitz, Bill, 2003. Latinos on the front lines: US military targets Latinos for Iraq and future twenty-first century wars. *Dissident Voice*, 16 October. Found at: http://tinyurl.com/37lasl8 (accessed 10 June 2010).

Bertelsen, Lance, 1989. Icons on Iwo. *Journal of Popular Culture*, Spring, pp. 79–95.

Betsalel, Ken & Mark Gibney, 2008. Can a film end a war? *Human Rights Quarterly*, Vol. 30, No. 2, May, pp. 522–525.

Biskind, Peter, 2004. *Down and Dirty Pictures: Miramax, Sundance and the Rise of Independent Cinema*. London: Bloomsbury.

Blackfive, 2004. Note to Harrison Ford. [Online] 20 December. Found at: http://tinyurl.com/394d8fe (accessed 7 December 2009).

Blanton, Gene E., 2007. The intellectual grunt (Part II). 1 June. Found at: http://tinyurl.com/2fsxuh6 (accessed 2 March 2010).

Boal, Mark, 2004. Death and dishonour. *Playboy*, May.

Bordwell, David, 1979. *Film Art: An Introduction*. New York: McGraw-Hill.

——, 2006. *The Way Hollywood Tells It: Story and Style in Modern Movies*. Berkeley, CA: University of California Press.

Bordwell, David, Janet Staiger & Kristin Thompson, 1985. *Classical Hollywood Cinema: Film Style and Mode of Production to 1960*. New York: Columbia University Press.

Bowles, Scott, 2010. 'Green Zone' can't change fortunes of war movies. *USA Today*, 14 March.

Brew, Simon, 2008. The Den of Geek interview: Daniel Myrick. [Online] *Den of Geek*, 12 June. Found at: http://tinyurl.com/24cuk2s (accessed 31 March 2010).

Brewin, Chris R., 2003. *Posttraumatic Stress Disorder: Malady or Myth?* New Haven: Yale University Press.

Brownfield, Paul, 2008. Daniel Myrick has a movie, and it's not horror. *LA Times*, 26 April.

Buckland, Warren (ed.), 2009. *Puzzle Films: Complex Storytelling in Contemporary Cinema*. Chichester: Wiley-Blackwell.

Burgess, Jean & Joshua Green, 2009. *YouTube*. Cambridge: Polity Press.

Burston, Jonathan, 2003. War and the entertainment industries: new research priorities in an era of cyberpatriotism. In Daya Kishan Thussu & Des Freedman (eds), *War and the Media*. London: Sage, pp. 163–75.

Buzzell, Colby, 2005. *My War: Killing Time in Iraq*. New York: Putnam Adult.

Caldwell, John Thornton, 2008. *Production Culture: Industrial Reflexivity and Critical Practice in Film and Television*. Durham, NC: Duke University Press.

Campbell, Duncan, 2003. Politics and war skew betting on the Oscars. *Guardian*, 3 February.

Caputo, Philip, 1976. *A Rumor of War*. New York: Holt Paperbacks.

Carruthers, Susan L., 2000. *The Media at War*. Basingstoke: McMillan.

——, 2006. Say cheese! Operation Iraqi Freedom on film. *Cineaste*, Vol. XXXII, No. 1, pp. 12–19.

——, 2007. Question time: the Iraq War revisited. *Cineaste*, Vol. XXXII, No. 4, pp. 12–17.

——, 2008. Noone's looking: the disappearing audience for war. *Media, War & Conflict*, Vol. 1, No. 1, pp. 70–6.

Cawelti, John, 1970. *The Six-Gun Mystique*. Bowling Green, OH: Bowling Green University Press.

——, 1976. *Adventure, Mystery and Romance: Formula Stories in Art and Popular Culture*. Chicago, IL: Chicago University Press.

Chambers, David, 2002. Will Hollywood go to war? *Transnational Broadcasting Studies*, Vol. 8, Spring/Summer. Found at: http://tinyurl.com/3a5pzdo (accessed 9 December 2009).

Chapman, Wallace, 2009. *Avatar* more an Iraq film than *The Hurt Locker*. 26 February. Found at: http://tinyurl.com/3aasqxl (accessed 10 March 2010).

Christensen, Christian, 2008. Uploading dissonance: YouTube and the US occupation of Iraq. *Media, War & Conflict*, Vol. 1, No. 2, pp. 155–75.

——, 2009. 'Hey man, nice shot': setting the Iraq War to music on YouTube. In Pelle Snickars & Patrick Vonderau (eds), *The YouTube Reader*. Stockholm: National Library of Sweden, pp. 204–17.

Cienfuegos, Ernesto, 2002. LA RAZA: the 'grunts' of the US Armed Forces. *La Voz de Aztlan*, 9 September. Found at: http://tinyurl.com/32ur55q (accessed 2 March 2010).

Clark, Doug, 2004. Editorial: Democrats revive Vietnam. *News & Record* (Greensboro, NC), 4 August.

CNN, 2004. Harrison Ford may lead charge in Falluja movie. 18 December. Found at: http://tinyurl.com/3x66sym (accessed 21 March 2010).

Coy, Patrick, Lynne M. Woehrle & Gregory M. Maney, 2008. Discursive legacies: the U.S. peace movement and 'Support the Troops'. *Social Problems*, Vol. 55, No. 2, pp.161–89.

Crawford, John, 2007. *The Last True Story I'll Ever Tell: An Accidental Soldier's Account of the War in Iraq*. New York: Riverhead.

Cronin, Theresa, 2009. Media effects and the subjectification of film regulation. *Velvet Light Trap*, Vol. 63, pp. 3–21.

Croteau, David & William Hoynes, 2005. *The Business of Media: Corporate Media and the Public Interest.* Newbury Park, CA: Pine Forge Press.

Darling, Cary, 2007. Hollywood goes to war. *Fort Worth Star-Telegram* (Texas), 23 September.

Dauber, Cori E., 2009. YouTube war: fighting in a world of cameras in every cell phone and Photoshop on every computer. *Institute of Strategic Studies*, November. Found at: http://tinyurl.com/3y6q5eb (accessed 16 March 2010).

Davey, Monica, 2004. For 1,000 troops, there is no going home. *New York Times*, 9 September.

DelVecchio, Rick, 2004. Why would 1,000 people crowd into a church to hear a talk by a linguist? *San Francisco Chronicle*, 18 June.

Democratic Underground, 2007. Why is there such a paucity of Iraq war films? Found at: http://tinyurl.com/37gm7fs (accessed 9 December 2009).

Derakshani, Tirdad, 2004. Harrison Ford may star in an Iraq-war movie. *Philadelphia Enquirer*, 17 December.

De Vany, Arthur, 2003. *Hollywood Economics: How Extreme Uncertainty Shapes the Film Industry.* London: Routledge.

Devine, Jeremy M., 1995. *Vietnam at 24 Frames a Second: A Critical and Thematic Analysis of Over 400 Films about the Vietnam War.* Austin, TX: University of Texas Press.

Dickensen, Ben, 2006. *Hollywood's New Radicalism: War, Globalisation and the Movies.* London: I B Tauris.

Dobbs, David, 2009. The post-traumatic stress trap. *Scientific American*, April, pp. 64–9.

Doherty, Thomas, 1993. *Projections of War: Hollywood, American Culture, and World War II.* New York: Columbia University Press.

Dubin, Steven C., 1992. *Arresting Images: Impolitic Art and Uncivil Actions.* London: Routledge.

Eberwein, Robert, 2010. *The Hollywood War Film.* Chichester: Wiley-Blackwell.

Edwards, Janis L. & Carol K. Winkler, 1997. Representative form and the visual ideograph: the Iwo Jima photograph in editorial cartoons. *Quarterly Journal of Speech*, Vol. 83, pp. 289–310.

Egan, Kate, 2007. *Trash or Treasure?: Censorship and the Changing Meanings of the Video Nasties.* Manchester: Manchester University Press.

Erb, Cynthia, 1998. *Tracking King Kong: A Hollywood Icon in American Culture.* Detroit, MI: Wayne State University Press.

Esmonde, Donn, 2008. Cote's spirit rules pages of new book. *Buffalo News* (New York), 16 November 2008.

Everhart, Bill, 2009. Summer comes earlier to movie season. *The Berkshire Eagle* (Pittsfield, Massachusetts), 1 May.

Farhi, Paul, 2008. The Iraq war, in Hollywood's theatre. *Washington Post*, 25 March.

Feeney, F. X., 2007. Pick *GI Jesús* (Film Reviews). *LA Weekly*, 25 January.

Fick, Nathaniel, 2006. Interpreting the grunts. *Los Angeles Times*, 19 March.

Filner, Bob, 2008. *Recognizing the contribution of Latino Americans serving in the armed forces.* Congressional Update, August. Found at: http://tinyurl.com/2vbq59e (accessed 2 March 2010).

Fiske, John, 1987. *Television Culture.* London: Routledge.

Fitzpatrick, Joann, 2005. Editorial: new rules on interrogation. *Patriot Ledger* (Quincy, MA), 4 May.

Fleming, Michael, 2004. U finds 'Glory' in Iraq war pic. *Daily Variety*, 16 December.

Frankel, Fred H., 1994. The concept of flashbacks in historical perspective. *International Journal of Clinical and Experimental Hypnosis*, Vol. XLII, No. 4, pp. 321–36.

Fryer, Alex, 2005. Drifter, soldier, author: a keen eye on Iraq. *Seattle Times* (Washington), 9 November.

Gaines, Jane, 2007. The production of outrage: The Iraq war and the radical documentary tradition. *Framework*, Vol. 48, No. 2, pp. 36–55.

Gardiner, Nile, 2009. Is *Avatar* an attack on the Iraq War? [Blog] *Daily Telegraph*, 12 December. Found at: http://tinyurl.com/35zbgwd (accessed 10 March 2010)

Gardner, Michael, 2009. Fight that turned tide: Veterans Day marks anniversary of U.S. assault to regain control of Fallujah. *San Diego Union-Tribune*, 11 November.

Garnham, Nicholas, 1990. *Capitalism and Communication: Global Culture and the Economics of Information*. London: Sage.

Geier, Joel, 2000. Vietnam: the soldier's rebellion. *International Socialist Review*, 9, August–September.

Gentle, Mary, 1995. *Grunt*. Harmondsworth: Penguin.

Gillin, Beth, 2005. The home front. *Philadelphia Inquirer*, 26 May.

Gilsdorf, Ethan, 2003. Lord of the Gold Ring. *The Boston Globe*, 16 November. Found at: http://tinyurl.com/36t3rhd (accessed 6 May 2010).

Glander, Timothy, 1999. *The Origins of Mass Communications Research during the American Cold War: Educational Effects and Contemporary Implications*. New York: Routledge.

Gledhill, Christine, 1985. History of genre criticism. In Pam Cook (ed.), *The Cinema Book*. London: British Film Institute, pp. 58–64.

Goffman, Erving, 1961. *Asylums: Essays on the Social Situation of Mental Patients and Other Inmates*. New York: Doubleday.

Goldberg, Vicki, 1993. *The Power of Photography: how Photographs Changed our Lives*. New York: Abbeville Press.

Goldman, William, 1983. *Adventures in the Screen Trade*. New York: Warner Books.

Gradus, Jaimie L., 2007. Epidemiology of PTSD. [Online] *US Department of Veterans Affairs, National Center for PTSD 1989–2009*, 31 January. Found at: http://tinyurl.com/389skq4 (accessed 21 March 2010).

Grajeda, Tony, 2007. The winning and losing of hearts and minds: Vietnam, Iraq, and the claims of the war documentary. *Jump Cut*, Vol. 49. Found at: www.ejumpcut.org/archive/jc49.2007/Grajeda/index.html (accessed 17 May 2010).

Grant, Barry Keith, 2007. *Film Genre*. London: Wallflower Press.

Griswold, Deirdre, 2004. The phenomenon of *Fahrenheit 9/11*: After countless imperialist wars, is a sea-change coming? [Online] Originally published in *Workers' World*, 29 July. Found at: http://tinyurl.com/2wts6je (accessed 18 February 2010).

Hagen, Ingunn, 1999. Slaves of the ratings tyranny? Media images of the audience. In Pertti Alasuutari (ed.), *Rethinking the Media Audience*. London: Sage, pp. 130–150.

Hallas, James H. (ed.), 2000. *Doughboy War: The American Expeditionary Force in World War I*. Boulder, CO: Lynne Rienner.

Hammond, Michael, 2002. Some smothering dreams: the Combat Film in contemporary Hollywood. In Steve Neale (ed.), *Genre and Contemporary Hollywood*. London: British Film Institute, pp. 62–76.

Hanlon, Michael E., 2000. Origins of 'Doughboy': an interim report. Found at: http://tinyurl.com/32okew3 (accessed 22 February 2010).

Hanson, Jarice, 2008. Selling the Bush doctrine. In Thomas Conroy & Jarice Hanson (eds), *Constructing America's War Culture: Iraq, Media and Images at Home.* Lanham, MD: Lexington Books, pp. 47–57.

Hariman, Robert & John Louis Lucaites, 2002. Performing civic identity: the iconic photograph of the flag raising on Iwo Jima. *Quarterly Journal of Speech*, Vol. 88, No. 4, pp. 363–92.

Hartley, John, 1996. *Popular Reality: Journalism, Modernity, Popular Culture.* London: Edward Arnold.

Harwood, Matthew, 2008. Evangelical grunts. *Guardian*, 27 June.

Herzog, Tobey C., 1992. *Vietnam War Stories: Innocence Lost.* London: Routledge.

Hess, Aaron, 2009. Resistance up in smoke: analysing the limitations of deliberation in YouTube. *Critical Studies in Media Communication*, Vol. 26, No. 5, pp. 411–34.

Hewitt, Chris, 2010. In the Zone. *Empire*, February, pp. 71–4.

Hightshoe, Carol (ed.), 2009. *Space Sirens: Full-Throttle Space Tales.* Denver, CO: Flying Pen Press.

Higgins, John, 1999. *Raymond Williams: Literature, Marxism and Cultural Materialism.* London: Routledge.

Hil, Richard, 2005. Life lottery: US military targets poor Hispanics for frontline service in Iraq. *New Internationalist*, May.

Holmes, Jonathan, 2007. *Fallujah.* London: Constable.

Horwitz, Allan, 2009. Post-traumatic stress disorder: the result of abnormal environments or abnormal individuals? In Gerald N. Grob & Allan V. Horwitz (eds), *Diagnosis, Therapy and Evidence: Conundrums in Modern American Medicine.* New Brunswick, NJ: Rutgers University Press, Chapter 7.

Hoyle, Ben, 2009. War on Terror backdrop to James Cameron's *Avatar. The Times* (Australia), 11 December.

Hulet, Craig B., 2004. *Bush reform of immigration policy has a hidden agenda.* [Online] duckdaotsu, 18 January. Found at: http://tinyurl.com/3yaadtw (accessed 2 March 2010).

Human Givens Institute, no date. *Traumas and phobias.* [Website] Found at: http://tinyurl.com/35kvmgy (accessed 22 March 2010).

Jeffords, Susan, 1994. *Hard Bodies: Hollywood Masculinity in the Reagan Era.* New Brunswick, NJ: Rutgers University Press.

'John', 2007. *No True Glory.* [Online] Op-For, 26 October. Found at: http://tinyurl.com/35zkkt3 (accessed 12 May 2010).

Kasama Project, 2010. Žižek on *Avatar'.* Found at: http://tinyurl.com/34ytbtl (accessed 24 June 2010).

Keene, Jennifer D., 2003. *Doughboys, the Great War and the Remaking of America.* Baltimore, MD: Johns Hopkins University Press.

Kellner, Douglas, 2009. *Cinema Wars: Hollywood Film and Politics in the Bush-Cheney Era.* Chichester: Wiley-Blackwell.

Kimball, Jeffrey, 2008. The enduring paradigm of the 'lost cause': defeat in Vietnam, the stab-in-the-back legend, and the construction of a myth. In Jenny MacLeod (ed.), *Defeat and Memory: Cultural Histories of Military Defeat in the Modern Era.* Basingstoke: Palgrave Macmillan, pp. 214–32.

King, Geoff, 2002. *New Hollywood Cinema.* London: I B Tauris.

——, 2005. *American Independent Cinema.* London: I B Tauris.

——, 2009. *Indiewood, USA: Where Hollywood Meets Independent Cinema*. London: I B Tauris.

Kinney, Katherine, 2000. *Friendly Fire: American Images of the Vietnam War*. Oxford: Oxford University Press.

Kirk, S. & S. Kutchins, 1992. *The Selling of DSM: the Rhetoric of Science in Psychiatry*. New York: Aldine de Gruyter.

Klenotic, Jeffrey, 2008. Staying in the moment: Hollywood, history, and the politics of 9/11 cinema. In Thomas Conroy & Jarice Hanson (eds), *Constructing America's War Culture: Iraq, Media, and Images at Home*. Lanham, MD: Lexington Books, pp. 85–106.

Klinger, Barbara, 1994a. *Melodrama and Meaning: History, Culture, and the Films of Douglas Sirk*. Bloomington and Indianapolis, IN: Indiana University Press.

——, 1994b. Local genres: the Hollywood Adult Film in the 1950s. In Jacky Bratton, Jim Cook & Christine Gledhill (eds), *Melodrama: Stage Picture Screen*. London, British Film Institute, pp. 134–46.

Kondracke, Morton, 2004. Despite similarities, Bush differs from Reagan in electability. *San Gabriel Valley Tribune* (California), 14 June.

Koppes, Clayton R. & Gregory D. Black, 1987. *Hollywood at War: How Politics, Profits and Propaganda Shaped World War II Movies*. London: I B Tauris.

Langford, Barry, 2005. *Film Genre: Hollywood and Beyond*. Edinburgh: Edinburgh University Press.

Lewis, Lloyd B., 1985. *The Tainted War: Culture and Identity in Vietnam War Narratives*. Westport, CT: Greenwood Press.

Longley, Kyle, 2008. *Grunts: The American Combat Soldier in Vietnam*. (New York: M E Sharpe.

Marken, Ellen, 1995. *The Romance of American Psychology: Political Culture in the Age of Experts*. Berkeley, CA: University of California Press.

Marling, Karal Ann & John Wetenhall, 1991. *Iwo Jima: Monuments, Memories and the American Hero*. Cambridge, MA: Harvard University Press.

Martin, Martin, Maggi & Laura Johnston, 2007. Right to shoot and not be sued? *Plain Dealer* (Cleveland), 14 July.

Massey, Anne & Mike Hammond, 1999. 'It was true! How can you laugh?': history and memory in the reception of *Titanic* in Britain and Southampton. In Kevin S. Sandler & Gaylyn Studlar (eds), *Titanic: Anatomy of a Blockbuster*. New Brunswick, NJ: Rutgers University Press, pp. 239–63.

Mathijs, Ernest, 2003. 'It may not be such a bad disease after all': AIDS references in the critical reception of David Cronenberg. *Cinema Journal*, Vol. 42, No. 4, pp. 29–45.

Mattis, General Jim, 2003. *Message to Marines at the start of the Iraq War*. [Online] American Veteran's Memorial, 19 March. Found at: http://tinyurl.com/35k2yzh (accessed 12 May 2010).

Mayes, Rick & Allan V. Horwitz, 2005. DSM–III and the revolution in the classification of mental illness. *Journal of the History of the Behavioral Sciences*, Vol. 41, No. 3, pp. 249–67.

McCrisken, Trevor & Andrew Pepper, 2005. *American History and Contemporary Hollywood Film*. Edinburgh: Edinburgh University Press.

McDonald, J. Fred, 1985. *Television and the Red Menace: the Video Road to Vietnam*. New York: Greenwood Press.

McDonald, Paul & Janet Wasko, 2008. *The Contemporary Hollywood Film Industry* Chichester: Wiley-Blackwell.

McGrath, Jacqueline L., 2009. Recent documentaries about the Iraq War. *Journal of American Folklore*, Vol. 122, No. 484, pp. 218–23.

Melton, Buckner F., 2004. A willing audience key to the success of Reagan's role as the reassurer. *The News & Observer* (Raleigh, NC), 13 June.

Montgomery, David, 2004. To oversee a tribute to the 'greatest generation', organizers tap an eclectic scholar. *Washington Post*, 24 May.

Moore, Alan, 1991. *The Complete Ballad of Halo Jones*. London: Titan.

Mr Disgusting, 2007. *The Objective*: Writer/Director Daniel Myrick. [Online] *Bloody Disgusting*, September. Found at: http://tinyurl.com/33ykhz4 (accessed 31 March 2010).

Muralidhar, Sudhir, 2007. Why are Iraq war movies box-office flops? *American Prospect*, 27 November.

Muse, Eben J., 1993. From Lt Calley to John Rambo: repatriating the Vietnam War. *Journal of American Culture*, Vol. 27, pp. 88–92.

Myers, Thomas, 1986. The tainted war: culture and identity in Vietnam War narratives. [Review] *Modern Fiction Studies*, Vol. 32, No. 2, pp. 293–6.

Neale, Steve, 1993. Melo talk: on the meaning and use of the term 'melodrama' in the American trade press. *The Velvet Light*, No. 32, pp. 66–89.

——, 2000. *Genre and Hollywood*. London: Routledge.

Newland, Paul, 2009. Look past the violence: automotive destruction in American movies. *European Journal of American Culture*, Vol. 28, No. 1, pp. 5–20.

Nolte, John, 2008. Hollywood loses the war in Iraq. [Online] *Pajamas Media*, 20 July. Found at: http://tinyurl.com/33mkgv3 (accessed 6 May 2010).

Norris, Matt, 2004. Battle for Fallujah. 20 December. [Online] *Cinema Blend*. Found at: http://tinyurl.com/32qeku3 (accessed 12 May 2010).

Novikov, Eugene, 2008. Iraq war movies and their box office deaths. [Online] *Cinematical*, 26 March. Found at: http://tinyurl.com/35jt3w7 (accessed 10 December 2009).

O'Donnell, Patrick, 2007. *We Were One: Shoulder to Shoulder with the Marines who Took Fallujah*. Cambridge, MA: Da Capo Press.

Onstad, Katrina, 2007. *Under suspicion* – Rendition: *a topical, well-intended, messy thriller*. [Online] CBCNews.ca, October 19. Found at: http://tinyurl.com/36segal (accessed 27 May 2010).

Ó Tuathail, Gearóid, 2004. 'Just out looking for a fight': American affect and the invasion of Iraq. *Antipode*, Vol. 35, pp. 856–70.

Parish, James, 2006. *Fiasco: A History of Hollywood's Iconic Flops*. New York: Wiley.

Petley, Julian, 1984. A nasty story. *Screen*, Vol. 25, No. 2, pp. 68–75.

Pfeiffer, Glenn, Robert Capettini & Gene Whittenburg, 1997. *Forrest Gump* – Accountant: a study of accounting in the motion picture industry. *Journal of Accounting Education*, Vol. 15, Issue 3, pp. 319–44

Pilger, John, 2006. *The Quiet Mutiny* (1970) [Video]. Oley, PA: Bullfrog Films.

Poe, G. Thomas, 2001. Historical spectatorship around and about Stanley Kramer's *On The Beach*. In Melvyn Stokes & Richard Maltby (eds), *Hollywood Spectatorship: Changing Perceptions of Cinema Audiences*. London: British Film Institute, pp. 91–102.

Poole, Oliver, 2008. Pentagon declares war on internet combat videos. *Daily Telegraph*, 26 July.

Propp, Vladimir, 1968. *The Morphology of the Folktale*. Austin, TX: University of Texas Press.

———, 1984. *History and Theory of Folklore*. Minneapolis, MN: University of Minnesota Press.

Radway, Janice, 1991. *Reading the Romance: Women, Patriarchy and Popular Literature*. Chapel Hill, NC: University of North Carolina Press).

Rahner, Mark, 2007. Brian De Palma sets his sights on Iraq with *Redacted*. *The Seattle Times*, 29 November.

Redd, Rea Andrew, 2008. Off-topic – War in Iraq: The Battle of Fallujah [review of Bing West, *No True Glory*]. [Blog] *Civil War Librarian*, 11 July. Found at: http://tinyurl.com/32su7vt (accessed 8 December 2009).

Reiland, Ralph, 2004. The big lie behind Moore's *Fahrenheit 9/11*. 3 July. Found at: http://tinyurl.com/2uhh6fb (accessed 18 February 2010).

Rich, Frank, 2005. The mysterious death of Pat Tillman. *New York Times*, 6 November.

Robb, David L., 2004. *Operation Hollywood: How the Pentagon Shapes and Censors the Movies*. New York: Prometheus Books.

Roberts, Randy & James S. Olson, 1995. *John Wayne: American*. Lincoln, NE: University of Nebraska Press.

Robnik, Drehli, 2002. Saving one life: Spielberg's *Artificial Intelligence* as redemptive memory of things. *Jump Cut*, No. 45, Fall.

Rosen, Gerald M., 2004. *Posttraumatic Stress Disorder: Issues and Controversies*. Chichester: John Wiley.

Rotten, Ryan, 2007. Myrick's new *Objective*. [Online] ShockTillYouDrop, 18 April. Found at: http://tinyurl.com/3ymtotm (accessed 31 March 2010).

Ryan, Michael & Douglas Kellner, 1988. *Camera Politica: the Politics and Ideology of Contemporary Hollywood Film*. Bloomington, IN: Indiana University Press, 1988.

Schechter, Harold & Jonna G. Semeiks, 1991. Leatherstocking in 'Nam: *Rambo*, *Platoon*, and the American frontier myth. *Journal of Popular Culture*, Vol. 24, No. 4, pp. 17–25.

Schiappa, Edward, 2008. *Beyond Representational Correctness: Rethinking Criticism of Popular Media*. Albany, NY: SUNY Press.

Schoenbach, Klaus, 2001. Myths of media and audiences. *European Journal of Communication*, Vol. 16, No. 3, pp. 361–76.

Sconce, Jeffrey, 2007. Movies: a century of failure. In Jeffrey Sconce (ed.), *Sleaze Artists*. Durham, NC: Duke University Press, pp. 273–309.

Scott, Wilbur J., 1990. PTSD in DSM-III: a case in the politics of diagnosis and disease. *Social Problems*, Vol. 37, No. 3, pp. 294–309.

Shephard, Ben, 2002. *A War of Nerves: Soldiers and Psychiatrists, 1914–1994*. London: Pimlico.

Shone, Tom, 2005. *Blockbuster: How the* Jaws *and* Jedi *Generation Turned Hollywood into a Boom-town*. New York: Scribner.

Simpson, Catherine, 2006. Antipodean automobility and crash: treachery, trespass and transformation of the Open Road. *Australian Humanities Review*, Vols. 39–40. Found at: http://tinyurl.com/3ycgu22 (accessed 6 May 2010).

Simpson, Christopher, 1996. *The Science of Coercion: Communication Research and Psychological Warfare, 1945–60*. New York: Oxford University Press.

Somosierra, Rev. Fr. Jessie, Jr., 2007. U.S. has naturalized 32,000 immigrant soldiers since Iraq war. *Agence France-Presse*, 25 July. Found at: http://tinyurl.com/34zcv4q (accessed 2 March 2010).

Soriano, Cesar G. & Anne Oldenburg, 2005. With America at war, Hollywood follows. *USA Today*, 8 February.

Spark, Alasdair, 1984. The soldier at the heart of the war: the myth of the Green Beret in the popular culture of the Vietnam era. *Journal of American Culture*, Vol. 18, No. 1, pp. 29–48.

Spicuzza, Mary, 2007. An army of uno. *SF Weekly*, 19 June.

Spurlin, J., no date. *Bosko the Doughboy*. [Online] Full Movie Review. Found at: http://tinyurl.com/3x2kpd3 (accessed 13 May 2010).

Staiger, Janet, 1992. *Interpreting Films: Studies in the Historical Reception of American Cinema*. Princeton, NJ: Princeton University Press).

——, 2000. *Perverse Spectators: the Practices of Film Reception*. New York: New York University Press.

Stewart, Garrett, 2009. Digital fatigue: imaging war in recent American film. *Film Quarterly*, Vol. 62, No. 4, pp. 45–55.

Stouffer, Samuel, 1949–50. *The American Soldier* (Four Volumes). Princeton, NJ: Princeton University Press.

——, 1962. *Selected Writings*. New York: Free Press.

Thompson, Anne, 2008. Big directors turn to foreign investors. *Variety*, 11 September.

Thompson, Kristin, 1999. *Storytelling in the New Hollywood: Understanding Classical Narrative Technique*. Cambridge, MA: Harvard University Press,.

Toplin, Robert Brent, 1996. *History by Hollywood: the Use and Abuse of the American Past*. Urbana, IL: University of Illinois Press.

——, 2005. The long battle over *Fahrenheit 9/11*: a matter of politics, not aesthetics. *Film & History*, Vol. 35, No. 2, pp. 8–10.

Trudeau, G. B., 2005. *The Long Road Home: One Step at a Time* (foreword by Senator John McCain). Kansas City, KS: Andrews McMeel.

——, 2006. *The War Within: One More Step at a Time* (foreword by General Richard B. Myers). Kansas City, KS: Andrews McMeel.

Ungar, Craig, 2004. *House of Bush, House of Saud: The Secret Relationship between the World's Two Most Powerful Dynasties*. New York: Scribner.

Universal Studios, 2009. Press Release. [Online] 25 September. Found at: http://tinyurl.com/3ywztd2 (accessed 21 March 2010).

Vicari, Justin, 2009. Post-Iraq cinema: veteran heroes in *The Jacket* and *Harsh Times*. *Jump Cut*, 30 November.

Vice, Jeff, 2007. Cast good, but *Kingdom* isn't. *Deseret Morning News* (Salt Lake City), 28 September.

Waller, Gregory A., 1988. *Rambo*: getting to win this time. In Linda Dittmar & Gene Michaud (eds), *From Hanoi to Hollywood: the Vietnam War in American Film*. New Brunswick, NJ: Rutgers University Press, pp. 113–28.

Ward, Dayton (ed.), 2008. *Space Pirates: Full-Throttle Space Tales*. Denver, CO: Flying Pen Press.

——, 2009. *Space Grunts: Full-Throttle Space Tales*. Denver, CO: Flying Pen Press.

Wasser, Frederick, 2001. *Veni, Vidi, Video: the Hollywood Empire and the VCR*. Austin, TX: University of Texas Press.

West, Francis 'Bing', 2006. *No True Glory: A Frontline Account of the Battle for Fallujah*. New York: Bantam

Wilkerson, David B., 2009. Studios feel pinch of slowing DVD sales. *Wall St. Journal*, 22 September.

Williams, Linda, 1991. Film bodies: gender, genre, and excess. *Film Quarterly*, Vol. 44, No. 4, pp. 2–13.

Williams, Raymond, 1979. *Politics and Letters: Interviews with New Left Review.* London: Verso.

——, 1980. *Problems in Materialism and Culture: Selected Essays.* London: Verso.

Williams, Raymond & Michael Orrom, 1954. *Preface to Film.* London: Film Drama Ltd.

Wills, Gary, 1997. *John Wayne's America: the Politics of Celebrity.* New York: Simon and Schuster.

Woll, Allen L., 1993. Hollywood Views the Mexican-American: from *The Greaser's Revenge* to *The Milagro Beanfield War.* In Robert Brent Toplin (ed.), *Hollywood as Mirror: Changing Views of 'Outsiders' and 'Enemies' in American Movies.* Westport, CT: Greenwood Press, pp. 41–52.

Wright, Will, 1975. *Six-Guns and Society: A Structural Study of the Western.* Berkeley, CA: University of California Press.

Young, Peter & Peter Jesser, 1997. *The Media and the Military: from the Crimea to Desert Strike.* Basingstoke: Macmillan.

Žižek, Slavoj, 2010a. A soft focus on war: how Hollywood hides the horrors of war. *In These Times*, 21 April. Found at: http://tinyurl.com/35zzb45 (accessed 24 June 2010).

——, 2010b. Return of the natives. *New Statesman*, 4 March.

Index